Angling Techniques

Angling Techniques

By Ján Sedlár

SUNBURST BOOKS

Designed and produced by Aventinum
English language edition first published 1995
by Sunburst Books, Deacon House,
65 Old Church Street, London SW3 5BS

© Aventinum, Prague 1995

Text by Ján Sedlár
Translated by Clare Krojzlová
Illustrations by Vlastimil Forejt, Bohumil Landa, Jiří Malý
and Pavel Amena
Photographs by Sláva Štochl, Kamil Sedláček and Jiří Vostradovský
Graphic design by Antonín Chmel and Pavel Gaudore

ISBN 1 85778 102 3
Printed in Slovakia
3/21/04/51-01

Contents

Introduction

I caught my first trophy fish — a magnificent silver salmon — with the first cast of my first real fishing-rod, complete with fixed reel and spinner. This unexpected and entirely fortuitous success has of course never repeated itself. Subsequent catches have required patience, the accumulation of a great deal of theoretical knowledge and years of practical experience. Although a certain amount of luck is welcome in every branch of sport, knowledge is more often the key. Success in fishing not only depends on an acquaintance with the principles of fishing and a certain amount of finesse in fishing technique, but also upon knowledge about fish behaviour according to their specific living conditions. Although the type of equipment carried by the fisherman does play a part in his success, its importance should not be over emphasized. A master fisherman will usually catch more fish with a homemade spinner than an inexperienced one equipped with the latest technical innovations.

Every would-be fisherman should first acquaint himself with the basic principles of the sport before even setting out for the water. For ease of understanding I have chosen not to undertake a detailed study of individual sport fishing species as the catching principles can usually be generalized. The technique for catching a barbel, for instance, can successfully be applied to catching a sturgeon; broad-snout, vimba bream, etc., can be caught in a similar manner to orfe. Preference has been given to fish which occur more commonly. Therefore the common roach or rudd is given more space than the huchen or sturgeon.

From time to time claims will be made regarding the phenomenal success of a revolutionary new change in fishing technique. However, as any old-timer will tell you, the only well-trodden road to success lies in the gradual accumulation of personal experience. Always listen to other people's advice of course, but, as with any sport, what suits one will not always suit another, so one suggestion should be weighed against another. In this book years of handed-down experience are weighed against the practical results of sport fishing in European waters, enabling us to answer the questions most commonly asked by sport fishermen, namely: Where do I go to look for a certain fish; when will I be most likely to catch it; and which is the most suitable tackle to use?

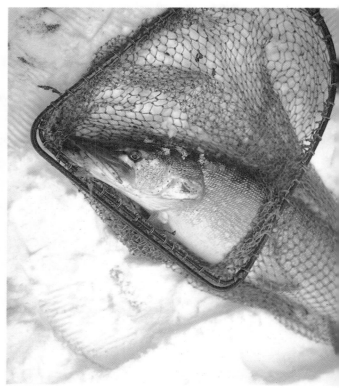

Sporting fishing tackle

Numerous manufacturers' fishing tackle catalogues provide such a wealth of detailed information that there is no need to devote attention here to the technical description of individual items of tackle. This chapter will address practical issues connected with the functional use of tackle and will attempt to answer the basic question of what the all-round sports fisherman should have in his tackle. The need to answer this fundamental question arises from the fact that, in current conditions of highly-developed fishing technique, there is no single item of tackle which may be regarded as universal. On the other hand, it is far from necessary to own every single piece of tackle on the market which the manufacturers claim that we cannot do without. It is hard for the average fisherman to orient himself in this confusing abundance of 'extra' and 'super' fishing aids, so we need first to make an objective assessment of fishing tackle.

RODS

The rod is the basic component of fishing tackle and has two main functions: it facilitates casting the lure and holding it in the required position; it maintains contact with the fish when it takes the bait, facilitating the hooking, playing and landing of the catch.

Today's assortment of rods (with the exception of classic built-cane fly-fishing rods) consists exclusively of man-made materials. Depending on the method of manufacture, these can be divided into solid and tubular rods. The former are stronger and, of course, heavier, and are therefore only made up to lengths of 260—270cm (102—106in). All longer rods are tubular. The latest graphite (carbon) rods are excellent, with faster and more positive action; they are for the time being, however, relatively fragile and require very careful handling.

Depending on the method of construction we can distinguish between assembled rods, consisting of two, three, four or more parts, and telescopic rods. Both types have their advantages and their weaknesses. The most serious disadvantage of assembled rods — the fitting together of the individual parts with the aid of metal ferrules — is gradually being eliminated, both with the aid of ferrules made of the same material used for the manufacture of the rod, and most recently and best of all with the fitting of the parts directly into each other, thus dispensing with ferrules altogether. Their advantage, on the other hand, is the fact that the rod rings can be spaced along them, so that the rod takes an evenly distributed strain when in use. The advantage of telescopic rods is their simple handling when dismantling and assembling, although in this case it is not possible to have the ideal functional distribution of rod rings.

Price differences between graphite and other man-made material rods are proportional to quality. It is definitely not necessary, however, to have a whole series of top quality rods. We should always bear in mind the purpose for which the rod is required. For fishing methods in which the rod is constantly held in the hands (fly-fishing, long rods for fishing with floats, and possibly even for sink and draw fishing) it is worth investing in more expensive, lighter, graphite rods, whilst in the case of rods intended for passive catching methods, one can save money by buying the somewhat heavier fibreglass rods, which are of adequate quality.

From a functional point of view, rods are classified into fly-fishing rods, spinning rods and rods for basic catching methods (i.e. bottom fishing, float fishing, etc.).

From the point of view of practical use, one should note the following features in rods: weight in relation to length, power, flexibility and the suitability of strain and action. The principle that the weight in grammes should not exceed the length of the rod in centimetres is now standard in contemporary ranges, and usually a 30—40% lower weight than length is called for.

The power of a rod in relation to the characteristics of its action expresses the mass of the optimal weight that it is possible to cast from the rod without reducing its qualitative properties. Occasional over-

Basic types of fishing rod: a) for basic fishing methods [with a float, on the bottom, fishing in the wind, and so on], b) for spinning, c) fly-fishing rods.

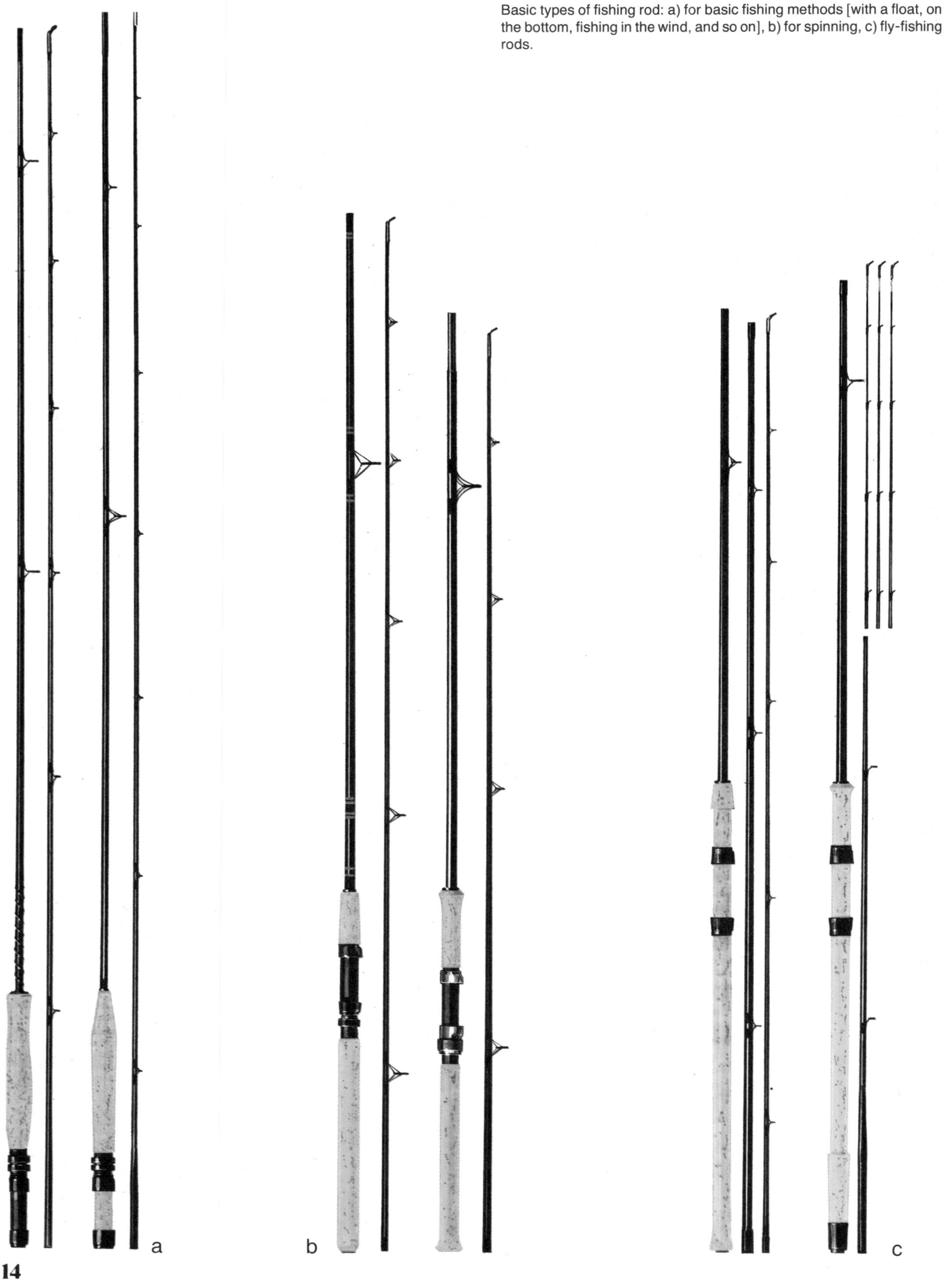

a

b

c

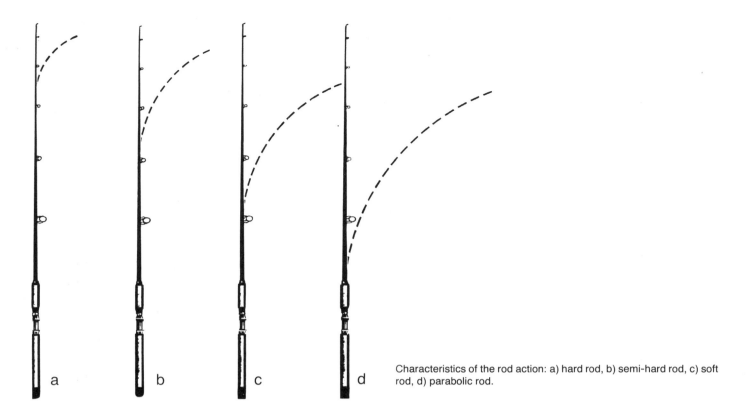

Characteristics of the rod action: a) hard rod, b) semi-hard rod, c) soft rod, d) parabolic rod.

loading by 10—20% is permissible, although this should not become the rule. The figures mentioned above, of course, do not refer to the weight of the catch. With a rod intended for a recommended weight of 10—30g (0.4—1oz), for example, one can also easily catch a fish weighing as much as several kilogrammes.

The action of a rod is the result of its basic characteristics — power, flexibility and elasticity — demonstrated by the bending of the rod at the maximum permitted strain. In practice there are several ways of indicating rod action. The DAM firm (FRG), for example, indicates rod action by means of 4 basic categories as follows:

a 1.5 — 2.0 rod bends through its entire length with the exception of the butt;

a 2.5 — 3.0 rod bends through two-thirds of its length;

a 3.5 — 4.0 rod bends in the top half only;

a 4.5 — 5.0 rod bends at the tip only.

In other words, rods may be characterised as soft (bends through entire length), semi-hard or hard (bends at the tip only). Rods may also be marked with the letters A to D (A representing the hardest action).

The action of a rod should not be confused with its power, which is expressed by the recommended weight. A rod for 100g (3.5oz) weight, for example, may be either hard or soft. The general rule is that rods for lower weights are generally harder, and those for heavier weights are softer.

The choice of a rod according to its action characteristic also depends on the fishing method. The advantages of rods with a harder action manifest themselves mainly during casting (accuracy) and also in their quick reaction to a take by a fish. While playing the catch, however, it is mainly the tip of the rod that is active, which diminishes its effectiveness, so we must compensate for this handicap by using a stronger line. In the case of rods with a softer action, reaction to a take is slower. This disadvantage, however, is compensated for by easier and safer playing of the catch owing to the fact that here the full length of the rod comes into play. In this case one can use a relatively fine line. The general rule is that for spinning, rods with a harder action are preferred; for float and bottom fishing a semi-soft action is chosen, whilst fly rods should have the softest action.

The smooth guiding of the line from the reel up to the tip of the rod is ensured by a certain number of rod rings and a single tip ring. The rings are the components of the rod which come under the most strain, and must therefore be of the best possible

15

quality and made of exceptionally resilient material so that grooves do not appear on them as a result of line friction. Today's range of quality rings completely fulfils these requirements, whether they are superlative Fuji rings made of aluminium oxide, or rings made of hard porcelain, as long as they are reliably secured against cracking with a plastic or metal outer covering. Depending on the method of catching, differently constructed ring types are selected. The shape and size of rings must conform to the reel type, and it is always necessary to take into account the smooth running of the line from the reel up to the tip ring. In the case of fly-fishing rods smaller rings on low fittings are suitable (S-shaped), facilitating the casting of the fly line. On rods for float fishing the rings must partially stand off, so that the line does not stick to the rod. The largest rings with the greatest stand-off are suitable for casting rods. Care must also be given to the distribution of the rings along the rod, as this affects both the lure-casting procedure and the strain on individual parts of the rod while playing the catch.

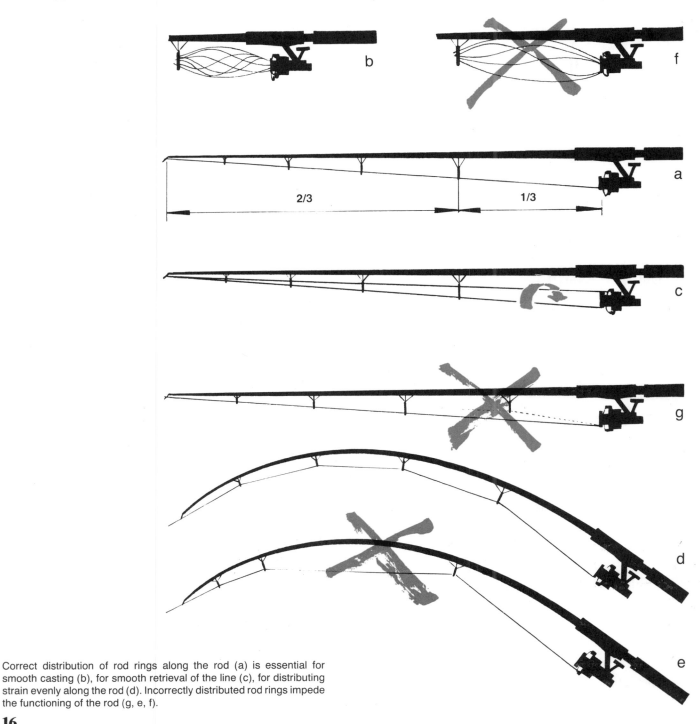

Correct distribution of rod rings along the rod (a) is essential for smooth casting (b), for smooth retrieval of the line (c), for distributing strain evenly along the rod (d). Incorrectly distributed rod rings impede the functioning of the rod (g, e, f).

Various types of rod butt: a) butt of one-hand rod, b) butt of two-hand rod, c) butt of fly-fishing rod.

The rod butt, whether made of cork or plastic, should sit well in the hand. Of the various construction methods for fixing the reel, all those which fix the reel firmly, so that it does not work loose even after long-term use, are acceptable. On fly rods the reel is placed on the lower part of the butt because of the fishing method. It is positioned higher on other rods, but always in such a way that the centre of gravity of the rod lies at the centre of the reel. Where it is not possible to counterbalance the rod in this way (as is frequently the case with longer rods, in which the front part is top-heavy), one can compensate for this by means of sufficient weighting of

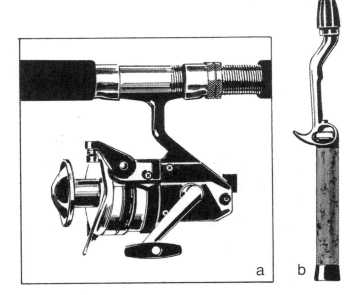

Methods of fixing the reel on to the rod butt: a) standard fixing of a common fixed-spool reel, b) butt for fixing a multiplier reel.

the lower part of the butt. A butt designed for fixing a multiplier reel is specially shaped.

Of all the factors which play a part in the selection of the optimal rod, the most important are the size of the fish, the predominant method of catching, the type of water, as well as the individual characteristics of the angler. Rods for basic catching methods (i.e. fishing on the bottom, float fishing, swimming the stream, etc.) should be longer. These facilitate lighter and more accurate casting and a more effective angle between the tip of the rod and the line direction, thus enabling swifter reaction to take. In the case of more passive catching methods, the weight of the rod is not particularly important, but active catching methods require the lightest possible rods. Normal rod length is considered to range between 3.5—6.5m (11½—21¾ft), longer rods only being used without rod rings; that is, as whiprods. Their strong points are indisputable, although handling them requires the good physical condition of the angler, training and experience.

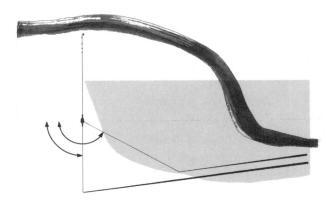

The advantage of relatively long rods lies in the fact that they enable instantaneous contact with the bait, the fisherman thus being able to react more readily to the take of a fish.

Spinning rods are selected either on the basis of the expected quarry, or on the weight of the lure. When catching with the smallest spinners, weighing 2—5g (0.07—0.2oz) one can successfully cast only with a finer casting which has a maximum stipulated weight of 10—15g (0.4—0.5oz). When using lures of average size and weight, a rod for a weight of 30—40g (1—1.4oz) should be chosen, whilst when catching with the heaviest lures the rod should be designed to take a weight of more than 50—60g (1.75—2oz). With all casting rods a harder action should be given preference. The rod length for catching with light and average weight lures ranges from 240—270cm (95—106in), and the rods are always for one hand. A rod for heavy lures may be longer than 3m (10ft) and is generally for both hands.

Fly rods must meet certain requirements over and above the usual ones. These mainly concern the casting of the lures (flies), which are practically weightless. When casting, therefore, the weight of the fly line combined with the specific properties of the rod have a significant effect. Fly rods also differ in the construction of the butt, but mainly in the fixing of the reel on the lower part of the butt. In this way the centre of gravity of the rod is shifted to the lower part, thus reducing hand fatigue. The S-shaped rod rings are fitted lower and on a fly rod there are usually 6—11 of them, which is more than on other types of rod.

A soft action is characteristic of a fly rod. If when under strain the whole rod regularly bends as far as the butt, all-through action, this is known as the 'English action' (top quality rods made of built-cane and some graphite rods). If the upper part bends more noticeably than the lower part, this is called parabolic action (products made of tubular laminate and some harder graphite rods). The speed of action of a rod also needs to be taken into account. This manifests itself in how swiftly hand movements are transferred to the fly-fishing line and the fly. Shorter and harder rods have a swifter action than softer and longer rods.

The most important properties of fly rods are classified in accordance with an international agreement among manufacturers, by means of the AFTMA (Associated Fishing Tackle Manufacturers) system. The basic characteristic is expressed in Arabic numerals, lower numbers indicating softer rods with slower action and vice versa.

When choosing a suitable fly rod it is also necessary to take into consideration the types of fish which one wants to catch, as well as the type of water. The finest rod is chosen for catching grayling, and can be somewhat harder for trout; when dry fly-fishing a rod with a swifter action is better; for fishing with dry flies and nymphs a slower action is sufficient; if the fisherman catches mainly in small brooks, a rod up to 240cm (95in) long is sufficient, whilst in more open waters a rod of around 3m (10ft) in length will be required. The most powerful (AFTMA over 7—8) and longest rods (even

more than 4.5m / 14¾ft), originally intended for salmon and large trout fishing, are recently finding much wider application as a result of a gradual shift in interest on the part of anglers towards more open waters, lakes and valley reservoirs, but chiefly due to the 'discovery' both of new 'fly' fishes (such as silver salmon and chub as well as pike-perch and pike), and of new effective lures (streamers and bucktails). Fly-fishing has thus acquired unlimited potential for further development.

Matching the fly rod with fly-fishing line is indispensable for correct functioning. Manufacturers' specifications for the characteristics of the rod or for the ideal accessories should be taken as obligatory. If in the case of a given rod a range of two categories of fly line is recommended, the heavier fly-fishing line (the higher number) is more suitable for the beginner as it is easier to cast. It is better to graduate to a lighter fly-fishing line, which facilitates more elegant fishing, only after obtaining practical experience.

REELS

Apart from catching with a whiprod, when the fisherman uses a piece of line tied directly onto the rod, a reel is an absolute essential for most catching methods. The functional value of a reel is tested mainly from the viewpoint of the required quantity of line and the potential for smooth and swift casting and retrieving, as well as from the viewpoint of being able to play the quarry smoothly and securely. In the former case the line container is the most important component, that is the spool of the reel, as

A simple ventre-pin reel, the so-called Nottingham reel.

well as its capacity, shape, the quality of the material and its execution (resilient material, smooth finish). For playing the quarry the most important role is played by the brake mechanism, the principle of its construction design and its overall execution. Additional important features of a reel are its operational speed (arrangement of gears), reliability and durability (quality of the materials, method of mounting of the gear mechanism) and smooth running (gear system).

There are several types of reel, which differ according to their constructional and functional design. The simple (Nottingham) reel is nowadays more valuable to the collector than it is for practical fishing, being so primitive that it can scarcely be used for fishing even with a short cast, and it is in any case incompatible with modern telescopic rods.

The current range of reels consists of three basic types: fly-fishing reels, multiplier reels (with a rotating spool) and fixed spool reels. Fly-fishing reels are intended exclusively for fly-fishing and according to their technical construction may be divided into simple ones, either with open or closed, sometimes even with replaceable spools, and automatic ones. For all other catching methods multiplier and fixed spool reels are equally appropriate.

With their precision of execution, simple construction principle and functional properties, multiplier reels rank among the classics. Their function is based on the principle of a rotating spool, with the gearing arranged in such a way that it turns several times with one turn of the handle, thus facilitating quick line retrieval. The gear mechanism freewheels during casting, the spool revolving lightly without resistance, thus enabling a sufficiently long cast to be reached. The most modern types of multi-

Fixed-spool reels with varied positioning of brake mechanisms.

plier reel are protected against line fouling by means of a sensitive brake mechanism. The line guide ensures the optimum and even winding of the line across the whole surface of the spool during retrieval. Direct guiding of the line from the tip of the rod to the reel, thanks to which the fisherman has constant and direct contact with the lure, is another valuable feature. Multiplier reels are not particularly popular with fishermen, as they are rather expensive, and perfect mastery of fishing technique with these is admittedly trickier than with fixed-spool reels. For catching large fish, however, a multiplier reel is certainly unrivalled.

Fixed-spool reels are functionally based on the principle of a fixed, stationary spool, from which the line falls freely during casting. During retrieval the line is evenly wound on to the spool with the aid of a rotating pick-up and a line guide. The process

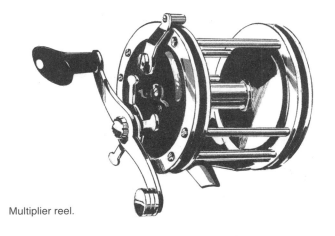

Multiplier reel.

of innovation in fixed-spool reels is currently proceeding at a revolutionary rate, both from the point of view of the use of more advanced construction materials (plastics, which enable reduction in weight with a simultaneous increase in quality), and from the point of view of new, more practical construction designs. One of the most promising designs, the outer spool, which covers the body of the reel, has eliminated troublesome catching of the line in the mechanism. The characteristics of the brake mechanism are also currently undergoing substantial improvement. Smoother regulation of the brake is facilitated by placing its controls in the more accessible lower part of the reel. Automatic or manual control of the pick-up, a hard-chromed rotating line guide, an outer spool with a safety peg facilitating spool changing, a double brake system with regulation on the lower part of the reel and with a high-speed brake, multi-component brake pads reducing overheating, easy assembly for use with either the right or the left hand, a folding pick-up and a folding handle for easier transportation, are all now regarded as common features of standard fixed-spool reels.

The latest type of reel is known as the cased reel, in which the spool is enclosed in a case, the line being guided over the upper part of the casing. The functioning of some models corresponds to the principle of fixed-spool reels, whilst others can be

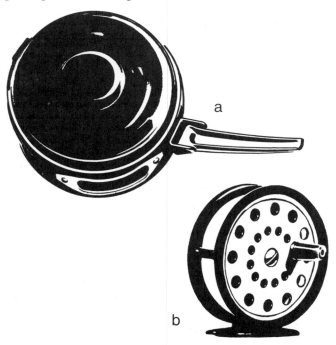

Simple (a) and automatic (b) fly-fishing reel.

used as multiplier reels. They are basically easier to handle than classical fixed-spool reels because during casting the line is released by means of a lever or push button, the line release automatically being activated when the handle is turned. Some types are equipped with an auxiliary finger brake, which can be used to increase the brake power, or with a brake on the handle, which can be used for gentle reduction of the brake power. All types of encased reels manufactured so far are intended only for lines up to 0.30 to 0.35mm (0.012—0.014in), and are therefore only suitable for catching smaller fish.

Fly fishermen basically have a choice of only two possibilities — classic mechanical or more advanced automatic reels. The mechanical fly-fishing reel is based constructionally on an originally simple wheel (Nottingham reel), its basic components being a case with a shaft, and placed inside it a narrow spool for winding the fly-fishing line. An essential addition to the reel is a handle and a controllable brake, ideally a silent one. Automatic reels are equipped with a spring which expands when the fly-line is being pulled out. With activation of the release mechanism — that is, during retrieval — the spring works in the opposite way, winding on as much fly-fishing line as has been released.

An automatic reel may be either vertical or horizontal. A vertical one, with the spool in the normal position, enables manipulation with either hand, while a horizontal one has the spool placed flatwise, this being intended for fishermen who hold the rod in the right hand and handle the fly-fishing line with the left.

When choosing a suitable type of reel, the fisherman endeavours to coordinate the reel with the rod and to consider spool capacity. Matching the reel to the rod is also desirable for correct rod balance, especially in the case of active catching methods. When assessing the required spool capacity, one should adopt a conservative approach, since 100 to 150m (330—500ft) of line is enough, with an adequate reserve, to play any quarry.

LINES AND FLY-FISHING LINES

The rule concerning the restrictive role of the weakest link in the chain applies, in the case of the fishing rod, above all to the line, the function of which is contact between the rod and the fish. The effectiveness of this contact is directly dependent on the sensitivity of the line, which is the reasoning behind the general rule of using the thinnest, finest lines possible.

The common denominator in the whole range of manufactured lines is the same basic material (polyamide 6, or modified polyamide 6) and, in principle, a similar technological procedure. The aim of constantly improving the quality of the physical and mechanical properties of lines, chiefly their resistance (especially in knots), softness, elasticity and colour, is another common factor. The market offers specialised types of line for various fishing conditions — hard, extra hard, soft.

The only information on the mechanical properties of a line which is provided by the manufacturer, expressing the resistance to tensile stress in kilograms (in other words, the strength of the line) applies only under laboratory conditions, that is when the line is dry. Polyamide line absorbs water relatively easily, which has a detrimental effect on its mechanical properties. It becomes more tractable and softer, its resistance gradually reducing by up to one fifth of the stated level. From the practical point of view, the so-called deformation of the line when pulled apart (expansibility), which may reach from 18 up to 30% of the length of the line, is also an important factor. Softer lines have greater expansibility (25 to 30%) than harder ones. Lines with extremely low expansibility (less than 17%) usually have reduced resistance in knots.

Of all the factors which reduce the resistance of line when in practical use, knots are predominant. The degree of negative influence on line resistance is directly dependent on the type of line and the execution or quality of the knot. Knots on the rod and line are a necessary evil, the proportions of which can nevertheless be affected by suitable assembly of the rod, the use of a line with relatively high knotting resistance and by choosing the appropriate type of knot. Line resistance is reduced by 15—20 up to 50% when knotted. It is a general rule that extremely strong lines (strong, extra strong) are less resistant when knotted than softened lines (soft, top knot). Hard lines, however, have a higher degree of basic resistance and are thus in fact of the same

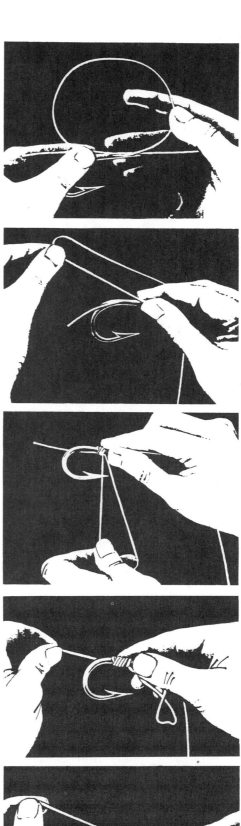

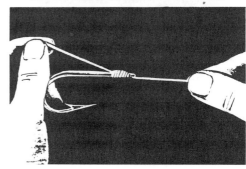

Basic procedure for tying the line on to a tanged hook.

value as soft ones in terms of strength.

The more the line bends in the knot, the greater is the reduction in the line's resistance. In fishing catalogues one can sometimes find knot types recommended for a certain type of line. Whether the line is tied into a knot while dry or damp also influences quality, thy latter option being preferable.

With long-term use the line also loses its properties under the influence of atmospheric conditions. Polyamide lines are particularly sensitive to sunlight, which after a certain time reduces their resistance, especially in knots. Lines should therefore not be exposed to the sun unnecessarily.

A drop in line resistance as a result of strain while fishing depends on the extent to which it is overburdened, and cannot therefore be quantified unequivocally. The elasticity of the line, that is its ability to return to its original state after straining, varies with different types of line, but is in no case absolute. Due to the effect of long-term strain, every line is permanently distorted, being elongated and weakened. This damage manifests itself mainly in the end part, which is most frequently in use. This distortion occurs mainly while playing the quarry or when attempting to extricate a hook caught in an obstacle. During normal use, for example sink and draw, or casting and pulling out the lure, distortion of the line is negligible. It occurs more often when using smaller sized lines than one should, which consequently take more strain.

The strength and functioning of the line while fishing are conspicuously affected by its working length, that is the length from the reel to the lure. The line will constantly soften with extension of the working length. If a line is extended by 1 m over a 10 metre distance, at a distance of 100 m it will be extended with exertion of the same force by 10 m, the line thus being substantially more elastic. During a take at a shorter distance, hooking will therefore be harder and the line will be less resilient to being pulled apart, which forces us to lower the intensity of the hooking action. At a great distance, hooking will be disproportionately gentler, thus proportionately reducing the risk of pulling the line apart, although one must hook more energetically. This needs to be taken into account when choosing a line. Hard lines with higher resistance are suitable for fishing at greater distances, where it is necessary

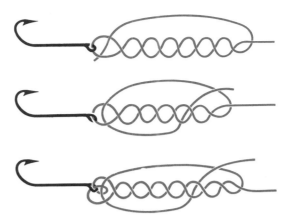

Tying the line on to a hook with an eye.

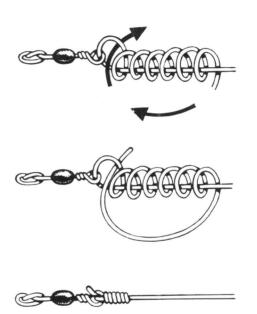

Procedure for tying a swivel on to the line.

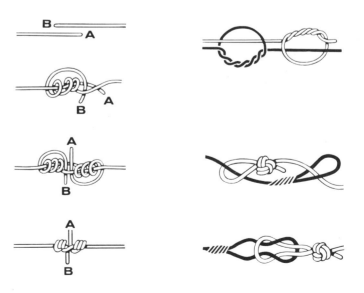

Methods for tying lines together.

to hook energetically and also when as thin and resistant a line as possible is required for catching. Softer lines are used for smoother, more accurate and longer casting, also being used for catching fish which are slower to take the bait and which escape after taking. Hooking is also gentler and more reliable with such lines, as is demonstrated to positive effect while fishing on the bottom with a more weighted lure, and when fly-fishing.

Undesirable mechanical properties of lines can be attributed to poor quality production. These undesirable properties include the tendency to twist, which may sometimes also arise from incorrect retrieval onto the reel spool, as well as the tendency of a line to retain shape. Lines with this shape retention usually retain for a long time the spiral shape in which they were stored over a lengthy period. Softer lines suffer less from this than harder ones. Lines of greater diameter are more inclined to foul and knot, which reduces their casting length. After lengthy contact with water during fishing, or being intentionally kept in water heated to 60°C, although the line does lose this shape retention, this is usually only temporary — until it dries out. It is better to discard these lines.

The effect of coloured line dyes has been proved in practice. In some cases, chiefly in reduced visibility, the effect of line dye is imperceptible, but generally it can make a difference, whether positive or negative. This also depends, of course, on the fishing method. When spinning, the fish has practically no opportunity to react to the line, as is also the case when fishing on the bottom, when the line blends in with its surroundings. During fishing in clear water, swimming the stream, or fly-fishing, however, the fish may notice the line, either on the surface or under the water. Logically, therefore, we must assume that the colour of the line should be identical with the shade of the water or background. Lines with a greenish tinge are thus suitable for clear mountain waters, brown tinged ones in waters which have biological sediment, smokey coloured ones in rivers with stony beds, etc.

Special mention should be made of the latest so-called fluorescent lines. These contain an optical brightening agent which turns invisible ultraviolet rays falling onto them into visible bluish-violet light. During daylight in the air, these lines are bright bluish-violet and more visible in the water to the fisherman, but a fish does not register this brightening effect, since its eyes can only perceive higher wavelengths.

The key principles for using lines are as follows:
— The reel spool should always be filled as tightly as it will fill itself when retrieving. If the spool is overfilled, the line fouls; if it is not completely filled, casting becomes more difficult and the necessary length of line may be missing if playing a heavier quarry.
— From time to time the most frequently used end of the line should be renewed, at first by cutting off the weakened parts (padding out the spool as required, so that it is full), later by rewinding the line the other way round.
— One should avoid unnecessary knots on the line.
— Spool capacity should correspond to the fishing method so that there is always a sufficient length of line in the event of playing a larger quarry. In normal cases 100—150m (330—500ft) is ample.
— Mechanical abrasion of the line can be prevented by frequent cleaning and maintenance of the rod rings and reel pick-up.
— The rod and line should be assembled with only the minimum number of knots. Preference should be given to more complicated and therefore stronger ones, and lines should be dampened before tying them. Only lines of very similar strength should be tied together.

Technical progress has also improved fly-fishing lines, so that the former silk braided fly-fishing lines are now pretty much museum pieces. Fly-fishing lines made of man-made fibres have replaced them, not just because they are comparable in quality, but mainly because of their lower price, good durability and more straightforward maintenance.

Fly-lines were originally classified according to diameter. Today the internationally recognized AFTMA system is used, the basic unit of which is the weight of 10 yards of fly-fishing line (9.14m). Information is indicated in Arabic numerals equivalent to that indicating rods. Numbering ranges from the lightest fly-fishing line no. 1 (3.9g/0.16oz) to the heaviest number 12 (24.7g/0.99oz).

When fly-fishing, two basic properties of the fly-fishing line are important — how it behaves in the water and what shape it is. According to their behaviour in the water, lines are distinguished as follow: floating lines — marked F, sinking lines — marked S, intermediate lines — marked I, and sinking-floating lines — marked SF.

According to shape, lines can then be divided into four groups:

1 Parallel ones, marked L-level, have the same diameter along their whole length. These are the simplest lines and therefore the cheapest, but can only be used for the least strenuous types of fly-fishing. Their strong point is that they can be shortened as needed without altering their character.

2 Double-taper (biconical) lines, marked DT, are from the practical point of view among the best. They are excellent for casting, due to their weight and low air resistance, and can furthermore be used from both ends. They are manufactured in AFTMA nos. 4 to 12. They are reinforced in the middle and equally tapered at both ends.

3 Single-taper or shooting-taper (rocket) lines, marked ST, resemble half a double-taper line, but are more solid and heavy, and are suitable for casting greater distances. They are good and accurate for casting, and because of their good sinking properties are mainly suitable for fishing with nymphs.

4 Weight forward (club-like) lines, marked WF, have a thin end followed by a shorter, markedly conically reinforced part and then continuing with a parallel, thinner part of the fly-fishing line. These are suitable for all types of fly-fishing, although they lose value after the actively used end has worn out.

The colour of a fly-fishing line should not affect fishing success in practice, if only because in fly-fishing a relatively long cast made of monofilament line is attached to the fly-fishing line. Inasmuch, however, as there is a need to match the fly-fishing line to the surroundings, the more suitable colour is sand grey or white, whereas blue and green fly-fishing lines have a contrasting effect.

Fly-fishing lines, in contrast with ordinary lines, come with complex information on the labels concerning their basic characteristic features. The theoretically and practically verified parameters stated by the manufacturer should of course be respected, the fly-fishing line always being matched to the rod and vice versa.

FISHING HOOKS

We do not always devote sufficient care to items

worth only a few pennies, but in the case of fishing hooks one should make an exception. The hook is after all the only indispensible part of the tackle. One can sooner manage without a rod or reel than without a good quality hook.

When selecting hooks, two contradictory requirements need to be reconciled: the need for easy, economical and reliable mounting of the lure and at the same time the need for sufficient strength. The first requirement is met by the finest, and thus the thinnest possible hooks, whereas the condition of the required strength, on the other hand, demands more solid material. A balance between these two can only be reached on the basis of top quality material and the optimal method of processing, so that the hook is not extremely hard and does not break under strain, but is also not too soft either, so that it does not become distorted. Particular notice should be taken of the point of the hook, which plays a key role in hooking. The force required for the point of a hook and the barb to penetrate a fish's mouth increases in geometrical progression in relation to the thickness of the hook. Other characteristics of the hook — its colour, the shape of the bend, the direction of the point, the length of the shank and the way in which it is finished off — depend on the fishing method and the kinds of fish to be caught.

On the hook itself, we distinguish the shank, which can be of varying length and finished off in a number of different ways (with a tang, an eye or just plain), the bend, which may also be shaped in different ways, the point and the barb. In some types there is no barb at the point, whilst in other types there are also barbs on the shank for more reliable holding of the lure. The length of the shank needs to be judged not only from the point of view of the lure (e.g. longer for earthworms, shorter for corn grains), but also from that of the hooking ability of the hook, which is determined by the value of the so-called angle of detriment. The value of the angle is dependent on the ratio of the length of the shank to the span of the bend. The principle that the hooking ability of a hook increases with the value of the angle applies here. During hooking, the point does not penetrate the mouth of the fish perpendicularly, but at an angle which is practically identical with the value of the angle of detriment. From this

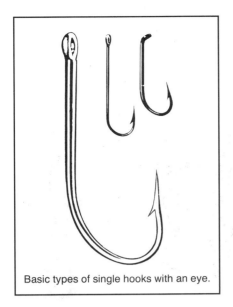

Basic types of single hooks with an eye.

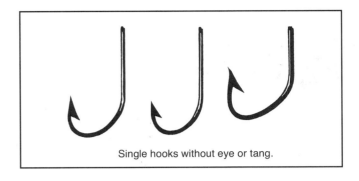

Single hooks without eye or tang.

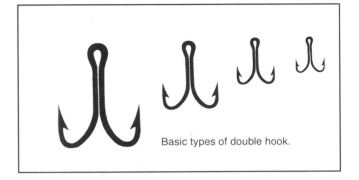

Basic types of double hook.

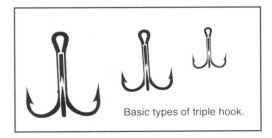

Basic types of triple hook.

information it is possible to deduce that in the case of fish which require more energetic hooking, a hook with a longer shank should be used, while for fish with soft mouths a hook with a shorter shank should be chosen. The colour of a hook can also affect its hooking ability to a certain extent. Silvery or golden hooks may be used for lighter lures (larvae, corn, potatoes), and darker shades for dark lures (earthworms, etc.).

The exceptionally rich assortment of hooks, which totals more than 30,000 types, may be divided into three essential categories. These are round band hooks, limerick hooks and snack band

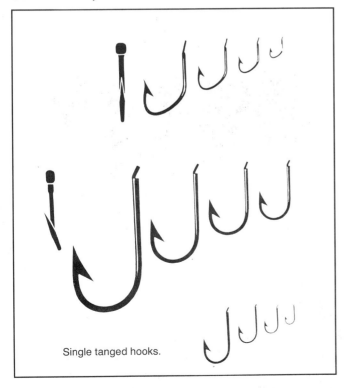

Single tanged hooks.

hooks. Each of these basic types features a whole assortment of hooks, differing in many details — shank length, shaping of the bend, points which are either straight or bend sideways, etc. Of the various alternative ways of numbering hooks according to size, the most commonly used is what is known as the old method (Redditch), in which a larger number indicates a smaller hook and vice versa. The size is determined according to the width of the hook span. Standard-size hooks are numbered from 1 to 16, outsize ones from 1/0 to 5/0.

Fly-fishing hooks for tying on artificial flies would be worth a chapter in themselves. With a view to easier mounting of flies, the most suitable shapes are those with an eye, although they may also be tanged or plain. The difference between hooks for dry and wet flies lies in the way in which the eye bends and in the thickness of the material used. Hooks for dry flies should always be thinner and lighter, so that they float well, which is also fa-

Some special hooks: a) a simple hook with small protective spring for fishing among obstacles, b) hooks for fishing for predators.

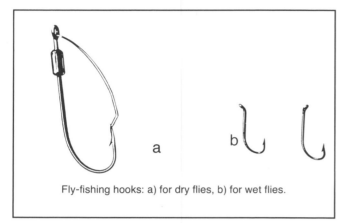

Fly-fishing hooks: a) for dry flies, b) for wet flies.

A selection of light, slender floats for fishing for white fish species in calmer waters.

cilitated by the eye being bent upwards. Hooks for wet flies and nymphs may also be made of thicker wire with the eye bent downwards, so that the fly naturally sinks below the surface. It is necessary, however, to be aware of the negative effect of the angle of the detriment, which is most favourable in hooks with the eye bent downwards. This above mentioned requirement is met by some of the recent types of hook with cranked shanks.

Double and triple hooks are essentially derived from single hooks.

FLOATS

When selecting a float it is necessary to take into account two of their key roles. These are, firstly, their potential for presenting lures to the fish in as natural a way as possible within any water course profile, and secondly the sensitive and timely signalling of a take by a fish. In addition to these, the float also facilitates more reliable placing of the lure, indicates the direction of movement of a fish when the angler is playing it, and keeps the line afloat.

For some fishing methods, for example in water with very fine mud or densely overgrown water, a float is an absolute must. Use of a float does nevertheless definitely contradict the principle of using the simplest possible rod and line assembly. In the attempt to compensate at least partly for this

Light but stout types of float for fishing for white fish species in swift waters.

fact, the fisherman is obliged to make great demands on the float, both in terms of its construction design and in terms of the material used, the dye preparation, sensitivity, etc. Floats should above all meet the requirement for maximum inconspicuousness in term of size, as well as appropriate hydrodynamic properties and colour.

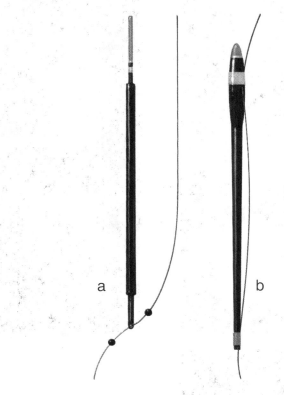

Methods for attaching the float on to the line: a) sliding float attached at one point, b) float fix-attached at two points.

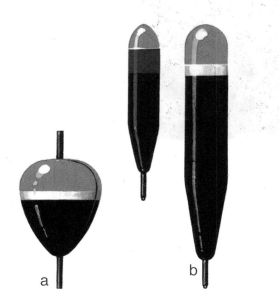

Basic types of float for fishing for predatory fish species with live bait: a) classic pike floats, which keep the fish-bait within a restricted space, b) slender float types, partially under-dimensioned, thus enabling the mounted fish-bait to move freely to a certain extent.

Depending on the fishing method, the depth of the water and so on, there are several alternative uses of floats. There are essentially two ways of attaching a float to the line, the fixed and the sliding methods. In fixed mounting the float is attached to the chosen place on the line with the aid of a suitable clip. In the case of larger floats, the line generally runs through the body of the float, being fixed by means of a small central pin. In smaller, more slender floats the line is generally led along the outer perimeter in such a way that it is caught on a small antenna in the upper part by means of a small rubber ring, tubing, etc., the line in the bottom part being caught in a special eye. Floats are fix-mounted for fishing in shallow waters, where the submerged depth of the cast is less than the length of the rod.

A sliding float is attached to the line at one or two points (eyes) in such a way that it can slide easily between them. Its maximum submersion depth on the line is determined by means of a stopper. The choice of a suitable type of stopper (cotton, line, rubber band and so on) depends on the diameter of the last rod ring, so that it does not make casting more difficult. A sliding float is used when fishing in deeper waters, where the submersion depth of the cast is greater than the length of the rod, or in shallower waters when casting a great distance.

The float has optimal sensitivity and stability when only that part protrudes above the surface which enables it to be observed. When selecting the colour of a float, practical considerations should prevail. The lower part of the float, which can be seen by fish, should be inconspicuous, whereas the upper part, which is intended to be observed by the fisherman, may have a more conspicuous colour. To this end, a small round head on the point of the antenna is advantageous, and it may also be changeable, so that the colour can be chosen to suit various light conditions. Yellow is the best colour in cloudy weather, orange in normal light and red in clear sunlight. For night fishing, floats with phosphorescence are used. These are visible for up to 45 minutes after initial illumination, for example with a torch. Even more reliable of course are so-called electro-floats with a permanent built-in source of electric energy. The most modern types have a life expectancy of up to 25 hours.

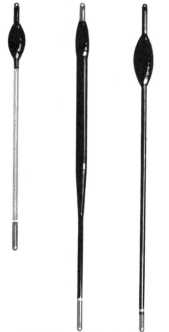

Special float types with built-in weight in the lower part of the body, used for fishing for white fish species from a distance.

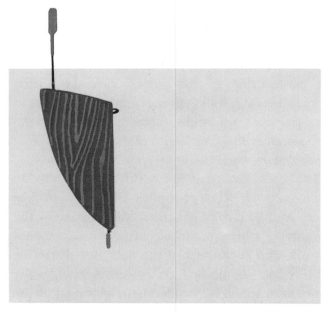

Flat, slab-shaped float for fishing for non-predatory fish species in waters with a very strong current.

a

b

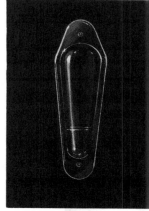

c

Glass balls of various colours:
a) spherical,
b) pear-shaped,
c) elongated.

Some special types of float are also useful for practical purposes. Floats weighted, either with lead or water placed directly into the body, may have either a fixed or an adjustable weight. Other types have a small telescopic antenna with adjustable length and bearing capacity. Spheres, made of glass or plastics, can be weighted as desired (filled with water) and are used for diverse fishing methods. Colourless glass spheres resemble air bubbles, and are ideal for catching the most wary fish, for example silver salmon or chub.

When fishing on the bottom without a float, many different bite detectors are used for signalling a take. These are attached to the line behind the tip of the rod, between the rod rings, or occasionally away from the rod, directly on the ground.

The bite detector must signal clearly the pluck of a taking fish, but without disturbing effect. During night fishing a strip of aluminium foil attached to the line works well as a bite detector. Various bell constructions are used for night eel fishing. Of the

28

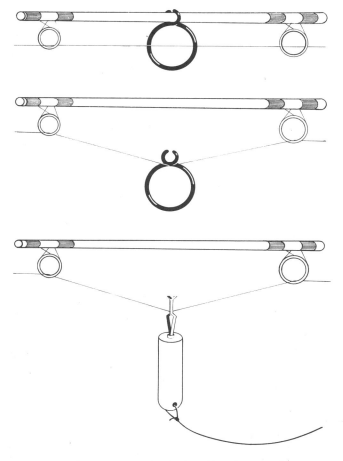

Basic types of bite detector, attached to either the rod or line.

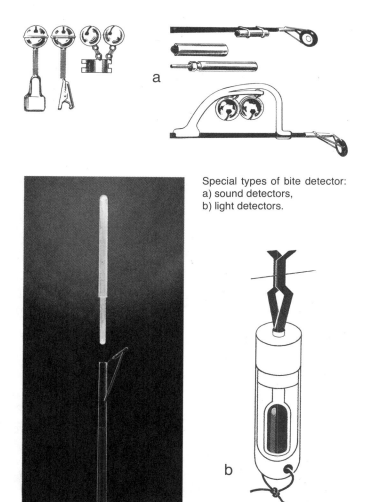

Special types of bite detector:
a) sound detectors,
b) light detectors.

technically more sophisticated acoustic-luminous bite detectors, those set up away from the rod are more practical.

WEIGHTS

In many fishing methods a weight is a necessary component of fishing tackle, generally taking the form of different shaped pieces of lead. The weight essentially fulfils three functions: it assists in casting what are usually light lures to the required distance, provides appropriate weight to the lure, accelerates its sinking into the water and holds the lure at the chosen position, which is essential, especially in swift waters.

When assembling tackle for catching smaller white fish, the most effective weights are small spherical pieces of zinc or drupe-shaped weights with a groove for attaching them to the line. In heavier tackle assemblies for fishing on the bottom, more solid zinc weights are used, usually with a central hole through which the line runs. The most suitable types of zinc weight seem to be those which can be attached to the line from the side, mounted with

the aid of a pin so as to be either fixed or sliding.

The attachment of the zinc weights can lead to damage and weakening of the line. One should therefore try to attach the weights with great care. The best weight is that which can simply be pressed on to the line with the fingers. Pliers are needed for harder weights.

The shape of the weight must be suited both to conditions and to the fishing method. When fishing in still waters with a harder bed, round or drupe-shaped ones are suitable, the weight of the zinc being determined by the required casting length only. In excessively muddy waters one should use a type which will not get stuck easily in the mud. When fishing on the river-bed in swift currents, spherical weights are not stable enough, so flat ones should be selected, perhaps with a small anchor. The weight of the zinc is in this case mainly determined by the strength of the current, rather than by the required casting length. When fishing with floated lures on the bottom in swift waters, a more oval-shaped

29

weight is suitable, for example pear-shaped. More unusually shaped weights are occasionally used when spinning. Their job is to prevent line-fouling, to lengthen the cast and to facilitate drawing in the deeper part of a water course. When fishing salmon-type fish by drawing the bait, head weights are attached to the fish bait to expedite fishing near the bottom, even in strong currents.

In many cases a zinc weight may be substituted, for example, with plasticine, harder clay, a piece of ice, etc.

For reliable reconnaissance of the bottom before fishing in an unfamiliar place, various types of plummet (plum line) are used.

Sliding weights for fishing both in still and flowing waters.

Special types of weight: sheet, wire, weights with clips, caps.

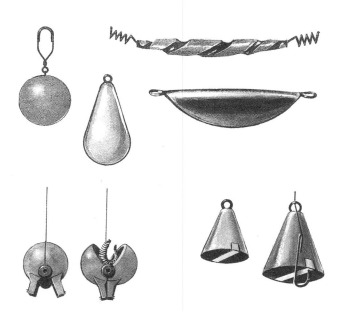

Weights for ascertaining the depth and profile of the bottom.

TACKLE ACCESSORIES

Swivels prevent line-fouling, and are therefore indispensable above all for sinking and drawing, although they may also be useful in other fishing methods, since they permit the use of more alternatives when assembling the tackle. The classic swivel has both eyes closed and can be mounted only by means of knots, which is a disadvantage in the case of steel wires. More practical, therefore, are swivels

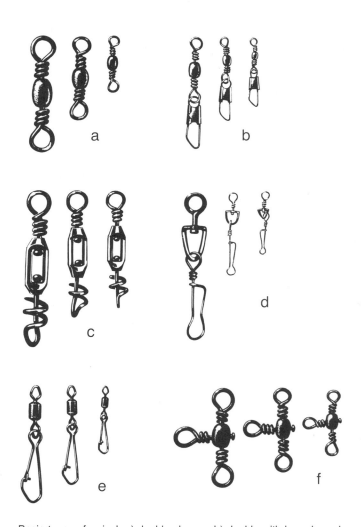

Basic types of swivel: a) double closure, b) double with lyre-shaped hinge, c) double with spiral hinge, d) pin-type, e) double with loop closure, f) triple closure.

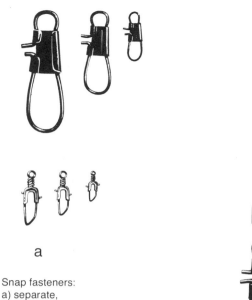

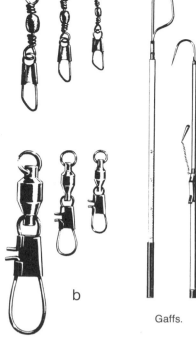

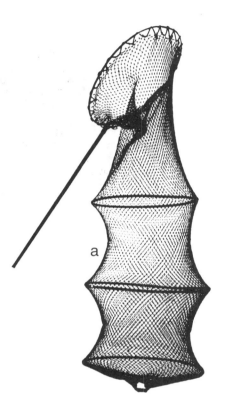

Snap fasteners:
a) separate,
b) combined with swivel.

a

b

Gaffs.

Nets for keeping live catches:
a) of fibre, b) of wire.

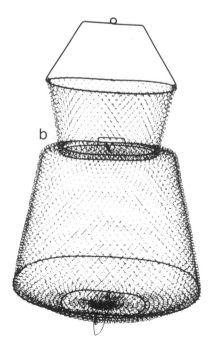

a

b

with one or two looped eyes and the type combined with a snap hook. In some fishing methods three-way swivels are used.

For fishing larger quarries which cannot be lifted out of the water with the rod alone, landing-nets and gaffs serve the purpose. Fly-fishermen use a special smaller fly-fishing landing-net with a small handle, whilst in other fishing methods a more substantial net is suitable, with a longer, ideally telescopic handle. Trophy catfish, however, cannot be caught without an appropriately strong gaff. Other tackle accessories are presented in the illustrations.

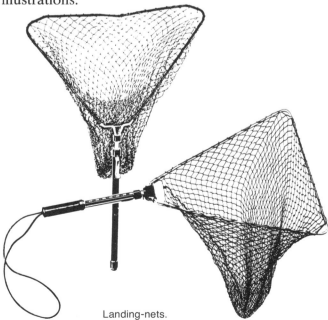

Landing-nets.

a

b

c

Containers for keeping live fish-baits: a) simple, b) with removable inner part, c) small aerating device.

a

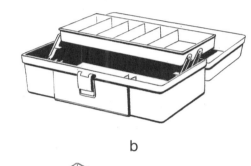

b

c

Boxes for fishing accessories: a) for storing artificial flies, b, c) suitcase-types.

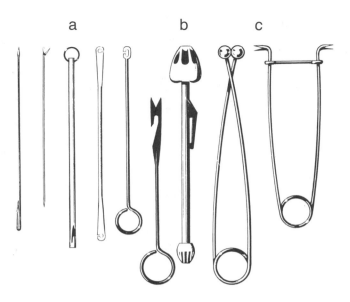

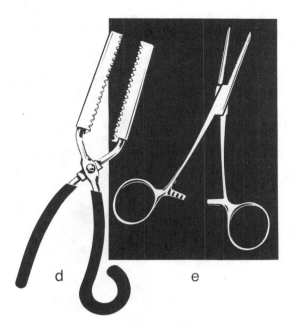

Auxiliary fishing accessories: a) sewing needles, b) hook removers, c) braces, d) small pliers, e) clamp.

Lures

When feeding, fish orient themselves by means of sight, smell and taste, as well as with the lateral line. Non-predatory fish use mainly the senses of taste and smell, which enable them to ascertain the suitability and quality of the food before swallowing it. Predatory fish react to their prey mainly by sight and also partly by means of the lateral line. They overcome the prospective morsel by attacking it, ascertaining its quality only later when tasting it. When catching non-predatory fish, therefore, only natural baits are used, whilst when catching predatory fish artificial lures may be used in addition to natural bait.

NATURAL BAITS

Natural baits may be divided according to their origins into two groups — animal and plant baits.

Baits of animal origin

The natural diet of the overwhelming majority of fish is of animal origin, so it is not surprising that animal baits are for them the tastiest morsels. This applies particularly to the larvae of water insects, which are the basic component of the fish diet.

The most accessible and effective bait are earthworms. Their effectiveness lies not only in their nutritional value and attractive appearance to fish, but also in the fact that they are found in water quite frequently as an occasional natural food, for example when there is rushing water, from underwashed banks and so on. The prime consumers of this meaty delicacy are the tench and the carp, although eel and barbel are often attracted to it as well.

Earthworms are relatively easy to obtain, although anyone who wants to use them for catching throughout the whole year is advised to prepare an adequate supply at the beginning of the summer. They can easily be collected at night after warm summer rains, when they come out of their holes, but they must not be startled either by noise or intense light. Earthworms can be found in every type of soil, although they are most abundant in well fertilised, cultivated soils in gardens and parks, on meadows, in rows of trees and so on. In dry weather, collecting can be facilitated by copious watering of vegetable or flower garden or a lawn. If necessary, it can also be facilitated by digging the garden, although with a pitch-fork rather than a spade, as a spade would damage the worms. Sometimes a thick stake can be driven into the ground and moved rapidly from side to side. The earthworms react to these vibrations by crawling out of their holes in panic, assuming that a mole is hunting in their vicinity. The catching of earthworms by means of detergents and other chemical preparations should be condemned as vigorously as possible, on account of its damaging effects on the environment.

The collected earthworms need to be stored carefully to ensure that they remain in good condition until the end of the season. The living organisms must be able to breathe and feed. They are stored in airy, spacious containers made of wood or porous earthenware, and placed in a cool, dark and sufficiently damp place, for example a cellar. An airy substrate (a combination of garden soil with compost, moss and sand) should be placed in the container, and the earthworms are placed on the surface of the substrate. From time to time the earthworms may be given supplementary food consisting of various kitchen leftovers, such as boiled vegetables, potatoes, crumbs and coffee dregs. The container is covered with openweave, moistened sacking.

On fishing trips the required quantity of earthworms should likewise be carried in an airy container, for example in linen bags, plastic containers with holes, or in a small glass jar, never in polyethylene bag. Fresh grass and moss should be put into the bag so as to maintain a damp environment. When at the water the earthworms should be protected from direct sunlight and drying out by the wind.

Among the commonest animal baits are worms living in manure — dung worms. These live practically everywhere a substantial pile of organic material is rotting in sufficiently warm and damp conditions. Collection is simple: the layers of rotting substrate are turned over with a fork and the dung

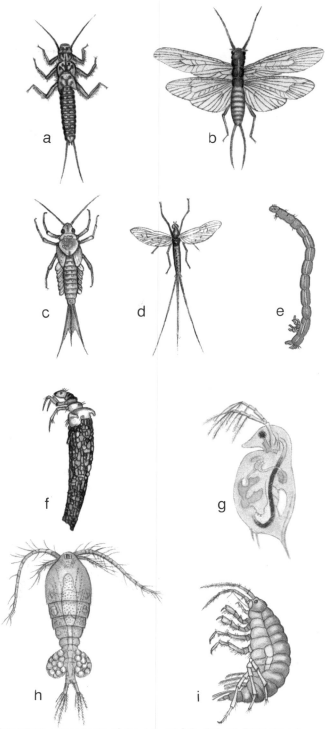

Important components of the natural fish diet: a) *Plecoptera* larva, b) *Plecoptera*, c) mayfly larva, d) mayfly, e) *Chironomidae* larva, f) bankbait larva, g) water flea (*Daphnia*), h) water flea (*Cyclops*), i) water flea (*Gammarus*).

tive baits are bone larvae. All that is needed to 'produce' them is a leftover piece of meat, on which grey flesh-flies obligingly lay their eggs. The larvae which hatch from these live on the meat and reach up to 1.5cm ($\frac{1}{2}$in) in length. Of course one can only take the liberty of breeding bone larvae in a remote corner of a largish garden in a suburban or rural area; it is not advisable to try this on the balcony of a block of flats. A valuable substitute for bone larvae are the larvae of the flour-beetle. These can be bred in leftover flour or bran, and breeding them does not involve so many hygienic issues as the breeding of bone larvae. Also, unlike bone larvae, breeding flour-beetle larvae is not limited by seasonal factors.

The most universal baits, used where all others fail, are the larvae of amphibious insects, the everyday diet of the majority of fish. The larvae of Chironomidae are excellent for catching carp-bream, roach, vimba bream, broad-snout, rudd, and so on, mainly at the end of the season, when the fish will make do even with smaller morsels. Barbel, carp and tench can also be caught regularly with this bait. When catching larger lowland fishes, the meatier mayfly larvae, particularly preferred by catfish, sturgeon and barbel, can be used. In flowing sub-mountain waters, any fish will readily bite bank-bait larvae. Collecting these larvae is not difficult. Mayfly larvae are easily collected in muddy river deposits, or in clay banks just above the waterline. Chironomidae larvae are caught in a mosquito-net fixed in a frame. Two to three spadefuls of muddy substrate are placed over it, the fine mud being gently washed off by the water flowing through it, the larger pieces together with the larvae being tipped into a container with water. From there the larvae are taken out with a strainer. Bank-bait larvae should be sought in shallow flowing water among stones. These baits, however, can only be kept for a limited period, so that one cannot make large stores of them. For a short period they are better kept in moistened moss rather than in water.

A wide range of dry land insects and their instars are also included in the category of baits of animal origin, for example wasp larvae, worms living beneath tree bark, grasshoppers, locusts, crickets, may-chafers, flies, horseflies, etc. The mole-cricket ranks as a special bait for catching catfish and bar-

worms picked out. Even simpler is to take parts of the substrate into a sieve and expose it to the sun. The dug worms try to conceal themselves from the sun, crawl down and fall through the sieve into a container placed below, into which some moistened moss has been placed. Among the most effec-

bel, while for catfish the horse-leech may also be used. Smallish land vertebrates (plucked birds, mice) may also be used as bait and poultry giblets can be put to excellent use in season (chiefly for chub), as well as pieces of liver and spleen. Various types of cheese (for catching barbel), home-made soap (for catfish), fillets of fish meat, etc., may also be included in this group of bait types.

We conclude this account of the selection of baits of animal origin with a paragraph specifically concerned with fish bait, the most important and effective of all the animal baits. The choice of fish bait is varied. One can consider using all species to which no stipulated catching length applies, but in case of other species the stipulated length must be respected. There are some general rules that apply when selecting which fish bait is suitable for catching which predators. One of these rules recommends giving preference to those species of fish which commonly occur where the predator is to be found. In general one can proceed on the basis of logical considerations, that for example when fishing for chub and perch, small fish from 3—4cm ($1\frac{1}{4}$—$1\frac{1}{2}$in) in length should be chosen, that is sunbleak, bitterling, gudgeon and loach. For catching silver-salmon, pikeperch, eel and burbot, 5—8cm (2—3in) long fish bait should be used. Pike will go for larger bait, so that one can regard 15—20cm (6—8in) long fish as normal. For a trophy catfish, we can even set out with a bait which would be more suitable for the frying pan rather than the hook. If one assumes the presence of large predators, one should not hesitate to use 25 to 30cm (10—12in) long fish as bait. One should bear in mind, however, that a predator will seek out the quarry which it can overcome most easily, so it is better to use a relatively slender fish as bait.

Obtaining fish bait is not usually a problem, either in summer or at the beginning of autumn; it is relatively easy to attract them to the rod and line or to the dip-net with suitable luring. An angler with some skill is able to catch them just before fishing for predators. However, he may make a store of them, although this gives him the problem of temporarily storing and transporting them, which in warmer seasons requires ventilation or changing water. A different situation occurs, however, in late autumn, when in fact the true fish predator season begins. At that time small fish gradually withdraw

into inaccessible depths, so one cannot manage without adequate supplies prepared beforehand. The fisherman should not overestimate his needs, however, and build up excessive reserves. The successful long-term keeping of small fish requires a sufficiently spacious area. There is a danger that the fish will suffocate if too many of them are stored in one place. The selection of fish should also be guided by how well they withstand keeping. Alburn and chub, for example, although ideal for catching predators, are better if they are not caught and stored on account of their sensitivity to storage. It is better to concentrate on hardier species, such as roach and rudd, and also goby. Most resilient to the rigours of storage, however, are German carp and tench.

Plant baits

The best animal baits are considered to be those which form part of the natural diet of the fish. This rule, with only a few exceptions, does not of course apply to plant baits. After all no fish ever encounters anything resembling boiled potato or corn groats under natural circumstances. If the angler wants to be successful in catching with plant bait, therefore, he should not leave it to chance and should familiarise the fish with the new type of food by luring beforehand. Correct methods of luring will be dealt with in a separate chapter.

The choice of plant baits is virtually endless, and obtaining them is even easier than with animal baits. In the worst case, a piece of bread can always be found — a small ball can be made of the crumb, the crust can be used as it is. There is nothing exotic among the most commonly used baits, which include corn, potatoes, bread, dough and so on.

The advantage of corn lies in the fact that it holds well on the hook, has an attractive appearance and smell and is easily obtainable. Fresh corn is ideal, although it can also be used boiled (soft, but not so that it will disinterate), processed, silaged and frozen. Corn grains may be mounted on the hook in various ways. It is equally effective to mount 1—2 grains on a largish hook, or 3—4 grains on a smaller hook, completely covering it. A larger hook, even if it is visible, ensures more successful hooking, whilst too small a hook can ruin hooking opportunities.

Potatoes should only ever be used boiled. Using a special knife, small balls can be cut out of them, or they can be cut into cubes, smaller potatoes being used whole as a lure. It is always better to under-cook potatoes a little rather than overcook them. Pieces of potato may simply be stuck on a single hook in such a way that the point and part of the shank is concealed in the potato. When casting further off is required, it is better to stick the potato on-to a smaller double or triple hook using a fisher-man's needle, so that it holds securely.

Bread and pastry are usually used only in an emergency if there is nothing else to hand. Many fishermen nevertheless use bread by choice; and it is true that for some fishing techniques bread and pas-try may be the ideal bait, for example when fishing for carp on the surface, or when fishing in excep-tionally muddy waters or in which the bottom is overgrown. The majority of other baits would sink with the weight deep into the mud during fishing, and thus disappear from the fishes' field of visibility. It is advisable to take a piece of bread from the crumb and squeeze only a part of it so that it will hold on the hook, leaving the edges hanging loose. This kind of bait will stay on the bottom and attract the attention of fish.

Dough and dumplings are prepared from both basic and supplementary ingredients. Among the former, one can include common kitchen types of flour, cornflour, fine barley groats, semolina, potato flour (which may be substituted with mashed pota-toes), and so on. Supplementary ingredients are chosen to improve the consistency of the dough, to emphasize its flavour characteristics and its colour. These may be eggs, honey, flax, hemp, processed cheese, colourings, crushed garlic, ground caraway and various aromatic additives.

Dough can be prepared in various ways. The ba-sic ingredients can be boiled until they reach the re-quired consistency and the supplementary ingredi-ents added after cooling, when everything is thor-oughly mixed together. The consistency of the dough may be adjusted by adding flour or water. Another way is first to mix together all the basic and supplementary ingredients and then to boil the sub-stance produced in the form of larger or smaller dumplings. Some doughs have a suitable consisten-cy in their raw state and do not need cooking at all.

From the large number of recipes for preparing dough, the following one is very effective in spite of being so simple: 200g (7oz) fine corn groats, 50g (2oz) flour, 2 dessert-spoons of corn or potato starch and 1 dessert-spoon of sugar, all thoroughly mixed together dry, and gradually poured into boil-ing water, stirring constantly. There should be just enough water to make the mixture sufficiently malleable, and it should be boiled only for a short time. After cooling the dough should be kneaded thoroughly. The corn groats provide the mixture with a conspicuous colour, so there is no need to colour it. It has a pleasant aroma, although adding a little honey to it will certainly do no harm. It holds superbly on the rod and line, and when fishing with a feed-trough it should be mixed with corn groats to a ratio of 1 : 1.

Manufactured pastas — spaghetti, macaroni, canelloni, etc. — should be used cooked for fishing. Peas are used quite frequently as bait, as well as beans (preferably white), kidney beans, soya, pearl barley and so on.

An enumeration of the most important plant baits would not be complete without mentioning some types of fruit. Cherries, morello cherries, plums, strawberries and so on are mainly suitable for catching chub. The fruit should be ripe, and as far as possible have a strong colour. Drupe fruits should be used whole as bait, including the stone and occasionally even with the stalk. When catching with soft fruit, hooking should not be delayed, whilst when using harder fruit one should wait a while until the chub has crushed it.

Grass carp may be caught with all the usual baits, but if one wants to specialise in catching grass carp, one should use green plants, lettuce leaves, boiled carrots, etc.

ARTIFICIAL LURES

Depending on the method of execution and the function intended, the wide range of artificial lures can be divided into two basic groups: artificial flies and artificial lures for spinning.

Artificial flies

By using artificial flies the fisherman imitates some important elements in the natural fish diet. These include predominantly imitations of amphibious

Dry flies commonly used for trout and grayling fishing.

and to some extent also dry land insects, and not only the adult individuals, but also individual life stages. The latter depend on the developmental characteristics of each insect species. In the case of insects with complete metamorphosis, the developmental cycle proceeds from the egg stage through larvae and pupae to the adult individual (imago). In insects with incomplete metamorphosis, which includes most amphibious insects, the larvae hatch from the eggs. These are similar in their basic characteristics to the imago and are known as nymphs. The nymph lives in water for varying lengths of time; in some species even for 3—4 years, gradually growing larger — it grows and sheds its epidermis from time to time. During this process it becomes more and more like the imago stage. The final shedding takes place on dry land, when the subimago changes into the adult insect.

Insects of all developmental stages constitute in practice the most important element in the diet of fish. Classic artificial flies should therefore imitate as closely as possible some of the development stages of specific insect species, and their function during fishing is based on the principle of perfect mimicry. The fisherman proceeds from the fact that fish on the bottom or very near the bottom feed on larvae or nymphs and pupae, in the water column or very near the surface they feed on hatching insects, and on the surface they feed on imagos which are either hatching or mating.

Depending on the fishing method, artificial flies can be divided into two basic groups: dry flies for fishing on the surface and wet flies for fishing in various water column profiles.

A dry fly imitates the living insect either by hovering freely on the surface or alighting on the

Wet flies used for trout and grayling fishing.

Nymph and standard streamer for trout and grayling fishing.

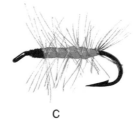

a   b   c

Basic types of artificial fly: a) hackless, b) wet fly, c) Palmer spider, d) dry fly.

d

surface. Its execution should be carried out as faithfully as possible, in terms of colour, size and body contours. It must be as light as possible and is therefore attached to a smallish, fine hook, sometimes with the eye bent upwards. It should give a slender, fine impression and be made of water-resistant material. During fishing the fly should be dried out between castings and greased occasionally so that it does not sink.

A wet fly imitates an insect drawn downwards into various profiles of the water column; the depth to which it sinks depends on which developmental stage of the insect it represents. Imitation imagos will logically be more successful in the upper layers of water, nymphs being used to fish at greater depths and on the bottom. A more substantial wet fly is usually made by tying absorbent material, and has narrower small wings which are continuous with

the body. It can also be attached to a double hook, and some types are weighted.

Artificial flies, both wet and dry, predominantly imitate those insect species which form the main part of the natural fish diet. These are chiefly mayflies, caddis flies, stone flies, Chironomidae, Simuliidae and Tipulidae. There are also inexhaustible possibilities for imitating land insects, mainly in places where the insects reach the water by natural means and the fishes are accustomed to them, for example grasshoppers in meadow streams and ants in woodland brooks.

Depending on their method of execution, dry flies may be either winged (with erect wings), wingless, or hairy — e.g. spiders (which likewise have no wings and are covered with hair all over the body). Wet flies are divided according to their construction into winged (imitating dead insects) and nymphs

Special flies imitating alevins.

Special streamers.

Fly twister.

42

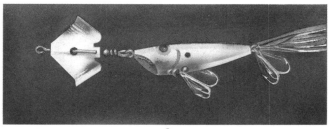

a

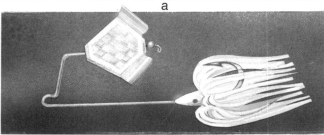

b

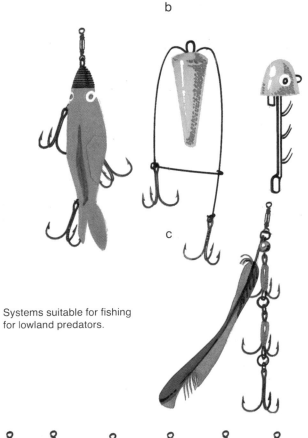

c

Systems suitable for fishing
for lowland predators.

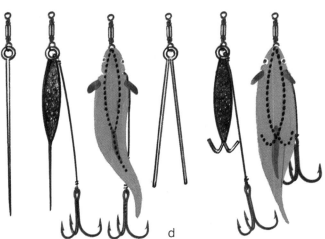

d

(imitating the initial developmental stages of insects). Sometimes streamers and bugs are ranked among wet flies, although they are not flies in the strict sense of the word. A streamer looks like a large artificial fly, although its task in the water is to imitate small fish. Bugs are of the same construction, but are manufactured of animal hair.

So-called fantastic flies form a special group, having no model in nature and being intended to provoke a fish to bite by means of their conspicuous colour, shape or a part of the body.

Flies may also be classified according to the species of fish which they are being used to catch, e.g. trout flies, grayling flies, salmon flies, silver-salmon flies, etc.

Artificial lures for spinning

Included in this rich and diverse group are lures which imitate the movements of the usual quarry of predatory fish. They imitate small fish, as well as some other types of animal (for example mice), which may be an occasional quarry of the predator. During sink and draw fishing the predator perceives the lure by sight (shape, colour), as well as with the senses of the lateral line (wave formation of the wa-

Tried and tested types of standard classic spoons.

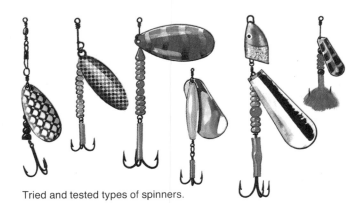

Tried and tested types of spinners.

Classic Devon
minnow spoon.

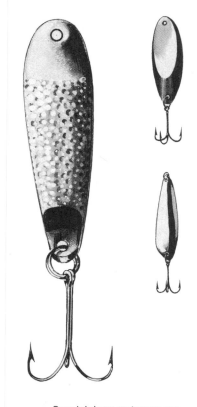

Special deep-water spoons.

ter, or the unusual sound effects of certain types of lure).

Artificial lures for spinning fishing form the richest assortment among fishing tackle, and there are no universally acknowledged criteria for their classification. Attempts to classify them into categories for catching individual groups of predatory fish are not particularly convincing, since it is not so much the type as the size of the lure which determines the catch. A more sensible classification of lures would seem to be based on their functional characteristics as follows:

— classic spinners, for which a rising and falling motion is typical during sink and draw. Their shapes may vary;

— rotating spinners, based on the principle of the rotation of the spinner itself on an axis which culminates in the hook. Devon minnows can also be classified in this group;

— wobblers made of wood or plastic, both floating and sinking, with one or more parts;

— special depth spinners and spinners for vertical sink and draw — pilkers and 'marmishkas'.

Many of these lures may be characterised as universal, suitable for all types of water, both deep and shallow, still and flowing, as well as for catching all species of predatory fish. In this group belong, for example, the majority of classic spinners, headed by the so far unsurpassed Heintz, as well as most rotating spinners. The colour of the lure should nevertheless be chosen carefully according to the character of the water. In clean, clear water, less conspicuous,

44

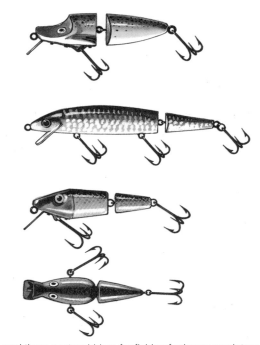

Two- and three-part wobblers for fishing for larger predators.

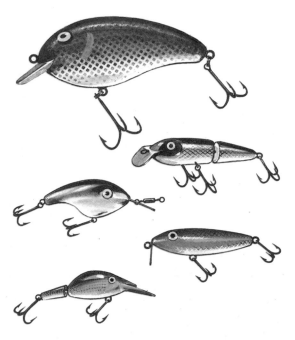

Floating wobblers which can be set for various depths.

matt colours are more suitable, whilst in cloudy water preference should be given to lighter and more conspicuous ones. Excessively shiny lures, however, tend to frighten off rather than attract even courageous predators.

The abundance of artificial lures and the advertising hype of manufacturers may confuse rather than guide the less experienced sporting fisherman. The choice of a lure should be based on its function during fishing, that is, when sinking and drawing. Predatory fishes cannot afford the luxury of choosing their prey according to which species they belong to. The sole criterion for them is its accessibility in terms of size and its attainability. An instinctive hunting method is typical for predators, in which there is little time for deliberation. An indecisive predator would probably die of hunger sooner or later. The purpose of the artificial lure, therefore, is to arouse the interest of the predator and provoke

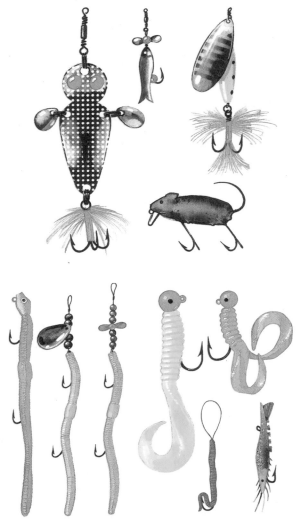

In waters spoiled by frequent sinking and drawing, less common types of lure can be successful.

45

it into attack. This is better accomplished by means of the correct movement of the lure during sink and draw and by its colour than by the finer details of its construction.

ESSENTIAL INFORMATION ON BAITS AND LURING

Within the context of sport fishing, the methods of luring fish have recently undergone considerable development. A decisive contribution to this progress has been made by competition sport fishing. The record catches of competitors — as many as several hundred fish per hour — although partly due to the success of individual fishing techniques, can largely be attributed to successful luring.

When luring, the angler must proceed from the knowledge that fish have substantially more effective senses of taste and smell than sight. Short-sighted fish can only see a morsel which is situated in the immediate vicinity, whilst on the other hand by means of taste and smell cells, situated both on the head and along the whole body, they are able to react with exceptional sensitivity to even the smallest concentration of aromatic substances. We do not, therefore, have to trouble ourselves too much with the colour of the lure, but must be all the more concerned to present the fish with the tastiest possible morsel.

Luring essentially serves two purposes. It should attract fish to the place which best suits us for catching, and gradually accustom the fish to food which they do not usually encounter and which we intend to use as bait. Of course it would be ideal to lure directly with what one intends to catch with. However we cannot afford to lure only with dung worms or bone worms and so on, because there are never so many at our disposal. One must therefore try to compromise. One should not spoil the fishes too much, instead using more accessible types of bait for luring, but if one has the chance one should add to these a pinch of the bait with which one intends to catch. This is not regarded as a condition for successful catching, however, but is simply a matter of arousing the interest of fish from a wider area and attracting them to the chosen place. The assortment

of lures may be regarded as identical with the assortment of baits, so the possibilities for luring are practically inexhaustible. If necessary one can even rely on just breadcrumbs, especially when one has a chance to add to them a sample of the bait, for example pieces of earthworms, bone worms, or larvae. It is quite common, however, to use a bait consisting of several items, the basic items being breadcrumbs, cornflour, crushed hempseeds, wheat, rye, soya or rice flour, mashed potatoes or potato flour. Most of these items should be used raw, with due care given only to sufficient fineness. Only the crushed hempseeds should be boiled, in order to emphasise their aroma. Depending on the circumstances, one can even add to the bait some items which fish do not consume. Earth may, for example, serve the purpose of a weight, the opposite function being served by an admixture of cork sawdust. Grated chalk enhances the effect of luring by clouding the water.

The assortment of basic bait items may be extended to include, for example, dried or fresh blood (excellent for catching tench and catfish), meatbone flour, germinated wheat (especially for catching German carp), silaged corn, ground peanuts or other oil-plant fruits, dried milk, horny tissue, fish flour, brewer's yeast, and so on.

We should mention here aromatic additives to baits. The most tried and tested ones include vanilla, aniseed, honey, rose oil, and extracts from fish and other aquatic animals. More adventurous fishermen even experiment with garlic paste, saffron, musk, Peruvian balsam, caraway decoction, and so on.

The effectiveness of industrially manufactured feed mixtures, which are becoming more and more specialised for both individual fish species and catching methods, in practice falls short of the advertised promises. Obviously they are not bad, but they certainly do not achieve miraculous results.

The composition of the bait must be suited to the fish species one intends to catch. If one is setting out for fishes which gather food from the surface layers of the water or in the water column, one needs a bait which will remain for as long as possible in the required water profile. This means that preference should be given to items which will float easily. One of the basic recipes for luring surface fishes recommends a mixture of 50% cornflour, 30% bread-crumbs, 10% ground hempseeds and 10% soil sieved as finely as possible. For fishes which gather food from the lower water layers, 30% each of breadcrumbs, cornflour and hempseeds, made up again with 10% earth, is recommended. For fishes which stay mainly at the bottom, breadcrumbs may constitute up to 70% of the mixture, cornflour 20% and earth 10%.

Here are several recipes for well-tried baits. For catching roach, rudd, German carp and other white fish:

— Mix 1 egg, 1 crushed clove of garlic, 1 teaspoon-ful of honey, 2 parts wheat and 1 part potato flour, with the minimum amount of water.

— Mix 1 part cornflour or semolina, 1 part water, 1 spoonful fat, 1 spoonful sugar, ½ spoonful vanilla sugar. For luring in darker water, add saffron colouring.

— Peel yellow-fleshed baked potatoes and knead while hot, adding potato flour and egg yolk.

— Moisten gingerbread and knead, adding a little honey.

Doughs are recommended for luring carp-bream. For example:

— Bring to the boil 3 litres (5¼ pints) water, ½ sachet of yellow edible dye, a small piece of vanilla and a few drops of aniseed oil. Add 1.5l (2½ pints) fine white breadcrumbs, 0.5l (18fl.oz.) fine corn-flour and 0.2l (7fl.oz.) dried milk. Boil for about 1 minute, stir, cover so as to make airtight and leave to cool. Luring should be carried out mainly in the early evening.

For catching tench:

— Boil 3 parts wheatflour, 1 part cornflour and 1 dessert-spoon sugar. When boiling, add a little fresh blood, for example from poultry.

— Stir without boiling 1 part mashed potatoes and 1 part wheatflour, peas, a little sugar and honey.

Although carp prefer corn, they will not decline other delicacies:

— Mix together in hot water corn groats, icing sugar and a pinch of saffron.

— Mix freshly soaked gingerbread with honey, add Peruvian balsam to taste and knead thoroughly.

Consistency is an important factor, as one must ensure that the bait will reach the required place safely and stay there as long as possible. The angler therefore moistens the bait only lightly when luring on the surface, just enough so that not too cohesive balls may be formed which will easily disperse on impact with the surface of the water. The deeper down the bait is required to disperse, the more cohesive it must be. If it is to sink as far as the bottom and dissolve slowly, the fisherman must moisten it generously, so that he can knead a thoroughly cohesive ball from it. Similar princi-

Ways of luring fish: a) those that keep near the surface, b) those that keep in the water column, c) those that keep to the bottom.

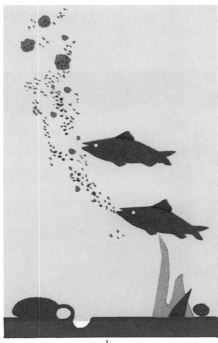

a   b   c

47

Common type of feeding-trough and method of mounting.

Using a suitable type of feeding-trough, it is also possible to fish in flowing waters.

When using a heavier feeding-trough, a weight can be omitted. A rubber ring between the feeding-trough and the stopper softens impact when casting.

ples must also be observed with regard to the swiftness of the current. The swifter the current, the more one should increase the proportion of weight, that is, earth. The actual technique of luring is simple, and mostly one should be able to manage by casting the lure by hand. Sometimes, of course, it is necessary to cast bait over a greater distance. From a whole range of technical aids, a simple sling may be regarded as one of the most tried and tested ones. One should not set limits, however, on technical inventiveness: small balloons, etc. may also be used.

One of the most popular recent developments in luring are feeding troughs, which have spread like wildfire in the fishing world. Every sword, however, is double-edged, and feeding troughs also have their drawbacks as well as their incontestable advantages. It is certainly a matter of taste, but many are of the opinion that the mass use of feeding troughs is a retrograde step in fishing. This specifically refers to the undesired effect that, with the aid of feeding troughs, the fisherman intentionally drives the fish away from the shore. Therefore anyone who does not want to submit to this latest trend cannot compete in many waters. Fishing rod manufacturers are undoubtedly those most pleased about feeding troughs. When fishing with a feeding trough, lighter rods in general are unsuitable, so there is likely to be a boom in heavier, stronger rods.

Much bad feeling within the fishing fraternity can be caused by the richness of a lure. I myself have

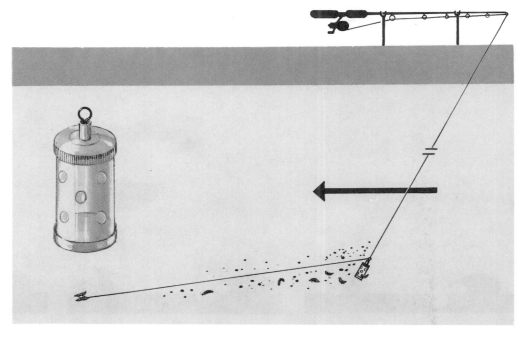

been a target of criticism several times from other fishermen when, after finishing a catch, I threw the remains of both baits and lures into the water. We would all certainly agree that it is necessary to lure in moderation, so as to tempt the fish and attract them to the required location, but not so much as to feed them. However, it is a question of defining the term 'in moderation'. Depending on the given conditions, the fish stocks in the water, the taste of the fishes and so on, sometimes only a few grammes of feed can be too much, whereas at other times one can throw half a sackful of bait into the water and the fish will still be searching for more. The richness of the lure is determined not only by the need to attract fish from a wide area to the required place, but also by the need to keep them there throughout the whole catch. The fisherman can of course only achieve this by retaining their attention with a constantly renewed supply of delicacies. Before actually beginning the catch, one should lure more abundantly; the first batch of bait may consist of three to four balls the size of a fist. After ascertaining that the fish are reacting to the bait, the angler reduces the batches to small balls the size of a pigeon's egg or even smaller, but throwing these at shorter intervals. We will address some of the more unusual methods for luring fish later in the accounts of how to catch specific fish species.

How to catch fish

In order to be really thorough, we would have to present in the introduction to this chapter at least the most essential information on the feeding habits of individual fish groups. We would learn which food is preferred by which fish, its requirements regarding the size of a morsel, which sensory organs it uses to orient itself when obtaining food, how it reacts to colour shades and scents, whether it obtains food actively or passively, what is its feeding rhythm depending on the time of day and season of the year, etc. Limitation of space, however, unfortunately does not permit us to deal with these basic issues in detail, so we shall limit ourselves to the most essential points in the course of dealing with other, more complex issues.

The foundation of success in sport fishing lies in the art of adapting oneself to the habits and needs of the fish. This determines selection of the most effective fishing method, the choice of the most suitable lures, and the use of the most suitable method for presenting them to the fish. This apparently simple approach has one drawback, however, which is that fish do not always behave according to a specific stereotype, and often have their whims. The carp may be taken as an example. Everyone knows that this fish prefers to seek food on the bottom, so that as a rule one also catches carp there. Under certain circumstances, however, the carp will begin to behave atypically, perhaps by developing an appetite for a tasty morsel on the surface. In this case the fisherman would try in vain to present it, for instance, with sponge-biscuit at the bottom, whereas it might take a dry bread crust on the surface.

In order to understand this problem area better, we need to divide fish species, depending on the nature of their nutrition, into two basic groups, the predatory and the non-predatory fishes. The difference between these two groups does not only lie in the food itself, but also in the way in which it is obtained. Predatory fishes require relatively large morsels, and when obtaining them orient themselves predominantly by sight and the sense of the lateral line (that is by some kind of 'hearing'), the other senses playing only a subsidiary role. Some predators are of course more active when obtaining food, for example the perch, silver-salmon or pike-perch; others are more passive, for example the eel. Non-predatory fishes require food in smaller morsels, and when seeking it are assisted mainly by the organs of taste and smell. Predators attack the prey instinctively without first ascertaining its quality, whereas non-predatory fish take their food with deliberation, after a thorough preliminary examination with the senses of taste and smell.

The division of fish into predatory and non-predatory categories is rather too general. If one were to take the criteria characterising predators literally, then only the hucho and the pike would qualify, these being exclusively oriented towards predatory means of obtaining food. Other predators, such as catfish, perch, trout, etc., will of course make use of every suitable opportunity for obtaining quarry by predation, but are nevertheless equally prepared to feed on small animals, thus qualifying for the category of omnivorous fishes. On the other hand, even the peace-loving carp has tendencies towards cannibalism from time to time.

From the point of view of selecting the correct fishing method, it is important to divide fishes according to how deep in the water they seek food, whether at the bottom, in the water column or at the surface. Among non-predatory fishes one may distinguish carnivorous and herbivorous ones, possibly also a group of fishes which live on the most minute planktonic organisms and a group which live on benthos, that is, the larvae of aquatic insects. In the following detailed sections on sporting fishing we have regrouped the traditional classification of fishing methods into fishing for predatory fish, non-predatory fish and salmon-type fish.

METHODS FOR CATCHING NON-PREDATORY FISH

One is able to select the most suitable method for

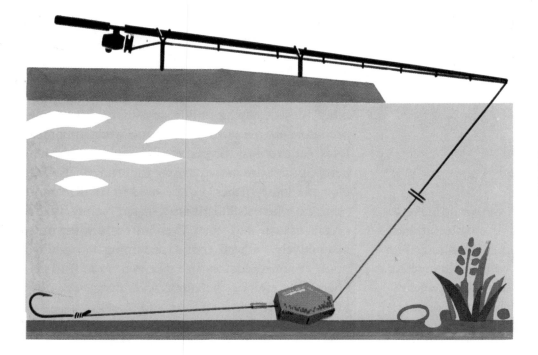

Standard rod and line assembly for fishing on the bottom. A sliding weight on the main line should be fixed with a reliable stopper.

catching various groups of non-predatory fishes on the basis of their habits, and, in particular, according to whereabouts in the water the fish stay, so that one can divide the basic fishing methods into three groups: fishing on the bottom, in the water column and on the surface.

Fishing on the bottom

In this simple fishing method, the bait, relying on its own weight or with the aid of a zinc weight, is cast to a certain place, where it remains for some time. One more or less expects the fish to find the bait of their own accord. Before swallowing the bait, however, a fish thoroughly investigates its credentials, so that in this fishing method only natural baits can be considered. Their selection must be made according to the food requirements of the fish one wants to catch.

Fishing on the bottom may be practised both in still and in flowing waters, both close to the bank and at a greater distance. The exclusion of a random occurrence, or the encouragement of one in this basically passive catching method, can only be accomplished by choosing a good vantage point and suitable luring. In some cases this method is indispensable, for example when catching barbel in a stronger current and more commonly when catching carp. It may also, however, be recommended in other cases, for example if the fish are suspicious of

a moving bait, or if one is catching at a well-stocked or otherwise hopeful position and wants the bait to remain there as long as possible; similarly when fishing in very varied terrain with a snaggy bottom, when the bait needs to be kept at the bottom.

Methods for assembling the rod and line vary depending on the conditions. Always, however, one should try to make the assembly as simple as possible, which is the guarantee of reliability. Preference should be given to lighter and therefore more sensitive assemblies. In still waters, a lure only, without a weight, may be cast to shorter distances, although a weight is of course essential when casting to a greater distance. The weight is limited only by the required casting length. For fishing in flowing waters, the weight has two functions — in addition to the casting requirements, it must also anchor the bait at the desired place. Its weight is determined by the strength of the current, as well as by the strength and length of the line being affected by the current. In the case of an assembly with a heavier weight, the stop between the weight and the hook is a particularly sensitive point; here only the most reliable stopper, for example one made of insulating tape, a swivel or a snap hook will function.

When fishing for some current-loving species, for example barbel or sturgeon, one really has only one option for assembling the rod and line — that is the

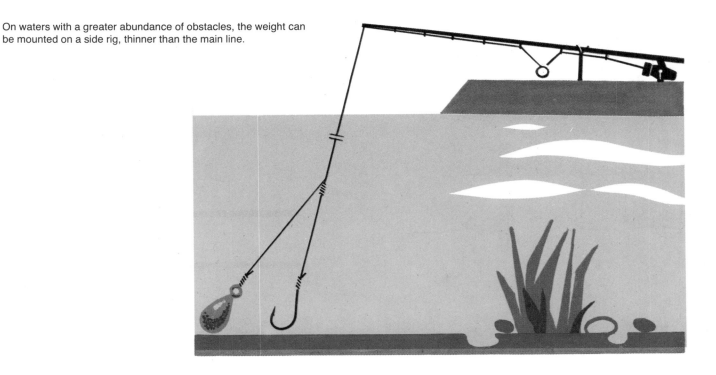

On waters with a greater abundance of obstacles, the weight can be mounted on a side rig, thinner than the main line.

classic assembly for catching on the bottom with a bite detector. One should choose as strong a rod as possible with a harder tip, so that it will not suffer from the weight of an exceptionally heavy weight. Both the hook and the weight may be directly on the main line with a sufficiently reliable stopper, or the weight may be mounted on a side rig. The former tackle should be chosen for lighter terrain, the latter where there is a danger of the rod and line being caught up in obstacles.

In flowing water, one should always cast at a slight angle to the stream. After casting, one takes the line in the fingers and observes when the lead weight takes hold on the bottom. Only then does one retrieve the line so as to obtain sensitive contact with the bait. Reliable securing of the baited rod and line, as well as the release of the reel brake, should go without saying, since if these are omitted it can have unfortunate results. One should detect the take at the tip of the rod; if technically possible,

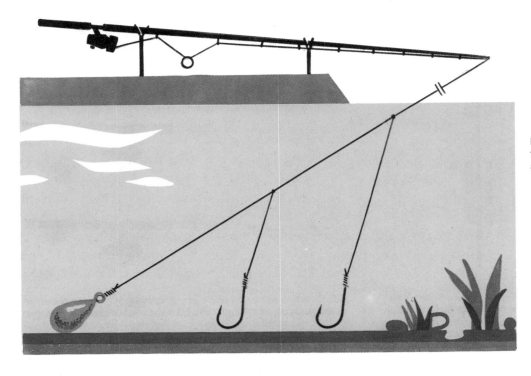

Rod and line for fishing on the bottom, assembled using two hooks and an end, fix-attached weight.

55

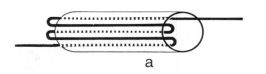

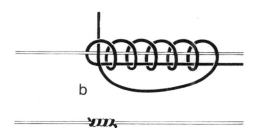

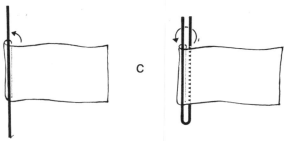

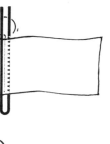

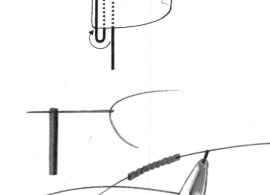

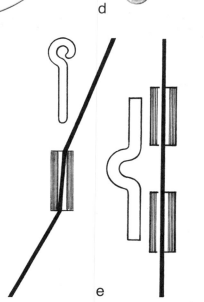

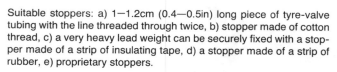

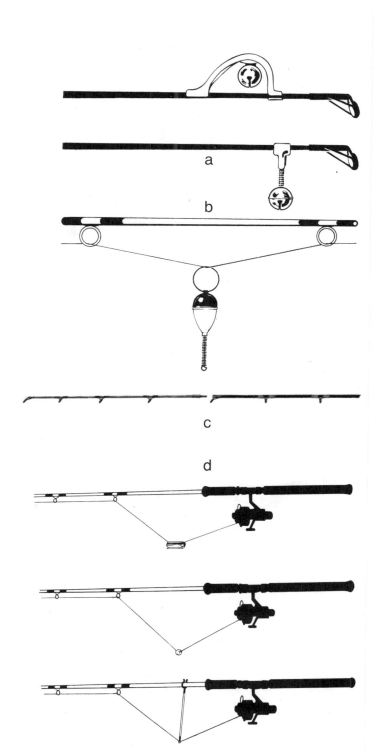

Suitable stoppers: a) 1—1.2cm (0.4—0.5in) long piece of tyre-valve tubing with the line threaded through twice, b) stopper made of cotton thread, c) a very heavy lead weight can be securely fixed with a stopper made of a strip of insulating tape, d) a stopper made of a strip of rubber, e) proprietary stoppers.

Bite detectors and methods for attaching them: a) at the tip of the rod (suitable for catching larger fish), b) on the line between the rod rings, c) detectors suitable for fishing for smaller, more sensitive fish with set tip and oscillating tip, d) emergency bite detectors (small balls of dough, small tube of aluminium foil, twig).

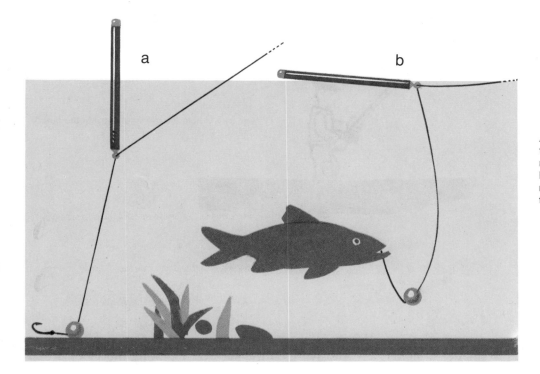

A float functioning also as a bite detector: a) when using the sinking method, the float reacts to the take by sinking, b) when using the lifting method, it reacts by emerging from the water.

the line may be equipped with a bite detector.

When fishing in still waters, one should not leave the bait on the spot after casting, so that it will not sink into soft mud. After reaching the bottom it should be slightly drawn up and the line tightened. When fishing for more sensitive species, which only signal a take in an inconspicuous way, it is necessary to use a more refined method of bite detection. This problem can be solved with an oscillating rod tip or a float. The latter in this case serves two functions —

apart from that of a signal it also prevents the line from sinking. Using a float offers several possibilities, which vary in function according to the distribution of weight.

The first is the so-called 'exposed' method, based on the fact that during the take the fish lifts part of the weight together with the bait. In this way the float becomes lighter, rises to the surface and lies flat. The bearing capacity of the float is always somewhat greater than the overall mass of the

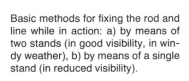

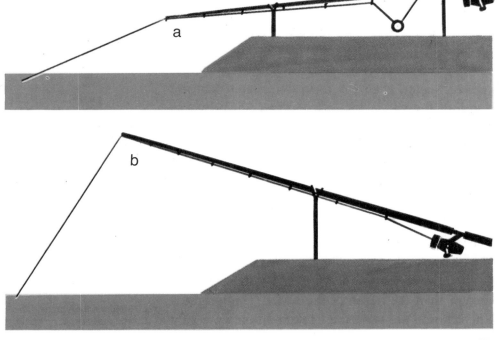

Basic methods for fixing the rod and line while in action: a) by means of two stands (in good visibility, in windy weather), b) by means of a single stand (in reduced visibility).

57

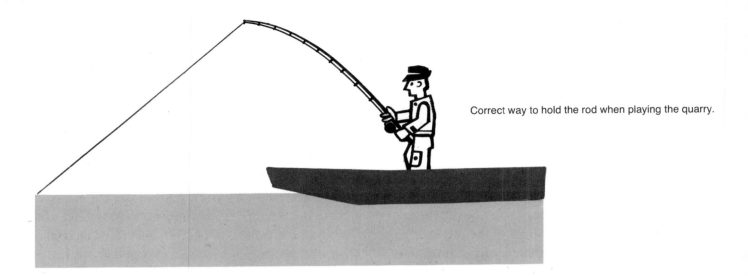

Correct way to hold the rod when playing the quarry.

weight, which consists of several smaller weights evenly distributed between the hook and the float. The bottom weight, when fishing for white fish, is attached approximately 15—20cm (6—8in) from the hook, for carp more than 50cm (20in). The submersion of the float from the top weight should be 50—80cm (20—30in) greater than the height of the water column. After casting, the fisherman gently straightens the line, so that the float can attain its normal position.

In the case of the similar, so-called 'sinking' method, the weight is somewhat heavier than the bearing capacity of the float. The main weight consists of two equal-sized weights, the mass of which is equal to the bearing capacity of the float, a third, smaller weight being placed between these two and the float and causing a partial overload of the float. The submersion of the float, measured from the central weight, is also in this case greater than the depth of the water, by up to 50cm (20in); by this distance the fisherman shifts the auxiliary weight towards the float. During the take, the bottom main weights rise, the overloaded float sinking deeper and staying submerged for the whole time that the fish is holding the bait in its mouth. The so-called 'lifting' method is very sensitive. Only one 'torpilka' (a drop-shaped weight), attached 3—5cm ($1\frac{1}{4}$—2in) above the hook, fully balances the float. The submersion of a float with a longer antenna is again greater than the depth of the water. The weight is lifted during the take, the lightened float emerging

and lying on the surface. Hooking must be carried out when the float begins to lean.

Float fishing in the water course

Whenever in doubt before fishing as to which meth-

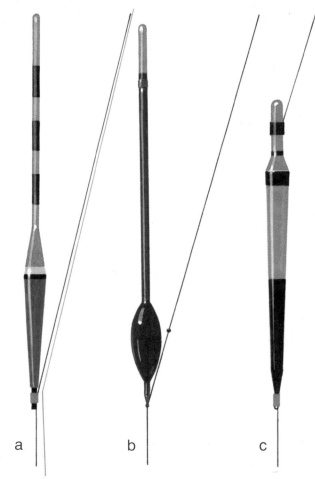

Methods for attaching the float: a) fix-attached at one point, b) sliding and attached at one point, c) fix-attached at two points.

58

od to try, I always decide on a float, and this is not only because float fishing has many effective and attractive alternatives and offers an opportunity to catch practically any fish, from a small year-old perch to a hundred kilo catfish. Apart from this, float fishing can serve as an excellent means for training the reflexes and action-readiness, and is also good experience for mastering other fishing methods.

When practising this fishing method, one should place great emphasis on suitable, fine and sensitive equipment. The minimum length of the rod is 3.5m (11½ft). Rods up to 7m (23ft) may have rings, but longer ones are better without rings, that is, simple whiprods. A standard rod equipped with a reel has its advantage in the fact that it facilitates casting to greater distances (although accompanied by an undesirable increase in weight, to the detriment of the

sensitivity of the assembly) and will give good service when playing an unexpected larger quarry, even at a greater distance. The advantages of the whiprod lie in its ideally light, simple, reliable and sensitive assembly (the weight can even be entirely omitted). This expedites light and accurate casting and reliable hooking, as well as accurate guiding of the float and bait in flowing water and also when it is windy and there are waves on the surface.

In both cases, however, one should choose rods with a harder action, enabling reliable casting and above all immediate reaction to the take. The risk of a harder rod, however, is the possible loss of a heavier quarry.

For float fishing, the fisherman should equip himself with a smaller, lighter reel with a broader spool and fine, sharp, solid hooks, and, when using plant baits, with a shorter reel. In the case of animal baits a longer pickup will be required. As far as the line is concerned, the thinner the better, on the one

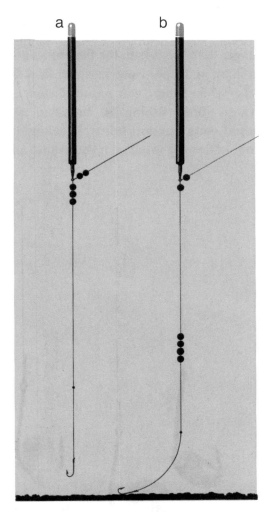

Standard rod and line assembly for fishing with a float in still and slightly dragging waters: a) if the bait is to sink to the bottom slowly, the weights are attached further away from the hook, b) greater weight situated closer to the hook speeds sinking of the bait to the bottom.

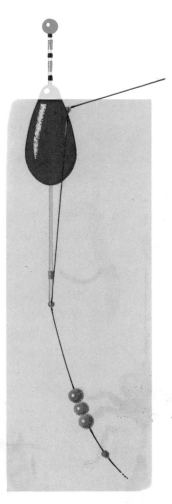

Standard rod and line assembly for float fishing in swifter waters with tiny spherical weights.

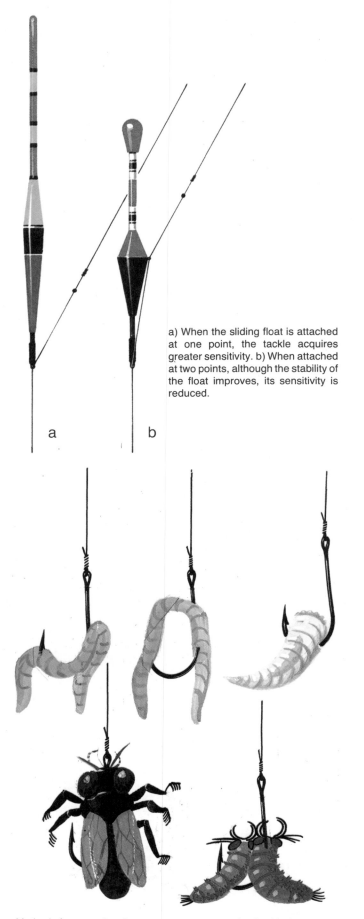

a) When the sliding float is attached at one point, the tackle acquires greater sensitivity. b) When attached at two points, although the stability of the float improves, its sensitivity is reduced.

a   b

hand for better handling, and on the other hand so that it is not conspicuous to the fish. There is no need to be wary of using the thinnest lines, from 0.10 to 0.118mm (0.004—0.005in), although this, of course, depends on the expected quarry. Softer types, inconspicuous in colour, for example sandy coloured, are more advantageous. The size of the float depends on the weight required. For still and slowly flowing waters one should choose, on the grounds of their lower resistance in water, more slender floats, which can be stouter in swifter waters, barrel-shaped, or possibly flat.

We can speak of classic float fishing if the float serves two functions simultaneously — keeping the bait at the required depth and indicating the bite of a fish. It may be practised in any type of water, flowing or still, shallow or deep. The choice of the suitable fishing variant depends predominantly on the depth of the water, its swiftness and the distance of the catching place. It is generally the case that, in shallower waters, if the rod is at least 50—60cm (20—24in) longer than the depth, the fisherman attaches a fixed float; in deeper waters a slider float is vital, as it is also when fishing at a greater distance.

In still waters float fishing is classified as a passive method, with the possibility of making it active by luring. In flowing waters it changes into an

Methods for mounting the most common natural animal baits.

Methods of mounting common plant baits.

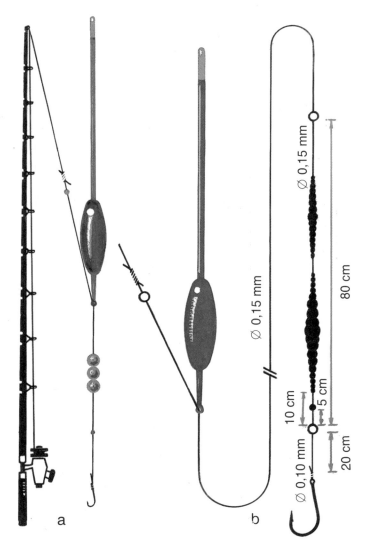

Ø 0,15 mm

Ø 0,15 mm

80 cm

10 cm

5 cm

20 cm

Ø 0,10 mm

a

b

Rod and line assembly for fishing with a float over a great distance:
a) overall view of the assembly, b) parameters in detail.

active method, regardless of whether a lure is used or not.

Float fishing in still waters

In addition to its positive aspects, we should also mention the disadvantages of float fishing. The float constitutes an undesirable intermediary between the rod and the hook, changing the direction of the line from the tip of the rod to the hook, and thus to a certain extent it slows down and therefore impedes hooking. When fishing in still waters one can partially counteract this with the simplest possible assembly of the rod and line, that is by attaching the float at one point at the lower end only, so that the straight direction of the line is retained.

The correct float, designed in accordance with the laws of hydrodynamics, should have the best possible bearing capacity (buoyancy), but at the same time a taking fish must not feel too much resistance. It must be characterised by reliable horizontal stability and ought to give a sensitive signal of even the slightest take. It must be well-balanced so that it will remain submerged with only a sufficient proportion of the antenna protruding from the water to make it visible. When fishing in still waters it is necessary to balance the float with great accuracy; we must include the weight of the hook and bait in overall mass of the weight. There are various possibilities for weighting the float, depending both on the character of the water and on how quickly the bait should sink to the required depth. Sometimes the bait is required to sink more rapidly, for example when one does not want the small surface fish to seize it. On other occasions it is better for the bait to sink more slowly and naturally.

When fishing further from the bank, one can only succeed by using an appropriate fishing technique, based on the principle of the so-called English far-off method. The fisherman uses a rod with a semi-fine action (also for gentler casting), for both hands with the handle at least 60—90cm (2—3ft) long and with adjustable reel clips. The guiding rod rings do not need to be of particularly large diameter, 8—10mm (⅓in) being sufficient. Nevertheless they ought to be on stands of the same length, 20—25mm (¾—1in). They are more densely fitted, 25—30mm (1—1¼in) apart, so that the fine line does not adhere to the rod. A normal, lighter reel is used, but with fast gearing. A special float with a longer (up to 30mm/1¼in) antenna (ideally the classic English float) is attached at one point, so that it will partially straighten the direction of the line and at the same time also sink it. The correct distribution of weight is the limiting factor. The classic assembly for fixed float fishing is clarified in the illustration.

The tackle should be cast as far overhead as possible, holding the rod at an angle of 75° during the flight. Correctly cast tackle assumes the shape of a broad parabole. During the flight phase, one should leave the tackle free checking the line with the finger just before impact with the surface. The tackle thus hits the water gently, in the order of bait, weight and float. After impact, the float is left to assume an upright position, and only then is the line gently straightened by dipping the tip of the rod into the water, so as to speed up the sinking of the line. If the line does not sink, it is possible to degrease it with a suitable preparation.

Fishing in flowing waters by swimming the stream

The basis of success in swimming the stream lies in the fact that the fish are presented in the most natural way possible with bait with which they are familiar, allowing the bait to float freely down the current. In order to stick to the rules of the game, fine, light tackle is chosen for fishing, depending, of course, on the fish being caught. The lightness of the rod is nevertheless important for the fisherman as well, because it is held in the hand constantly when fishing with this method. The choice of weight depends on the strength of the current and the profile of the water in which one wants to fish. In general one fishes just above the bottom, where fish in natural conditions have the best available choice of food, although one can sometimes fish in the upper layers of water as well. A roundish zinc weight should be chosen, which it is possible to let drift downstream; a small glass ball may also be used.

One fishes either from the bank or by wading, casting at an angle downstream. Fishing while wading is more effective, since it permits the fisherman to search every potentially promising fishing place, and a skilful fisherman is able to allow the bait to drift a greater distance downstream by manoeuvring it; the fish are then more trusting of the bait. One should not be afraid of the water clouding when wading, since slightly cloudy water may on the contrary attract the fishes' attention as it will lead them to expect food. After casting, the bait is allowed to sink to the desired depth and then to be carried by the current by a gradual release of the line. With the free hand the line should be handled in such a way that one is able to feel constant contact with the bait. This is essential for immediate hooking when there is a take. The take is of course also signalled by the float.

The actual technique of swimming the stream may be one of two alternatives, depending on the character of the water. In slightly flowing waters, in which the difference in intensity between the upper and lower currents is negligible, the fisherman gently eases out the line, thus enabling the float to move slightly ahead, so that it can help pull both the weight and the bait. Even during this action, how-

ever, the fisherman holds the line straight, so that he can react quickly to the take.

In more swiftly flowing waters, in which the difference in intensity between the flow of the upper and lower layers is more pronounced, it is not necessary to speed up the movement of the bait, partly because it might seem suspicious to the fish. In such a situation one chooses the variant in which one checks the movement of the float. The fisherman directs it with the rod, and with the aid of the line slows it down in such a way that it does not overtake the bait; thus it does not speed up its movement but, on the contrary, checks it a little where necessary.

The fishing method, or way of guiding the bait, is, apart from the factors already mentioned, also dependent on the baits used. With dung worms, etc., one should preferably catch at the bottom; with grasshoppers and similar insects, in practically any water area. If fishing with aquatic insect larvae, however, one can guide them through the water in various ways, here and there lifting the bait from the bottom to the surface even with a sharpish jerk, thus imitating the movements of hatching insects. Round fruit, on the other hand, is allowed to roll freely along the bottom.

In smaller, fairly shallow streams, one can fish by swimming the stream by wading even without a float, and if using a heavier bait also without a zinc weight. This method is recommended for lower water levels. In this method, also, the bait is allowed to drift freely downstream on a slightly tightened line. When the bait stops, the fisherman moves it ahead a little by gently lifting the tip of the rod.

Fishing on the surface

With the exception of silver-salmon, all sport fish only sporadically come near the surface, so that fishing on the surface can only be considered occasionally. Fishing on the surface may be carried out in several ways, although one must always bear in mind that the fish may be more suspicious than usual in a less familiar environment. In such a case, the optimal assembly of the rod and line is that without a float and using bait of greater weight, so that it can be cast on its own without sinking. A crust of bread, for example, or a may-beetle could serve as such a bait.

When dapping, the angler uses the bankside vegetation as cover.

Dapping

During the execution of this interesting fishing method, the bait is guided along the surface in such a way that it will alternately skip and float. The precondition for success is to get the bait to the desired place in such a way that the fish are not startled in the slightest. For this, one must be equipped with a long, fine rod, and above all have an opportunity to hide in the bank vegetation. For this reason, only brooks or rivers with a thicker bank growth are suitable for dapping. This is not only because one must hide in a suitable place, but above all because the fish in these conditions are used to a supply of food from trees, from which dry land insects fall, and sometimes also various fruits. If therefore, they are presented with bait which they take as normal, this usually results in an excellent catch.

When carrying out this method, one does not use either a float or a weight, and a reel is optional. The bait, a grasshopper or other insect, is gently lowered towards the surface, gently shaken, submerged for a moment and again lifted to the surface. By trembling the rod, the bait is gently shaken. Hooking must take place as soon as one feels a fish taking.

Fishing in the wind

This fishing method is based on a similar principle to that of presenting unweighted bait. It may be practised in more open waters, with accessible banks. Larger fish are always more cautious and feel most secure when they are far from the bank. To get unweighted bait to this greater distance is a real art. To do this one must be equipped with a good, flexi-

ble, long rod, as thin a line as possible and not least a favourable wind from behind. The bait, which is usually a crust of bread, is moistened for a moment before casting, so that it will be easier to cast. During its flight through the air it will dry out and will not sink. The fisherman turns his back to the wind and, while casting, holds the rod more upright, so that he can make use of the strength of the wind. After the impact of the bait on the surface, he only straightens the line slightly so as not to check the bait; the wind and waves carry it along freely. He should try, however, to keep a substantial proportion of the line above water, without much bulging. It is necessary to accomplish hooking quickly, at the moment one observes the water under the floating crust breaking into waves, with the surface of the water closing over it immediately afterwards. A prelude to a take may often take the form of small fish catching sight of the bait and going for it. Their attempts can often cause larger fish to lose their tempers and suddenly take the bait from under their noses. If the bait remains on a calm surface on the same spot for any length of time without visibly arousing the interest of the fish, it is better gradually to move it elsewhere, possibly even with a jumping motion. This often has a provocative effect on the fish. Sometimes, however, a larger fish may even take without prior warning, without one being given notice by a shoal of smaller fish and the wave movement under the surface. The line should therefore be held in the fingers of the left hand, so that one can hook without hesitation. But be careful: the line

63

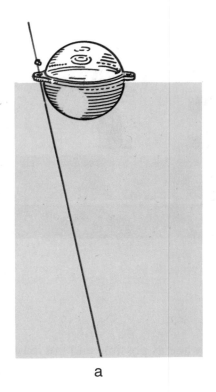

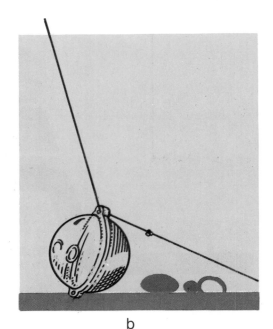

Basic methods for using a glass ball: a) a ball partly filled with water fulfils the function of both weight and float, b) a completely filled ball functions as a weight.

a

b

is very thin and hooking should therefore be carried out with maximum sensitivity. Sometimes it is enough just to hold the line a little more firmly and the fish will hook itself.

Fishing with the aid of a glass ball

A glass ball is one of the very useful aids by means of which it is possible to fish by more than one method. It is mainly given preference when the fish are for any reason suspicious. The use of a glass ball is universal — empty, it functions as an unweighted float, partly filled, as a weighted float, while a more filled one assumes the function of a weight, and at the same time that of a detector. The only disadvantage is its relatively low visibility, although even this can basically be regarded as a plus, because the fish see it as an air bubble floating on the water. Multi-coloured balls are more visible to the fisherman, but on the other hand are more conspicuous to the fish.

A standard glass ball is equipped with a valve for filling it with water, sometimes with two valves, as well as with two clips on the peripheral ring. It can be used not only for fishing on the surface, but also on the bottom, and even during classic fly fishing with either a dry or a wet fly. Depending on what one is aiming for, a glass ball may be attached either as a fixed or as a slider float, both at one and at two points. A good idea of the possibilities for using a glass ball is presented in the illustrations.

METHODS FOR CATCHING PREDATORY FISH

Basically two fishing methods are used for catching predatory fish, these being passive fishing with live fish bait, and active spinning.

Fishing with live fish bait

The passive, sedentary fishing method with live small fish is much more effective for catching predatory fishes than sink and draw; using fish bait, one is bound to be successful up to a point. Fisherman's ethics, however, suggest that where conditions are suitable, one should choose the more sporting method — sink and draw — which after all gives the fish a greater chance. Using a small live fish, one should fish only in more difficult conditions, for example in waters where there are few areas which are not overgrown.

Under these conditions, however, one must go for the fish with brute force, not being able to afford the luxury of tiring and playing the fish for a long time. The tackle therefore needs to be thicker and stronger. Here the rod is the decisive factor, of appropriate strength, with semi-soft action, and definitely at least 3—3.5m (10—11½ft) long, in very overgrown waters up to 5—5.5m (16—18ft). With such a rod it is easier to cast the bait to the selected place and safely to play the quarry among the obstacles. A line of 0.25—0.35mm (0.01—0.014in) will suffice, thicker ones being necessary only when one expects an unusually large quarry. The generally valid principle of the advantage of simple assembly of the rod and line cannot always be adhered to when fishing with small live fish. Indispensable components of the rod and line are a float, steel stranded wire, a snap hook or swivel and generally also a zinc weight. Above all, one must always undertake the most careful luring with the bait fish, which serves two purposes: it does not give predators on the look-out cause to suspect the bait, and it facilitates movement over a wider area for the fish bait, which increases the probability of it attracting the attention of a predator. These conditions can be met if the individual components of the rod and line are not over-dimensioned. Above all one has to use common-sense when selecting a float. It should not be viewed as an adornment of the rod and line, but as a practical item. We expect the float to retain the fish bait within the delineated area, without restricting its movement. The fish bait must be able to move freely. Large multi-coloured 'pike floats', often as big as a fist, are more likely to frighten off a predator. An under-dimensioned float, ideally of a slender shape, is preferable in every respect; it is a good thing if the fish bait draws it here and there a few centimetres below the surface. The fish bait thus works for us, provoking predators within

Fishing for predators with fish-bait mounted on a single hook is more sporting and more considerate of the fish.

a wider vicinity. Anyway after a while the float compels the tired fish bait to obey. If there is a danger, however, that the fish bait together with the sunk float might become tangled in obstacles, one should select a larger float.

Stranded steel wire with the function of a side rig is only essential when fishing for pike, which would bite through the line. It is sensible practice, however, also to use stranded steel wire when fishing for other predatory fishes, for there is always the chance that a pike will take, and moreover the stranded wire serves superbly well when cutting grass in which the tackle has become entangled. Only up-to-date types of stranded steel wire should be chosen, however, as these are the most flexible and do not have a disturbing effect on the rod and line. Their strength, or bearing capacity, needs to be adapted to the overall assembly of the rod and line; in this case also the rule applies about the limiting effect of the weakest component in the assembly. Stranded wire is most reliably attached to a strongish swivel or snap-hook, which at the same time functions as a good stopper for the weight. The latter is not a vital item of tackle, as some fish baits tend to sink towards the bottom of their own accord, so that they need not be weighted. The mass and size of the weight are selected according to casting requirements. The question of suitable hooks is open to debate. Many anglers prefer double or triple hooks to be on the safe side, because the hooking action will definitely take in the harder mouth of a predator. This certainty, however, is sometimes in

Rod and line assembled in the usual way for fishing for predators with fish-bait: a) overall view, b) method for attaching triple hook on to stranded steel wire.

a   b

Simple mounting of fish-bait without sewing, by piercing one shank of the triple hook either under the back or through the mouth.

direct conflict with fishing ethics, because if one catches an undersized fish it is almost impossible to dislodge the triple hook from its pharynx. We do not want to condemn fishing with double or triple hooks; after all, even the regulations permit this. However, we should like to recommend sometimes also trying a simple hook, or even one without a barb. We cannot promise richer quarry; on the contrary, one may even spoil hooking, but one should nevertheless be able to know how to lose in sport. After all, every predator saved in this way is worth it! One day — perhaps not so far in the future — we will get him, by which time he may have grown into a sizeable fish.

The assortment of hooks for fishing for predators is exceptionally rich and facilitates an adequate choice for the various methods of mounting small fish. Apart from the selection of standard hooks, numbered 1, 2 and 3, which are suitable for fishing for predators, there is also a whole range of special types, designed for reliable mounting of small fish. There are, for example, double hooks with an additional safety pin for stitching through the fish bait, and triple hooks with shorter shanks or hooks without barbs. The hook is chosen according to the predators for which one wants to fish and according to the size of the fish bait that one is using.

The fish bait may be mounted on the hook in several ways. All these methods nevertheless have one common denominator: one should try to damage the fish bait as little as possible, and it must be

sufficiently agile, so as to have a chance to move naturally and to survive on the line as long as possible. A smaller fish bait is either gently mounted on the single hook by the mouth, or by piercing it under the dorsal fin. Then, of course, casting must be carried out very gently, otherwise the fish bait would come off the hook during casting. The fisherman must also gently and skilfully move around and pull out the fish bait, because if it becomes antangled in grass or a branch he will lose it. A single hook with a smaller fish bait is used for fishing for perch, pike-perch, chub and silver-salmon. When fishing for pike and catfish, it is better to choose a somewhat larger fish bait, mounted on a single hook in the same manner. More common, of course, is mounting fish bait on a double or triple hook under the dorsal fin in one of two possible ways: by simply piercing the skin with one shank of the hook, or by stitching under the skin. The former method is quicker, but the fish bait can easily work itself off during more energetic casting. When stitching under the skin, one must proceed with the greatest possible care, so that the fish bait does not suffer or become weakened unnecessarily. The fisherman takes hold of it firmly in his left hand and guides the fishing needle close under the skin along the whole length of the backbone from one side of the dorsal fin, in such a way as not to injure the musculature. The needle should emerge just in front of the dorsal fin. Using the needle, a stranded steel wire should be guided under the skin, the needle

More laborious but more reliable mounting of fish-bait by sewing under the back section.

then being pulled out of the stranded wire loop, the end of the loop being firmly pressed between the fingers and guided through the eye of the hook and finally also over one shank of the triple hook. The stranded wire is then carefully pulled back a little, so that the lower part of the hook is also concealed under the skin of the fish bait. One shank of the hook thus protrudes upwards, the other two closing round the back of the fish bait.

The procedure is similar with a double hook. When mounting the fish bait 'sharp', when both shanks of the hook protrude upwards, one can hook soon after a take by a fish. When mounting the fish bait 'blunt', when the shanks of the hook enclose the fish bait from the sides, one must not hook until the predator has swallowed the bait sufficiently deeply. When carrying out the former method, the caught fish cannot be seriously injured, which is important in the case of smaller fish, which are put back in the water.

The fisherman must adapt himself to predatory fish, so as to be able to bring the bait into their vicinity. One must bear in mind that fish behaviour is affected by a whole range of factors, the daily and seasonal periods, the weather, etc. It is thus essential constantly to work on one's technique and to discover the laws of characteristic fish behaviour in certain conditions. It would be difficult to offer generally valid instruction, so we are restricting ourselves to characteristic examples.

In summer, fish withdraw downwards into the depths, only moving upwards into the upper layers of water and into shallows at dawn and dusk. In autumn and in cooler water they seek out the deepest places. Just before and during a storm, all fish will stay close to the surface, whereas when there is higher atmospheric pressure they remain near the bottom.

Various fish species will also behave in various ways. Pike-perch and catfish, for example, prefer deeper waters, pike favouring shallower water and staying near the edges. Every angler who observes life in the water will in time be able to guess what kind of mood the fish are in at the given moment.

There is one mistake which fishermen commonly make, mainly when fishing for pike, and that is to position the fish bait too shallow. As has already been mentioned, large fish are less trusting than small ones, and therefore feel safer at a greater depth. With shallow positioning of the fish bait, one will thus probably catch more specimens, but definitely smaller in size. If one positions the fish bait deeper, on the other hand, one will not reach such a large number of quarry, but the smaller number will be compensated for by the quality of the trophy.

One should also learn to cast the fish bait correctly. The first moment after casting may be a very important one, since the fish bait can at that moment easily catch the attention of a predator. One must therefore immediately be prepared for a possible take. One should cast with care, so that the fish bait does not come off and in order not to stun or damage it by too violent a pull or impact with the surface. Immediately after casting the line should be tightened slightly and care should be taken not to foul it among plants. After correct casting, the fish bait is startled and desparently tries to free itself from the float and the tackle in general, after a while growing tired and calming down. If, however, it catches sight of a predator, it will make another effort to escape, which the float signals by

Live-bait presented to a predator just at the surface.

means of more lively movement. One should then increase vigilance and wait for the moment the float stops moving again. This indicates that a predator has attacked and is trying the taste of the fish bait. After a brief interval, the float slowly sinks and begins to disappear into the depths. The predator is allowed to swim off a metre or so, the necessary length of line being paid out. As soon as one is sure that the fish does not intend to get rid of the bait, the line is tightened a little, the brake mechanisms setting on the reel is checked and hooking should proceed energetically but carefully.

One can naturally also encounter a different reaction on the part of the fish. Frequently a smaller pike will go for the bait but is not capable of swallowing such a large prey. It will take it into its mouth and swim here and there with it helplessly. In this case the float will only sink a little and surface again after only a moment. It is better not to hook in this moment, but to try to rescue the fish bait from the attacking predator.

Examples of some less common methods for catching predators can be found in the accompanying illustrations. We should particularly like to draw attention, however, to one alternative in especially difficult waters with an abundance of obstacles. In this case one requires two floats for the assembly of the rod and line. The main float is a glass ball, attached to a side rig in such a way as to stay about 10—20cm (4—8in) below the surface and to keep the tackle upright. The auxiliary float is attached directly to the main line in such a way as to stay on the surface, serving the function of a bite detector. The mounting of the fish bait itself by the paternoster system is common.

Less common is fishing with small live fish bait on the bottom or just above the bottom. Pike-perch and catfish are mainly fished for in this way, in view of their way of life. During the warmer season of the year, however, this method can also be recommended for pike fishing. In this case also, one can choose from several possible assemblies of the rod and line, for example without a float, with a fish bait weighted with zinc on a longer side rig, or with an auxiliary float positioned between the fish bait and the weight. Using live fish bait, one can also fish swimming the stream just below the surface. For this purpose, the rod and line is assembled without using either a float or a zinc weight, and a place must be chosen for fishing where the fish bait can be allowed to drift downstream.

Sink and draw fishing

Sink and draw fishing is based on the principle of guiding — drawing — the lure through the water in such a way that it will imitate as closely as possible some element of the natural quarry of predatory fish. Predators live predominantly on smaller fish, imitations of which prevail in the range of lures for sink and draw fishing. Less typical baits may also be successful, however, resembling various amphibious and land animals, for example mice and so on.

This concise definition of sink and draw appears simple at first sight. It might seem that in order to master this fishing method it is enough to be skilled in the basics of fishing technique, which enable one to cast far and accurately, and then only to turn the handle of the reel with enough patience and wait for the chance take of a fish. In fact, fishing by sink and draw is quite demanding. Together with mastery of technique, it also requires the fisherman to have a sound knowledge of the life habits and behaviour of fish, and not least also a special instinct, one could say a 'nose', for the fish.

One must above all start from the assumption that predatory fish are guided predominantly by sight and by the senses of the lateral line when identifying prey. By sight they register the prey directly, and by the lateral line indirectly in such a way that they perceive the disturbance of water caused by the movement of the prey, registering not only the direction of movement of the prey, but also its intensity. The lateral line thus functions as a perfect radiolocator. In good visibility the sense of sight is more effective for perceiving prey, in poorer visibility the lateral line senses are more effective, although in fact both senses work together. This means that when fishing by sink and draw it is necessary to make use not only of visual but also of aural effects.

One must make sensible use of the natural tendency of predatory fish to be lazy in the sense that, when obtaining prey, on principle they choose the line of least resistance. In practice this means that, although a fish predator is able to seize any normal prey, it will nevertheless give preference to

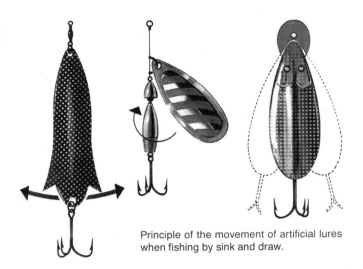

Principle of the movement of artificial lures when fishing by sink and draw.

a quarry which is more easily accessible, that is a less vigorous, sickly small fish with reduced reactions and agility owing to the effects of disease or injury. So in sink and draw fishing one should guide the lure in such a way that it imitates the movement of a sickly quarry. A sickly small fish hangs behind a healthy shoal, swimming more quickly and then more slowly, trying to reach the surface, then again falling tiredly towards the bottom, stopping for a moment and then making another attempt to get away. The drawn lure should imitate all of these movements.

The probability of success when drawing the lure in a slower and interrupted manner also increases because of the fact that the lure then remains in a predator's field of vision for a longer time. We must reckon with the fact that a predator on the look-out must be able to catch sight of the lure, and that it will in any case take it a moment to make a decision and prepare to attack. Drawing the lure too fast can simply make it travel round the fish's mouth without giving it a chance to attack.

The question of accurate imitation of the natural food of predators by means of artificial lures is in practice given too much stress by fishing tackle manufacturers. Any even slightly experienced fisherman knows that success in sinking and drawing lies predominantly in the correct guiding of the lure, and not in the extent to which its appearance corresponds to the original. After all, it is unlikely that an attacking catfish in the semi-darkness will first check on the accurate rendering of the eye colour of a small, artificial mouse.

Another precondition for success when sinking and drawing is an adequate amount of optimism. One should not be dissuaded by the first unsuccessful casts, since after all even master fishermen will not hook a fish at every cast, or even perhaps with every twentieth cast. If one knows of a place where predators are definitely to be found, one should fish it thoroughly. It may be that a predator has seen the lure during the first casts, but did not have time to

Correct alternating movements of the lure when sinking and drawing: a) with a spinner, b) with a wobbler.

69

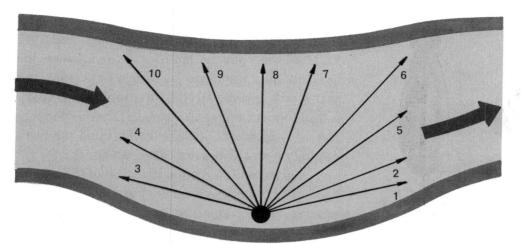

Procedure for fan-shaped combing of the water by spinning.

go for it. It has nevertheless aroused its attention, and if the lure appears again after a moment a little further away, it will probably be prepared to take. A change of lure or alternating the depths in which one fishes may be equally effective.

Mastery of casting technique, above all sufficient length and accuracy of the casts, is a prerequisite even for beginners, and yet one can often see that many fishermen have difficulties with accuracy of casting. This deprives them of many takes and moreover they will lose spinners caught in obstacles which they hit instead of the intended place. Accurate casting is exceptionally important. Predators instinctively take refuge among obstacles, and the only fisherman who can get to them is one who skilfully guides the lure as near to them as possible. There is no unequivocal answer to the question of how far to cast; sometimes one must cast several dozen metres, at other times a couple of metres will do.

Initially one should try to fish through the water which is nearest to the bank as long as the water is deep enough of course and there are fish in it. If one were to start by casting far off, one could easily frighten off a fish which happened to be close to the bank. One should cast through the chosen sector in a fan shape from a single point. During individual casts, rhythm and depth are varied when guiding

the lure. After one has thoroughly fished through the nearest vicinity, the casts should be extended, and again one starts to cast through in a fan shape, casting furthest off last.

After exhausting all the possibilities, including changing the rhythm of sinking and drawing and changing lures, one looks for a new position, which does not have to be too distant from the first one. If the chosen section of water is really good, it is enough to move along only a couple of metres, and it does not matter at all if some casts from the new position overlap the previous ones.

Many anglers make the mistake of not concentrating as much during the retrieval of the last few metres of line as in the beginning. They think that after many casts a predator cannot any longer be on the look-out near the bank. It can happen, nevertheless, that during a long cast a predator catches sight of the lure, but there is something suspicious about it. It starts to pursue it, and in its excitement goes as far as the bank, perhaps even as far as the shallows. If one happens to see it, one should try to provoke it to a take by changing the rhythm in which the lure is being guided. If not observed in time, it can happen that the predator will rush at a spinner which has already been drawn from the water, leaving behind only a rippling surface.

During drawing, the tackle is under exceptional strain, as it is in constant use. For lighter sinking and drawing when fishing for trout, chub, perch, pike-perch, silver-salmon, as well as smaller pike, a light-

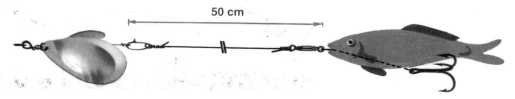

Combination of a spinner with dead fish-bait for spinning.

70

a) When pike fishing by spinning, a rig made of stranded steel wire is essential. b) One can venture for pike-perch even without stranded steel wire.

A lighter artifical lure may be combined with a weight, which facilitates both better casting and guiding of the lure in deeper water.

er rod, 1.8—2.4m (6—8ft) in length, with an adequately hard, flexible tip, should be chosen. For heavier sinking and drawing when fishing for catfish, huchen and larger pike, the rod must be more solid, harder and up to 2.5m (8¼ft) in length. A good casting rod must be sufficiently fine, in or-

der to cope with constant intense strain. Nevertheless excessive fineness is detrimental, since it is difficult to hook with such a rod. It must not be too heavy, so as not to tire the angler unnecessarily. It must be sufficiently resilient, to suit the purposes both of casting and playing the quarry. A great deal also depends on the rod rings, which affect the smoothness, and thus also the length and accuracy, of casting. Larger rod rings on stand-off rod ring fittings are more suitable. The butt of the rod must sit well in the hand. The reel must be securely fitted, so as not to work loose. Adjustable fitting of the reel enables the centre of gravity of the rod always to be at the point where the reel is fitted.

A solid and at the same time light reel, with a fluent action and faster gearing (about 1 : 3.5) and a reliable smooth brake mechanism, is absolutely essential. A good spool ought to have an absolutely smooth, slanted edge and should be completely filled with line. A shallow and broad spool is therefore more suitable. The line must wind onto the spool evenly for the sake of smooth casting.

Line thickness usually varies when sinking and drawing; however, one should try to use as thin a line as possible, by means of which it is possible to accomplish longer casts, even with a lighter lure. When fishing for smaller fish, a line up to 0.25mm (0.01in) thick will suffice. A line up to 0.30mm (0.012in) can only be justified in difficult waters with many obstacles, when one has to play the hooked fish within a limited space. When fishing for chub, perch and similar smaller fish, on the other hand, a line 0.20mm (0.008in) thick will do. In this case, however, the angler uses a rod with a very fine tip and a sensitively set reel break, which enables him to hook sufficiently abruptly within the limits of the line's bearing capacity. When sinking and drawing for catfish and larger pike, a line 0.35—0.40mm (0.014—0.016in) thick is necessary, as one fishes with heavier lures and with a harder rod, and one also expects to hook a larger fish. Only in lighter terrain in completely open water and with a tremendous amount of optimism can one set out for catfish with a line 0.25mm (0.01in) thick.

If the fisherman wants a truly sporting experience when sinking and drawing, he should try fishing with the thinnest possible line in all cases. In so doing, although he increases the risk of losing a larger

71

quarry or the lure by catching it in an obstacle, he will be compensated by more frequent takes, because the radius of action of the catch will increase. For the sake of faster reaction to the take, preference is given to harder types of line, which are less elastic and sufficiently firm when knotted.

Vertical sink and draw is a variation of sinking and drawing. It consists, quite simply, of the alternate sinking and raising of the lure in the water column perpendicularly, that is vertically. It is only possible to fish in this way in waters which are deep enough. If the bank is steep enough and the necessary depth can be found right by the bank, it is possible to fish from the bank, otherwise fishing is carried out from a boat anchored in deep water. This fishing method was originally practised on frozen waters at openings cut or drilled in the ice. Winter depth fishing can be explained by the fact that in winter the fishes withdraw into the depths. In the warm season of the year the use of vertical sink and draw might seem illogical, since according to all our information, fishes tend to keep to shallower,

A special rod and line for winter fishing through holes in the ice.

warmer water. Experience shows, however, that even in summer many fish stray into the depths and can be caught there. This applies particularly, of course, to the so-called deep water fishes, that is perch, pike-perch and some salmon-type fishes.

The technique of vertical sink and draw is not demanding. The rod ought to be short and hard, the so-called 'winter rod' and the reel as simple as possible, since the lure is not cast, but only sunk and drawn out. The lure is at first allowed to sink of its own accord as far as the bottom. When using heavier lures, impact on the bottom will be clearly registered; in the case of lighter lures, one must follow the straightening of the line more carefully. The lure is then alternately drawn out and allowed to sink again. It depends on the circumstances whether one prefers to concentrate on the bottom section, or the middle and upper layers of water. The lure is drawn

up energetically, by 50—60cm (20—24in) at each draw, and with short intervals between the individual phases. After three to five seconds, when the lure sinks downwards of its own accord, the draw is repeated. Sometimes it is more effective, instead of a single unbroken draw, to use over the same distance several shorter ones, one shortly after the other. At other times the lure should be shaken in a single place, possibly alternating all methods.

Not only a beginner but even an angler who knows his way about frequently has difficulty registering a take in time and reacting to it. If a fish takes during the draw, the take is exceptionally energetic and the fish usually hooks itself. The ensuing hooking is then only to secure the quarry. More difficult, however, is to register a take in the phase in which the lure is sinking. This can be discerned only by a tightening of the line, which in the moment of the take lightens up, so that one cannot even feel the weight of the lure. Hooking must follow immediately, otherwise the predator will quickly recognize the deceptiveness of the lure and get rid of it.

The choice of lures for vertical sink and draw is practically limitless. In addition to special artificial lures, classic spinners can also be used, as well as, possibly, combinations of artificial lures with natural ones (a dung worm, larva, piece of fish fillet, and so on mounted on the hook of the spinner). Insects and some types of artificial fly may also be used.

In the more open, deeper waters of lakes and valley reservoirs, where there is no danger of catching the drawn tackle in obstacles, another variation of the classic sink and draw method is used — with the aid of a boat.

FLY-FISHING

Classic fly-fishing used to be limited solely to catching salmon-type fish and grayling with an artificial fly. Recently, however, it has been discovered that many lowland fishes can be caught equally successfully by fly-fishing. New more all-round modifications of fly-fishing, as well as new types of lure, have become prevalent, so that this privileged branch of sport fishing is finally acquiring a mass character, whilst fly-fishing tackle is becoming common, even for the majority of lowland fishermen.

The basis of fly-fishing technique lies in as close an imitation as possible of the fish insects at all developmental stages. Not only the size, shape and colour must be closely imitated, but also their natural movements on and below the surface.

The following basic types of fly-fishing may be distinguished according to the type of lure used:
— dry fly-fishing;

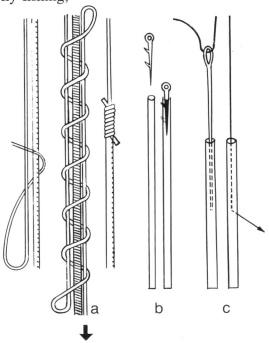

Methods for attaching the line on to the fly-fishing line: a) by special knots, b) by an eyelet, c) by sewing through with a needle.

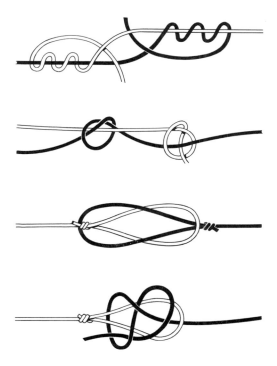

Types of so-called elastic knots for joining lines of different thicknesses.

— wet fly-fishing;
— fishing with nymphs;
— fishing with streamers and bucktails.

The choice of a suitable fishing method is dependent on the behaviour of the fish, particularly on which insects form the basic component of their diet and in which water profile they gather food. This in turn is affected by a whole range of factors — the season of the year, the time of day, the weather, the clearness of the water and so on.

The choice of a suitable place for fishing should be made according to the accessibility of the terrain and the assumed or known places where fish gather. One should try to choose a place where one can get at the fish from a shorter distance (5—15m/16—50ft), but without the fish being able to see the angler. The actual fishing technique should then be chosen according to the terrain and the casting length.

In order to get the fly into the field of vision of the fish, it is necessary to have some acquaintance with fish behaviour. In summer, for example, one expects to find both trout and grayling in the swiftest sections of the flow, mainly around obstacles, which provide the fish with a feeling of security. In the cooler seasons of the year, less swift, dragging sections suit the fish better. One can look for fish in these places even in summer at dusk.

It is necessary to emphasize several main principles of fly-fishing technique:
— In general, but especially when dry fly-fishing in smaller, cleaner brooks, the fly should be cast against the current. This is based on the fact that a fish takes up a position against the current, where it waits for the food to come towards it.
— The fly is not cast directly into the place where the fish is, but always 1—3m (3—10ft) upstream from it (according to the strength of the current), allowing it to float down freely to the required place.
— One should not try to fish unnecessarily far off, the optimal distance being 8—12m (26—40ft). At this distance there is an opportunity to approach the fish unobserved and to supervise the guiding of the fly, the take and hooking.
— Casting must be fluent. First the fly should hit the surface, then the rig and then the fly line.
— Impact of the fly with the water should be as gentle as possible, so as better to imitate insect behaviour.

— Lifting the fly from the surface should likewise be carried out with care. Before pulling up the fly line the fly should be pulled in slightly, and only after a short pause should one start to shorten the fly line.

— When fishing against the current the fly should be guided in such a way that the current does not pull down the fly-fishing line. Otherwise the fly would ripple the water and lose its effectiveness.

— If these is a mixed population of trout and grayling in the brook, casting should be carried out diagonally against the current. A hunting trout will pursue a fly against the current as soon as it spots it; however a grayling will not hurry, will let the fly float past it and if it likes it will only then turn and go for it down the stream.

Dry fly-fishing

Dry fly-fishing should always be given preference when the fish are hunting insects on the surface. Their so-called ringing can be discerned both by ear, when a hunting fish smacks the surface, as well as by sight from the rings forming on the surface. The optimal conditions for dry fly-fishing are thus in gently flowing waters in which one can easily find out what kind of appetite the fish have, and where one also has an opportunity for visual supervision of the take. As far as the conditions will allow, one should fish against the current, or possibly at least diagonally against the direction of the current. The fly is cast as gently as possible to fall neatly on the surface, and should be allowed to drift downwards, while proportionately to its speed shortening the fly-fishing

Knots for tying artifical flies onto the line.

line (either by retrieving or gathering in by hand). The downward drift of the fly should not be interfered with; a checked or accelerated fly would not behave naturally and would ripple the water. A soft and gradual impact of the fly, rig and fly-fishing line can be achieved by slightly lifting the tip of the rod just before the fly hits the surface. In this way the fly is slowed down a little, so that it will alight on the

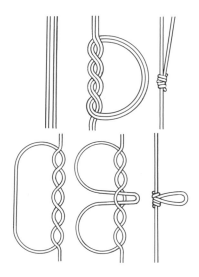

Tying of loops for attaching several flies.

water with a natural movement. Immediately after impact the rod should be dipped again and one should concentrate on handling the fly-fishing line.

One can fish using up to three flies simultaneously, although more experienced anglers do not generally make use of this possibility, and usually fish with two flies; if the fish are taking, even one fly is quite sufficient.

Polarized glasses are invaluable when following a take, although in some cases one can rely only on the movement of the fly-fishing line. One should not be too hasty with hooking, particularly if a grayling bites. Hooking is only secure when the fish, after having seized the lure, turns round and goes head first towards the bottom. Hooking should be carried out energetically, always, however, with consideration for the relatively fine hook and thin rig. After being in the water for some time, the dry fly usually loses its positive qualities, and must therefore be dried from time to time and greased as required, so that it does not sink. A correctly greased fly keeps its original shape perfectly, floats superbly and gives a natural impression. The fly is

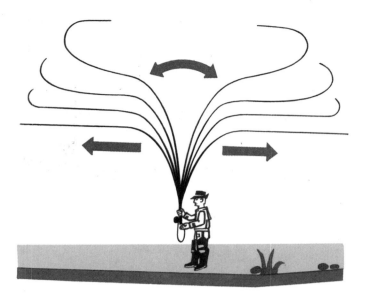

Basic positioning the fly-fisherman and movement the fly-fishing line.

For dapping, a somewhat longer rod is used. The angler fishes down the stream, allowing the fly to drift freely and raising the rod high in front of the point where he senses the fish to be, and then

Procedure for false casts with gradual releasing of the fly-fishing line.

dried by means of false casts, always behind where the fish is, so as not to startle it.

Dapping is a variation of dry fly-fishing. One can try this if for some reason one has been unsuccessful with classic fly-fishing, for example in extremely changeable weather, when the water level has dropped and so on. One must also avoid unnatural movements when using this method and should try to imitate the bobbing movements of insects. Mayflies, for example, fly quickly, alighting gently on the water and taking off again abruptly. Bank-baits, on the other hand, fly sluggishly, falling rather than alighting on the surface and being unable to take off again.

Pulling in and holding the fly-fishing line.

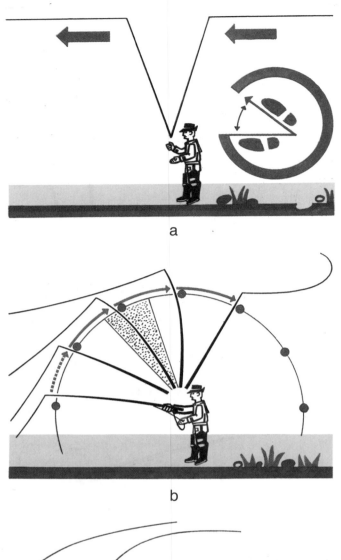

a

b

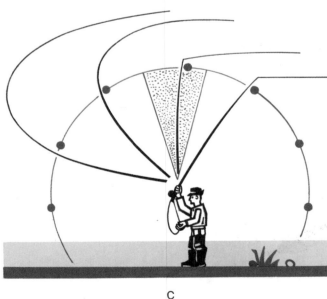

c

Vertical fly-casting method: a) basic position, b) lifting the fly-fishing line out of the water, c) casting.

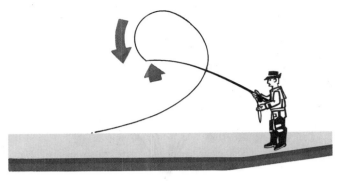

Casting the fly-fishing line with a rotating movement.

wobbling the tip so that the fly makes short little jumps on the surface.

In more open waters, where it is not possible to get the fly to the required distance by normal casting, one should try fly-fishing with the wind coming from behind, that is by fishing in the wind. A longer rod is also used for this method. So as better to make use of the force of the wind, another, auxiliary, usually somewhat larger 'gliding' fly is attached beside the fly, serving as the lure.

Wet fly-fishing

One resorts to wet fly-fishing when the fish do not show any interest in food on the surface, but are hunting only in the water column, where the flash of their bodies or their shadows can be seen. After the fly has alighted on the surface, the line and fly-fishing line overhang should be corrected, allowing the fly to descend freely through the water column, so as to create as realistic an impression as possible. If the fly has complete freedom of movement, the water current will carry it to the place where the fish are waiting for food which has drifted down. The classic wet fly represents a dead adult insect which is just hatching. In this case it is also possible to fish with two to three flies. The tail fly is usually submerged, the first suspended one floating in the surface, and the third bobbing just above the surface. When carrying out pure wet fly-fishing, all the flies may be submerged.

It is more of a problem to obtain a certain catch when wet fly-fishing, so that each section of the water is combed systematically, giving preference to the most promising places.

One problem with wet fly-fishing is difficulty in spotting a take, often because the water is not clear, or because there is a swift current. Polarized glasses are a useful aid in such conditions, although one is mainly dependent on following the movement of the fly-fishing line at the point where it sinks under the surface. For better orientation, the fly-fishing line may be marked in colour approximately 3m (10ft) from the rig.

For some unknown reason wet fly-fishing, compared with dry fly-fishing, is sometimes considered

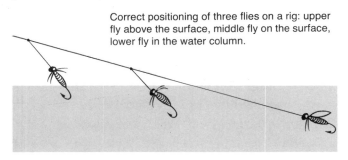

Correct positioning of three flies on a rig: upper fly above the surface, middle fly on the surface, lower fly in the water column.

to be rather a comedown, although this view is unnecessary conservatism. Wet fly-fishing, with the exception of minor details, is equally demanding, its advantage being that it can be practised almost without restriction throughout the whole fishing season, in clear as well as in slightly cloudy water, when the water level is rising as well as falling, and in both warm and cool weather.

Fishing with nymphs

If we proceed systematically from an analysis of the natural diet of fish, then fishing with nymphs — that is, with imitations of the developmental stages of diverse insects — must logically be considered the most effective method. This is because it is nymphs which form the daily diet of trout and grayling, whereas adult insects, imitated by classic flies, are for them special food. This is understandable for the reason that the developmental stages of insects remain in the water for several years, whereas adult insects have a 'mayfly' life in the true sense of the word, and are available to the fish only as seasonal fare.

Apart from this, fishing with nymphs is also attractive for the reason that neither complicated tackle nor any special technique is necessary. It can even be practised with a common rod used for fishing for white fish. The principle of the method is essentially identical to the technique for wet fly-fishing. A certain difference lies in the fact that mounted nymphs are somewhat heavier and larger, so they sink more quickly to the bottom. Nymphs are

cast downstream, diagonally downstream, as well as upstream, again always higher upstream from the place where the fish are assumed to be, so as to get into their vicinity inconspicuously using the water current. The actual movement of the nymph depends on the species of insect in question, although in general the mobility of nymphs is restricted and their movement is more or less passive.

Formerly, fishing with nymphs was only carried out with sunk fly-fishing lines, whilst nowadays floating fly-fishing lines are also used. With a sunk fly-fishing line one fishes in more open, deeper waters, combing mainly the deeper water hollows. Casting is carried out diagonally against the stream. A take may only be detected if the fly-fishing line is held in the fingers, or by the fly-fishing line stopping. The choice of the type of sinking fly-fishing line depends on the water — the stronger the current, the quicker-sinking the type of fly-fishing line required. For fishing in still waters, a combined fly-fishing line may be used, of which only part is sinking.

The advantage of fishing with a floating fly-fishing line, in contrast to the above method, lies mainly in the fact that one can more reliably detect the take of a fish. Casting is carried out at right angles or diagonally against the stream. The free bulge of the fly-fishing line should be continuously pulled in, so that one can react immediately to a take. A take is detected either from the silhouette of the fish or from the fly-fishing line, which checks a little, or deviates from its direction. Sometimes undulation of the water around the rig is also visible.

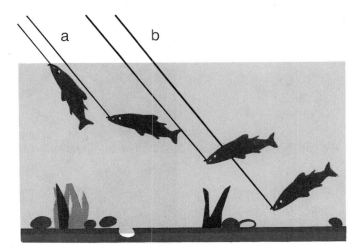

The optimal moment for the take is when the fish is heading towards the bottom with the captured quarry; a) premature hooking, b) hooking at the right moment.

77

Fishing with streamers and bucktails

This technique is somewhat of a hybrid between classic fly-fishing and spinning. Streamers, both in their shape and in the material used, resemble flies, although when in use in the water they resemble more closely young fish, having the advantage that they can be sunk and drawn through the water relatively slowly, so that the fish are given sufficient opportunity to react. They are therefore used for fishing mainly in spring and autumn, when the fish are generally more lazy.

Casting is carried out in the same manner as when fly-fishing. When the streamer has sunk to the bottom, the angler gradually draws it towards himself by jerking jumps 30—40cm (12—16in) long. The dragging of the fly-fishing line with the hand is combined with moving the rod tip up and down, by means of which more provocative movement of the lure is achieved. The lure is always cast upstream from the target spot, so that it has a chance to sink to the bottom before reaching the desired location. Casting is carried out at right angles to the stream, or diagonally against the stream. The risk of catching the lure in obstacles is minimal

The occasional angler may fish with a standard fly-fishing rod. A specialist, however, will give preference to a longer (over 2.7m/9ft), stronger (AFTMA 8—10) rod with parabolic action — which, amongst other things, enables smoother casting. A somewhat over-dimensioned reel with a reserve of line is also suitable, as one must be prepared for takes by larger trout, as well as by silver-salmon — especially at the end of autumn, when they are moving to the depths — chub, pike, and even pike-perch. One must consider this possibility when assembling the rod and line. When trout fishing, a cast 0.20 up to 0.30mm (0.008—0.012in) thick is used, when fishing for lowland predators up to 0.35mm (0.014in). If one specialises in pike, a standard stranded steel wire pays off, in spite of the fact that it will affect the performance of the streamer.

When fishing with bucktails, it is practically a question of fishing by sink and draw. If one does not have a fly-fishing rod, fishing can be equally successful with a standard, longer and finer casting rod. For the sake of more fluent casting and quicker sinking of the lure, the bucktail may be weighted with a tiny zinc weight.

The principles of fishing for individual fish species

We have acquainted ourselves with fishing tackle, with both natural and artificial lures, and have explained the principles of various fishing methods. It might seem that one can now set out for the water without fear of failure, that one knows how to go about fishing.

The most important thing, however, is still to come — that is, our acquaintance with individual fish species, with their way of life throughout the year, with their nutritional requirements, and with their special moods, which we must come to know. How to go about catching an individual fish species, which lure to use to outwit it, and how to play it — all this will be dealt with in the following chapters.

FISHING FOR NON-PREDATORY FISHES

Carp

The carp is one of those fish species which have best adapted themselves to the process of technical progress, and its presence is on the increase in most waters. This is on the one hand the result of the adaptability of the carp, but on the other hand man can also take some of the credit, constantly creating for it new habitats by building various types of water reservoir and introducing it into every suitable area of water. The carp is a thermophilic fish, which means that the intensity of its life functions is very sensitively influenced by the temperature of its environment. The fish is active in seeking food within a temperature range of 7—8°C (44—46°F) up to 26 to 28°C (79—82°F), depending, of course, on ecological conditions. Above and below the stated limits it becomes indolent. The carp is a gourmet in its food demands. The main components of its natural diet are small animals inhabiting the water column and bottom. During spawning, however, it has uncompromising requirements, demanding a temperature from 18—20°C (64—68°F) and a high quality, non-muddy, grassy substrate. The numerical strength of the carp can therefore only be maintained in many waters by introducing new fish regularly. The thermophilia of the carp can serve as a reliable guide when seeking out a suitable vantage point for fishing, as well as when choosing the fishing method and effective bait.

In brooks and rivers, the potential gathering place of carp can be determined relatively simply. Logically they can be assumed to be in calmer, deeper parts, that is in meanders, in water hollows, above and below weirs, at river junctions, at tributary estuaries, in whirling sections, and sometimes even in bankside parts of rivers reinforced with free-standing boulders. In rivers with excessive sediments of impurities, the carp is sometimes forced to change its typical gathering places for swifter sections with a more favourable oxygen balance. In enclosed waters, mainly in water reservoirs, the carp's behaviour is dictated by the instinct for self-preservation. It generally occurs in places where it has a feeling of security as well as sufficient food. In much frequented waters the instinct for self-preservation compels carp to keep well away from the banks.

The daily rhythm of the carp consists of a certain stereotype, characterised by periods of intensive feeding and relative calm. In the summer season the former period has two phases: it takes place in the early morning and later during evening hours. The carp devotes the short summer nights and long days to resting and digesting food. In the cooler autumn season, food consumption is more or less evenly distributed throughout the day.

The nocturnal, but above all the daytime siesta period, however, should not be taken literally. Even if relatively sated, carp will not disdain any accessible morsel, and only in exceptional cases will it refuse food on account of being over-full. Sometimes in summer, carp may also manifest atypical feeding activity during the day, not seeking food at the bottom as usual, but swimming upwards to the surface for it. The sunning of carp on the surface on hot summer days is probably one of the ways they

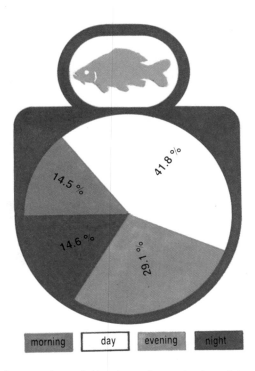

morning · day · evening · night

The effectiveness of carp-fishing depending on the time of day.

sary to suit the basic fishing methods to the behaviour of the carp, which means either fishing on the bottom or just above the bottom.

When putting into order of importance the most effective baits for carp, one should put in first place corn, both on its own and as a basic component of groats and combined baits. After this come boiled potatoes, groats and dough, bread and baked items. One of the most natural baits — the earthworm — is well behind these in terms of its effectiveness. Of the other, less common baits, successful ones are, for example, grains (boiled wheat, husked grain), pulses (peas, kidney beans, haricot beans), bone and flour worms, rice, pastas and not least also fish bait, the spinner and fillet of fish. On the basis of personal experience we can even recommend trying halved ripe plums and similar aromatic fruits, or dough made of crumbled bread with an admixture of ground red pepper and a whole egg.

The effectiveness of the lure also depends on the season. At the beginning of the growing season, one should give preference to baits of animal origin; at the end of the growing period, when carp are preparing for overwintering by forming necessary fat reserves, fat-forming glycid baits are preferable — carp encounter these in the wild, in the form of the

spend their siesta, which they are nevertheless quite willing to interrupt at every opportunity for seizing an attractive morsel. However, this behaviour may also indicate a deterioration of the oxygen balance in the water. It occurs in the second half of the summer in shallower, muddy and excessively overgrown reservoirs without sufficient inflow of water. An oxygen deficit caused by the processes of decay in mud becomes critical mainly in the early hours of the morning, increasing progressively from the bottom to the surface. Only the appearance of sun rays encourages the photosynthetic activity of aquatic plants, as a result of which the water is supplied with oxygen and the conditions for the feeding activity of the carp then return to normal.

In smaller, shallower reservoirs the movement of carp after food can even be followed with the eye. The carp leaves a tell-tale track of its movement by clouding the water, by causing escaping air bubbles released from the mud, as well as by the movement of the aquatic plants. Occasional jumping of the carp out of the water is not a good omen, since their interest in the lure at such moments is minimal.

The conclusions to be drawn from all this information are unequivocal. Carp must be fished for in places with sufficient food, during the period when they are feeding most intensively, and using lures corresponding to their natural diet. It is also neces-

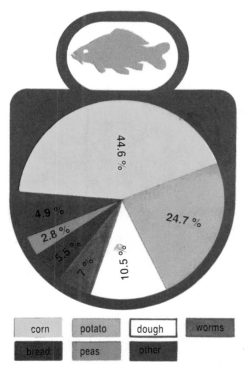

corn · potato · dough · worms
bread · peas · other

Graph showing the efficiency of various baits when carp-fishing.

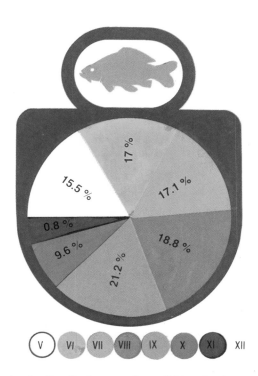

Graph showing the effectiveness of carp-fishing at various seasons of the year.

Carp can also be enticed with baits of the sandwich type: a) a combination of dough with one grain of corn, b) an earthworm and a grain of corn.

seeds of aquatic river and lakeside plants.

We must admit, however, that these considerations are nonetheless somewhat theoretical, in that they can only be valid assuming that the locality in question is one in which the carp have not yet come into contact with humans. In fact the majority of waters today are stocked with pond carp which are already partly 'domesticated'. Today's carp makes practically no distinction between natural food and substitute food. With corn, for example, one can fish successfully throughout the whole fishing season, although this will be most successful when it is ripening naturally, in the middle of July.

The optimal size of the bait is a debatable point and one which can be regarded as a matter of taste. Proponents of larger bait proceed from the assumption that carp, with their accordion-like protrudable mouths, can seize even a larger morsel, also justifying their choice with the fact that the hook will be more thoroughly disguised in the bait and that the carp will have no reason for suspicion. Another advantage of larger baits is that smaller fish will not dare to go for them. Those who prefer using smaller morsels justify this by saying that the natural food of the carp consists of small animal larvae and even smaller plankton, so that a small bait is more logical for the fish.

The question as to how much the hook should be concealed in the bait so that the carp does not become suspicious is important. Too much caution, however, is needless and may be a cause of unsuccessful hookings, for example on occasions when the point of the hook is also hidden in the bait, or if too small a hook is used for the sake of camouflage. It will undoubtedly bother the carp less if it can see 1—2 grains of corn on a half-exposed hook, than if it finds a whole necklace composed of 6—8 grains densely mounted on the hook among scattered grains of corn during luring.

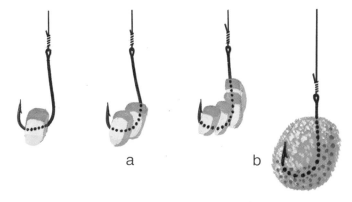

Universal and effective baits for carp-fishing and methods for presenting them: a) one, two or even more grains of corn are mounted on to the hook in such a way that the point remains free; b) a boiled potato may also be mounted on a single hook with a wider curve. If the angler is casting further off, the potato is sewn through on to a double or triple hook in such a way that the hook is completely concealed in the potato.

83

Carp is mostly fished for in shallower waters, so it can be assumed that the colour of the bait will play an important role in the orientation of the fish. Practical knowledge about the effect of the colour of the bait may be evaluated as follows: in shallow waters in the cooler season of the year (up to 12 °C/54°F) in clear weather, a lemon yellow colour is suitable, and in cloudy weather blue. In the warm season in sunny weather in the morning and early evening red is better, during the day a naturally coloured bait, and in cloudy weather green. When fishing in deeper waters the situation varies. In cool but sunny weather orange is the best colour, red when it is raining; in warmer sunny weather, violet, when the sky is overcast, green.

What kind of tackle to use for carp

As one of the most attractive sport fishes, the carp definitely deserves special fishing tackle appropriate to its proverbial love of combat. This requirement, however, sometimes comes into conflict with the tendency to give preference to the finest possible tackle for catching all fish, since by using fine tackle one gives the fish an equal chance to fight for its life, thus emphasising the sporting aspect of fishing. We must nevertheless be tough in our approach to carp. For one thing the angler is not usually at the water alone and must bear in mind that playing a carp with tackle that is too fine will cause such a commotion that it will foul up all the neighbouring rods and lines. Another thing the angler must bear in mind is that a large, prime specimen could bite, and then he would be sorry to lose the catch of a lifetime.

A specialist carp fisherman needs above all two identical carp-fishing rods for fishing on the bottom with a weight and possibly also with the aid of a feeding-trough. The ideal length is between 2.8 and 3.2m (9—10½ft) with a semi-soft action (B) and a recommended weight of at least 60—80g (2.1—2.8oz). The above requirements are best met by two, at most three-part assembled and relatively heavy rods made of either solid or tubular thick-walled laminates. One also needs any kind of more solid fixed-spool reel of average size, with particular emphasis on increased resistance of the reel with a capacity of 150 to 180m (500—600ft) of line 0.30mm (0.012in) thick. Depending on the character of the water and its diversity, as well as on the as-

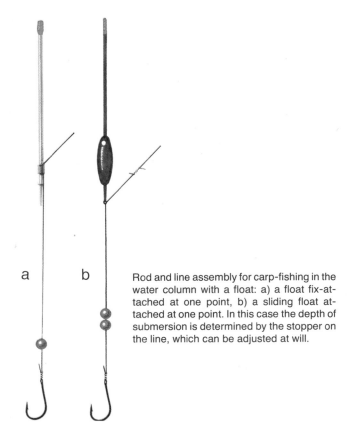

a   b   Rod and line assembly for carp-fishing in the water column with a float: a) a float fix-attached at one point, b) a sliding float attached at one point. In this case the depth of submersion is determined by the stopper on the line, which can be adjusted at will.

sumed weight of the quarry, one should use softer lines with sufficient knotting resistance from 0.22 up to 0.30mm (0.009—0.012in) thick, and thicker ones only in extremely difficult conditions, for example in excessively overgrown waters with many obstacles, inaccessible terrain and so on.

When fishing with a float, lighter rods from 4.2 up to 4.5m (13½—14½ft) long are more suitable with a semi-soft action (B—A), and a weight of 30—40g (1—1.4oz). These may also be telescopic if they have a sufficient number of equally distributed rod rings, so that when playing the quarry all parts of the rod are evenly strained. The reel used should be the same as for fishing on the bottom, but the line may be finer, from as little as 0.18—0.20mm (0.007—0.008in) up to 0.25—0.28mm (0.010—0.011in), since the finer, longer rod increases its bearing capacity. This type of rod is also entirely suitable when fishing for carp on the surface with a crust of bread; in this case, however, a fixed-spool reel may be substituted with a simple centre-pin reel and a thinner line should be used.

Carp hooks are chosen within a range of nos. 2—3 up to 5—6 of the size scale, but when fishing at a distance even larger hooks are more suitable, ensuring hooking. More important than the size of the hook is the quality of the material and its construc-

tion. The hook should be as fine as possible, but should have perfect bearing capacity, and a sufficiently solid and pronounced barb, which is particularly important when tiring a quarry over a longer period. Colour is irrelevant, more significant being the shape of the curve and the length of the shank, mainly in relation to the bait used. A longer shank is necessary when fishing with earthworms and so on, and a regular curve of the hook when fishing with corn or peas.

A weight on the rod and line should be regarded as a necessary evil when fishing for carp. Every weight detracts from the sensitivity of the rod and line and increases the possibility of the carp becoming suspicious. Every technical improvement replacing the classic weights, for example the use of ice cubes, special methods for mounting weights and so on, is therefore welcome. In the attempt to minimalise the mass of the necessary weight it is better to opt for thinner lines, since the mass of the weight increases in geometrical progression with the thickness of the line.

How to fish for carp

Three basic fishing methods can be considered when fishing for carp: fishing on the bottom with or without a weight, fishing in the water column with a float, and fishing on the surface with or without a glass ball.

The basic fishing method is fishing on the bottom, the principle of which lies in the bait being positioned on the bottom either by means of a weight or simply by its own weight and with or without a float. The principle of simplicity should be observed during assembly, as well as the lowest possi-

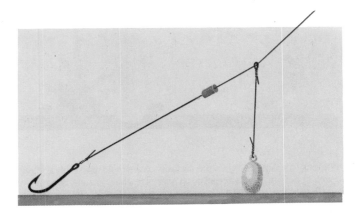

Classic rod and line assembly for carp-fishing on the bottom with a weight. In the case of a heavier weight, preference is given to a more reliable stopper made, for example, from a rubber band.

a

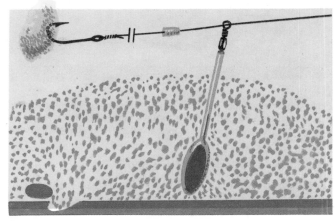

b

In the case of a classic rod and line assembly, the tackle may sink deeper into the mud in water with an excessive mud layer, which will render both observation of the take and hooking more difficult. Under these conditions, the rod and line are better assembled with a weight of the inverted buoy type (b).

ble weight of the rod and line. It is thus ideal to fish to shorter distances without a weight. When casting to medium distances of 20—30m (65—100ft), one can manage with a split weight mounted firmly on the line; for casting further off one selects a larger, sliding weight. Zinc weights of various sizes are mounted on 100—150cm (40—60in) lengths of line in such a way that the smallest is placed 30 to 40cm (12—16in) from the hook, the other progressively larger weights being mounted at regular distances apart. The size and shape of the larger weights depend on the character of the water and the bottom, as well as on the length of the casts. They should either be mounted as sliding weights directly with the aid of stoppers, or on a cast.

After being cast, the bait should be allowed to sink to the bottom, the line bulge then being straightened so that one has contact with the bait. When fishing without a detector the line should be kept taut. Between the rod and taut line there

87

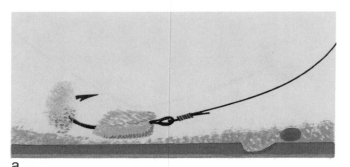

a

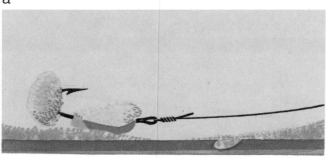

b

Sinking of the bait into the mud can also be prevented by means of a small polystyrene ball stuck on to the shank of the hook (a), or by choosing a bait which will hover in the water, for example a pressed roll (b).

should be a 90° angle. When using a detector which is attached with a 15—25cm (6—10in) bulge only behind the tip of the rod or among the rod rings, the rod can follow the direction of the line. In good visibility and mainly when there is a wind, the rods are positioned horizontally, as low to the ground as possible. In twilight the tip of the rod may point upwards, so that it is easier to observe.

On hot summer days, carp often put themselves on display just under the surface. Fishing for carp on the surface calls for a true master, who can convey the bait over a relatively long distance in such a manner that it will remain on the surface as long as possible. In this case the bait is most often a piece of bread crust or fresh roll. Every potential weight would have to be compensated for by a float, so that one tends to give preference to a larger piece of crust, which is briefly dipped in water before being cast. During the flight through the air the crust dries out and so remains on the surface. Casting lengths may also be increased by casting downwind. A rod for fishing on the surface should be finer and longer, the thickness of the line up to 0.18 to 0.20mm (0.007—0.008in); the bait may be large, so as also to serve partly as a lure.

One should not allow oneself to be put off by the apathy of the carp during the first moments after casting the bait. Their interest will manifest itself

only after a while, when small fish begin to take bites from the bait. Then one must be on guard, and at any moment expect their feeding to excite the interest of even the most phlegmatic carp, which with a noisy smacking of its mouth will whip the morsel from under their noses. When fishing on the surface, even the specialist fly-fisherman may come into his element.

Fishing for carp in the upper layers of water as well as on the surface may only be considered in cooler waters, supplied by springs of cool tribut-

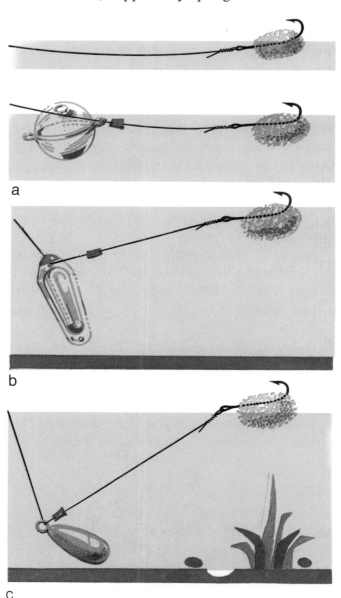

a

b

c

Methods for carp fishing on the surface: a) a simple assembly without a weight or float, with a bread crust serving as bait, is suitable for fishing close to the bank; b) if it is necessary to cast further off, the rod and line are assembled with a glass ball, ideally colourless, and partially filled with water, or c) with the aid of a sliding weight, in such a way that the distance between the stopper and the hook is greater than the depth of the water, so that a light bait, for example a bread crust, will float to the surface.

aries, when the water temperature in the lower layers does not exceed 10—12°C (50—54°F) even in summer. One is advised to take with a pinch of salt handed-down tales of carp takes. The carp's reaction during the take can vary greatly, and each of these ways could be characterised as typical. Sometimes a carp behaves itself well, at first chewing the bait in its mouth in order to let us know it is there by means of the wobbling of the detector and to give us enough time for hooking, only then starting continuously to tighten the line. However, it often simply grabs the bait and makes off with it so unexpectedly that one hardly manages to save the rod and line from being pulled under. Of course, certain rules apply for establishing the ideal moment for hooking. Under normal circumstances, the angler should not be too hasty with hooking at the very first hints of disturbance from the detector. It is necessary to wait for a regular, continuous pull from the fish. Another general rule is that when using softer baits it is advisable to hook sooner; in the case of harder ones, mainly corn, one should wait for a continuous pull. This also depends on the season of the year or the temperature of the water. Carp are never apt to take so eagerly at the end of the fishing season as in summer, and therefore at this time one should hook at the first tentative hints of a take.

Playing a hooked carp, which ranks among the most combative species, may also be variable, likewise depending on the environment and origin of the fish. It is a pity that pond carp have inherited so little of the combative spirit of their wild ancestors. Even among pond carp, however, stubborn escapes several dozen metres long are no rarity, so that when playing them with what is as a rule fine tackle it is inadvisable to act precipitately. In the first phase of playing one should allow the carp to get away to a greater distance if possible, making use of the flexibility of the rod and line to tire it. In doing so one should take great care to hold the rod at the correct angle and not to lose contact with the fish even for a moment. As soon as one notices that the fish is losing strength, one should shift to counterattack and finish the combat by netting the carp with a fairly solid landing-net.

Tench

In their requirements for a living environment, tench and carp are like brothers. In waters which they inhabit together, the tench has never attained the popularity of the carp, however. Nonetheless in some waters the tench is truly sovereign, although this is usually the case in debased waters — in excessively overgrown, shallowish and muddy ones, remote river branches and similar waters, where an unfavourable oxygen balance makes existence impossible for more demanding fish species.

In spite of the fact that calmer, warmer, muddy and overgrown waters are the chief domain of the modest and unbelievably adaptable tench, it is able to thrive even in the harsher climatic conditions of cooler valley reservoirs after being introduced there. In flowing waters, it avoids the swifter sections, inhabiting slightly dragging currents with more dense vegetation cover only in summer. It always, however, gives preference to still, shallower waters and feels most secure in a labyrinth of underwater vegetation.

It feeds in a similar manner to other carp-type fishes on the small larvae of aquatic insects, from time to time also enjoying a plant diet. It spawns relatively late, only when the temperature of the water reaches 22—23°C (71—73°F). It grows quite slowly, even in favourable conditions only reaching the weight of 1kg (2.2 lb) in the sixth or seventh year of its life and for the most part much later. For this reason quarries weighing more than one kilogram are considered quite remarkable, and over four kilograms outstanding.

Fishing for tench is most successful in the warmest season of the year, from May to August. An evaluation of the effectiveness of various baits confirms the carnivorousness of the tench, and qualifies earthworms as a universal bait. The effectiveness of other usual baits cannot be evaluated unequivocally as it depends on regional conditions. Among these baits are pastas, groats, larvae, potatoes, bread, husked grains, peas and wheat, and among less common ones the artificial fly and the spinner.

It shouldn't be a problem for the angler to deduce the probable gathering places of tench, seeking them out in every type of water in shallow, muddy and densely overgrown corners. Tench behave inconspicuously, but when seeking food in the mud they release rings of gas bubbles in a similar way to carp. Another sign of the feeding activity of tench is the clouding of the water here and there.

The more modest body size of the tench is not always a good guide when choosing tackle, which should not be too fine. An assembly for catching carp-bream may only be used when fishing in more open waters or reservoirs without a continuous growth of aquatic vegetation. In such atypical places, however, one usually catches tench accidentally while fishing for other fish.

One should only concentrate on tench fishing in those areas where it occurs in large numbers, that is in muddy and overgrown waters. In such places one is forced to cast the bait to smaller water openings in the tangled vegetation, where the trumps are in the hands of the hooked tench, fighting for its life. In these conditions one should have no compunction about fishing with a firm carp-fishing rod and a line 0.30—0.35mm (0.012—0.014in) thick, so that that one can hold the fish on a tight rein after hooking, tire it and catch it within a very small space. A thicker line shouldn't affect the tench, the waters in such places usually being cloudy and less clear. A zinc weight and float may nevertheless be a nuisance while hooking, so that it is necessary to assemble even more robust rods and lines with care. This also applies to the hook, which should be entirely hidden in the relatively small bait. When fishing with smaller earthworms one should use a size 8—10 hook, and if bone worm larvae are the bait even smaller sized hooks are suitable, whilst in the case of larvae of aquatic insects sizes 14—16 will do.

Since one is fishing in still waters, a weight is only necessary for casting and can be minimalised. In this way the size requirements of the float, which is attached at one point, are at the same time also reduced, thereby achieving a straight direction of the line from the rod to the bait, the tackle therefore being more sensitive. Fishing with a sliding float cannot be considered in practical terms. In calm weather a more slender, longer float should be used, and with greater undulation of the water a conical one. For greater rod and line sensitivity a divided weight should be chosen. In windless weather the weights should be evenly distributed, whereas if there is a choppy surface the lower part of the line should be weighted more so that the bait will remain at the required place. Tench approach the bait confidently and spend some time chewing it in the mouth. A take may be signalled in various ways. Generally the float sinks continuously after shaking hesitantly; sometimes it leans to one side and lies on the water, in the same way as during a carp-bream take. A scarcely visible wobbling of the float may, however, also be caused by tench colliding with the line in search of food. On such an occasion one must not be precipitate with hooking, so as not to startle the shoal.

When selecting baits and when luring one should observe the principle that too little is better than too much. During the period in which tench have the greatest appetite, that is, at the beginning of summer, the baits may be larger; dung worms, for ex-

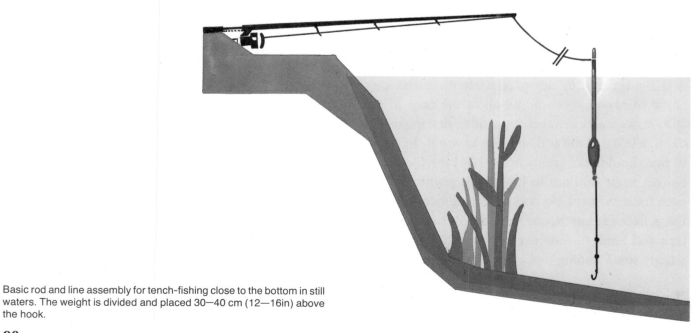

Basic rod and line assembly for tench-fishing close to the bottom in still waters. The weight is divided and placed 30—40 cm (12—16in) above the hook.

ample, may be put to superb use. Later, when the appetite of tench is gradually subsiding, one should try to butter them up with smaller morsels; in cooler water one is most likely to succeed with the small larvae of aquatic insects. The same rules apply to luring. Tench are more prone to over-eating than other fish species, among other things because they have no competition in their gathering places from other fish which could join them in picking up the lure. Luring is therefore more or less symbolic, only with the intention of arousing the interest of the fish, and may therefore be finer, for example in the form of roasted hempseeds with a few smaller grains of corn or wheat. The attention of fish may also be attracted by simply stirring up the mud.

In some cases tench may have their appetites awakened by luring in such a way that they will obligingly rise to the food as far as the surface. On such occasions one can even fish successfully in the upper water profile on the assumption that the hooked bait falls slowly to the bottom with the thrown bait. The rod should be held in the hand with a finger on the line, so that one can react immediately to the slightest take.

A hooked tench will stubbornly try with substantial force to escape into the densest growth. A large fish on a fine rod and line will generally succeed. It cannot be retrieved from the growth by brute force, and it is equally useless to expect the fish to change its mind after a while and give up. In such a case one has only one option: to attempt to raise the fish from the bottom and direct it head upwards by re-peated energetic pumping movements. The line should be held constantly taut, so that the fish does not escape even deeper into the tangled growth, and when lifting the rod and line one should carefully hold on to the spool of the reel.

Winter fishing for the pronouncedly thermophilic tench cannot be recommended. In winter tench are absolutely indolent, lying buried in the mud and waking only under unusual circumstances. The contrived disturbance of fish from their winter sleep, for example by stirring up the mud for the purposes of sport fishing, is not in accordance with the rules of fair-play.

Carp-bream

At the first encounter with carp-bream, one has the impression that from its distinctive body one can tell the environment in which it lives, the food it likes to eat, how it obtains it and its swimming capabilities. Appearances are deceptive, however. Looking at the apparent clumsiness of the carp-bream, one would exclude the possibility of its existing in flowing waters and would condemn it to a life in still waters only. It is true that the carp-bream mainly inhabits all types of more open, deeper, and enclosed waters, but at the same time it has claimed a living space in flowing waters as well. It will nevertheless still not venture into swift sections with rapids, as it would have problems moving there. It regards calmer, dragging currents as its standard habitat.

The prognosis for the future existence of the carp-bream is favourable. There is evidence of this, for example, from the dynamic increase in the long-term average. Unlike carp, which heads the list of

On warm, windless summer days, one can even look for tench, with suitably chosen bait, close to the surface.

catches and which owes its leading position mainly to man the husbandman, the carp-bream has worked its way up to second place largely on the strength of its own characteristics. Besides an overall adaptability, these can mainly be seen in the unique ability of the carp-bream to lay roe on various substrates, for example grass, the small roots of aquatic vegetation and trees, on finer twigs, on clean largish rocks, and so on. It knows how to take care of its young in every environment, even those which are not entirely suitable, and in most waters is thus not dependent on the help of man. It spawns in May and in cooler conditions in June, always in groups of large numbers and ostentatiously loudly.

In spite of its modest requirements, the carp-bream is nevertheless a gourmet, orienting itself predominantly towards animal diet elements. Its specially formed, accordion-like protrudable small mouth moreover limits it in its food-gathering possibilities to smaller sized prey, exclusively from the bottom. It is therefore also necessary to judge with forbearance its relatively modest rate of growth. In average conditions it reaches a weight of 1kg (2.2lb) only in its eighth or tenth year. On the list of the causes of its slower growth probably also figures a high price for feeling safe, contingent upon as numerous a species community as possible. Family solidarity inevitably leads to merciless competition for food, and in extreme cases of excessive over-reproduction it can result in degeneration of the whole carp-bream population in some waters. Nevertheless in most waters the carp-bream knows how to assert itself, so that even in average conditions catches weighing 4—5kg (8¾—11lb) may be regarded as normal.

One has to make use of the character traits of the carp-bream when sport fishing. The sport fishing rules for carp-bream are in many respects completely different from the technique of fishing for other white fish species. Carp-bream may be fished for practically throughout the whole year. On account of its shyness it is sought out in deeper, calmer waters, and one can only outwit it with the tiniest baits, which it is even able to find sunk in the mud. The most important difference, however, lies in its special manner of obtaining food. Other fish species are constantly on the move when seeking food and also consume the presented morsels in

motion. A bait consumed in motion is always clearly signalled by the take in the true sense of the word. The intensity of the take varies with different fish species, the common denominator, however, always being smooth movement of the bait and thus also of the line and possibly of the float as well. In the case of the carp-bream, the discovery of the bait is a ceremony, determined by the shape and position of the mouth. When discovering a morsel, a carp-bream must stop, positioning itself with its head almost at right angles to the bottom, and with its telescopic small mouth sucking the food, even possibly with an admixture of mud. It then straightens itself out again into a horizontal position, motionlessly chewing the bait in its mouth as if separating the edible parts from the ballast, and thus of course also from the hook, which if possible it spits out. It does this so gently that the line hardly sways, so there can be no question of a classic take. One can only succeed in outwitting a cunning carp-

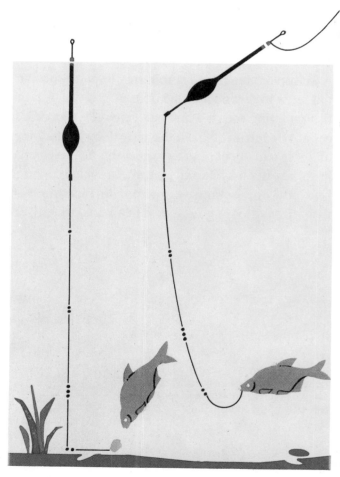

Typical pike-perch take: when the bait is being seized, the float stands upright and does not react; when the morsel is being tasted, the lightened float slowly emerges and leans sideways. It never submerges or moves away, as happens during the takes of other fish species.

bream in two ways, depending on the fishing method: either with a special way of assembling (weighting) the rod and line when fishing with a float, or with a specially sensitive method of attaching the detector.

When assembling the rod and line for float fishing, when the float only fulfils the task of a sensitive detector, one proceeds from the principle that the carp-bream, when gulping down the bait and regaining its horizontal position, will be forced to lift part of the weight as well as the bait. The lightened float, hitherto submerged up to the tip of the antenna, pops out of the water and lies on the surface. This is pre-eminently the sign of a typical carp-bream take, to which the angler reacts by hooking. The rod and line is assembled in such a way that the length of the line from the float to the bait will be greater than the height of the water column (in flowing waters even more than in still), and part of the weight is attached close to the hook, approximately 6—7cm (2½in) away.

When fishing for carp-bream, one can only succeed using the finest and most sensitive tackle, which is limited by the thickness of the line, up to 0.18—0.20mm (0.007—0.008in), and the hooks up to no. 8 during the period of the greatest appetite of the fish, and at other times even smaller. The rest of the tackle, including as far as possible a longer rod with a semi-soft action, must be in accordance with these limits. The use of the lightest possible assembly is limited by its relatively small range. A wary carp-bream usually keeps away from the reach of a light assembly. The angler can, of course, adapt himself to the fish and fish for it in its usual gathering places. This is not the ideal solution, however, because with the excessive distance the weighting

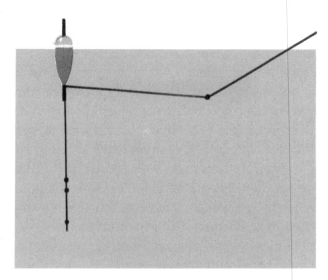

In strong wind, the submerging of the line under the surface can be assisted by a tiny weight.

requirements increase in geometrical progression, at the expense of the sensitivity of the rod and line. It appears, therefore, to be more sensible to try to attract the carp-bream nearer by luring. The angler must maintain absolute silence both before and during fishing. When fishing for carp-bream, the angler can only consider the basic fishing on the bottom method, with several alternatives for assembling the rod and line, depending on the given conditions. Whenever possible, fishing with a simple whiprod should be given preference, although of course only a standard assembled rod and line can be employed for fishing from a distance. In both cases either a float or a suitable type of detector is used. One decides between a fixed or a sliding float depending on the circumstances, a fixed one being preferable. If the float is attached at one point one achieves more sensitive contact between the rod and the bait,

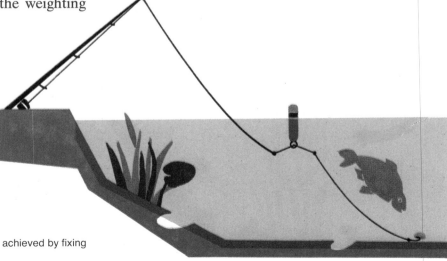

A superbly sensitive rod and line assembly can be achieved by fixing the float with two weights.

which is especially important with carp-bream, and moreover more advantageous for better stability of the bait. A float attached at two points, however, fully meets the demands of fishing at shorter distances with a longer rod, from which the line is directed towards the water in a more favourable, perpendicular direction. A float attached at one point can be fixed, for example, with two weights in the lower part at a distance of 5cm (2in) from the float.

When fishing without a float, its function is partly fulfilled by a detector. Of the various technical designs, a seesaw-type detector seems to be quite effective. This is either an 8—10cm (3—4in) long, thin goose quill, or a porcupine spine with an eye at the lower end. It is attached to the line by means of a small ring of tubing or of rubber tire valve tubing exactly in the centre, so that it will create an equal-armed lever — a seesaw, which will react sensitively to the slightest impulse. The seesaw is mounted close behind the tip of the rod. A floating detector is also suitable — a quill attached to the line at both ends. After casting, the angler straightens the line so that the detector will form an obtuse angle with the line. During a take the angles align themselves into an inclined plane, and during a very gentle take only the rear section of the detector will seesaw.

The most favourable season for carp-bream fishing is summer, especially July, although this does not mean that one should not set out for it in spring or autumn. Then it does not have a particularly wide choice of food in the water and will certainly

not disdain a good morsel. Earthworms are the most popular bait for carp-bream fishing, especially smaller dung worms. Dough, the larvae of both aquatic and land insects, bread, corn, potatoes, cheese and oat flakes are also effective, and carp-bream can often be deceived even by a spinner. As a subject for experimentation, we recommend giving preference to earthworms at the beginning of the season, insect larvae in summer and plant baits in autumn.

Barbel

The fact that when classifying courses, swift varied sections of brooks and rivers in the sub-montane belt were named the barbel belt, most aptly characterises the qualities of this noble fish. The barbel is gradually losing its once pre-eminent position in many waters. It is not certain whether its decline can be attributed just to water pollution. In many rivers, barbel do not stay in the cleanest sections; on the contrary they are often found precisely in the places where the water is dirtiest — under sewage outlets and outlets of other organic waste products. They are also sometimes found in whirling sections with a thick layer of sediments, and for the sake of a morsel of food, which is abundant there, may lower their high hygienic demands.

Such cases are not typical, however. The barbel remains a fish of swift, more varied courses with hard sandy, gravelly or clay substrate and is not prepared to adapt itself to excessive pollution. Owing to its way of life it is restricted to the bottom. Animal elements from the river bed prevail in its diet, although it also occasionally enjoys plant food, and larger, older fish will sometimes seize smaller fish.

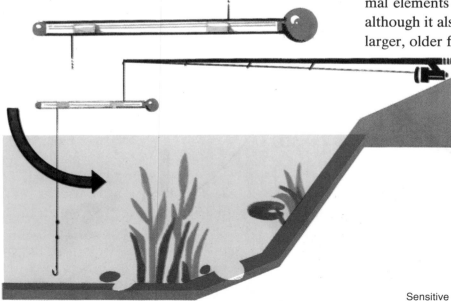

Sensitive balance-beam bite detector for pike-perch fishing.

98

One cannot speak of permanent barbel gathering places. The barbel is exceptionally restless and wanders tirelessly almost the whole year round. It only keeps to a permanent place in winter, when it gives itself over to winter sleep and does not take food. However, as soon as the first spring torrents wake it, it resumes its nomadic life, moving from place to place, motivated sometimes by the search for a suitable spawning place and at other times by lack of food or by the rise and fall of the water level. In some cases it can cover as much as 8—10km (5—6¼ miles) in a day. During the interruptions to its wanderings, it of course keeps to its typical gathering places. Sometimes it will completely disappear from certain sections, whereas a couple of days later one cannot catch any other fish than barbel in the same place. It is persistent in maintaining its daily routine, being active from dusk until late into the night and reluctant to show itself during the day, with the exception of times when the water is cloudy, when it will uninterruptedly indulge in titbits which have drifted down.

It spawns in May to June; its roe is slightly poisonous prior to spawning. It reaches a weight of 1kg (2.2lb) relatively late, only in the eighth or tenth year of its life, growing to 2kg (4.4lb) after fifteen years.

One must speak of the sporting qualities of the barbel with the highest appreciation. Any angler who can boast of at least fifty percent success with hookings certainly knows his craft. The virtuosity with which a barbel is able to denude a hook is unparalleled in the fish world. One can also search in vain among fish species for a quarry which is its equal in combative spirit.

The ideal season for barbel fishing is at the beginning of spring, in April, and in late summer, in August and September. In November and December, barbel are already tucking themselves down for their winter sleep. Of the relatively rich choice of baits, earthworms are definitely the most effective. The proportion of quarries caught with other baits is more or less the same, with possibly more success being achieved with the larvae of both land and aquatic insects, peas, husked grains and wheat. A traditional speciality for barbel fishing — cheese — is not in fact particularly effective. Among other things, various doughs, bread or bread crust, oat-

The barbel is able to denude a hook completely, so each bait must be securely attached.

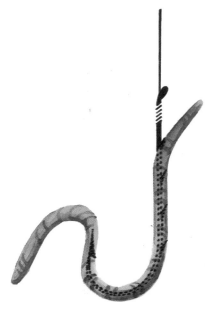

The bait holds best on a barbed hook.

flakes, corn, various drupe species, mole-crickets, leeches, salami, bacon and the offal of domestic animals additionally figure here. Universal baits may be used all year round, but the seasonal character of other baits should be respected, for example fruit and land insects. The relatively high effectiveness of fish bait and spinners is well established; older fish will sometimes directly seek out this type of bait. The fry of white fish species may also serve as a good thrown bait.

99

The usual fishing method, fishing on the bottom with a weight, is based on knowledge about the way of life of the barbel. In contrast with the usual principles, when choosing suitable tackle one must definitely cut back on the demands for lightness and fineness of the rod and line. The tough combative spirit of the barbel can only be confronted with more resilient, harder tackle. The 2.5—3m (8—10ft) long rod should be strong, with semi-soft action for a weight of 40—80g (1.4—2.8oz), the reel fixed, with a capacity of 120 to 150m (390—490ft) of line 0.25—0.35mm (0.01—0.014in) thick. In view of the barbel's gathering places being in swift sections, round weights must be exchanged for flat ones which will hold the bait in the desired place more securely. Hooks should of course be used, depending on the bait, from sizes 2 up to 6 with various shank lengths, longer for earthworms and so on.

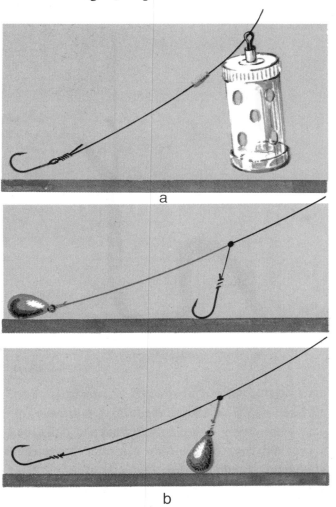

a

b

Basic methods for assembling the rod and line for barbel fishing in swift waters, with appropriately heavy weight: a) standard assembly with hook, stopper and weight, b) assembly with weight on a thinner rig, for fishing in water where there is a risk of the line becoming caught up.

100

There are two ways of assembling the rod and line. In easier terrain, where there is less risk of the rod and line becoming caught up, preference is given to the simplest and thus also the most reliable attachment of both the hook and the sliding weight to the main line. In more difficult terrain, the weight should be fixed to a separate, thinner rig.

Giving preference to bulkier baits in the expectation of more successful hooking is debatable, as is the threading of earthworms throughout their whole length on a hook with a longer shank, or sewing some baits, for example mole-crickets, on to a triple hook. There is no doubt about the attractiveness of sandwich-type baits (e.g. larvae with peas, earthworm with husked grain and so on), but the barbel has no difficulty coping even with these, as it is a magician at denuding hooks, and one is more likely to get the better of it by being prompt when hooking.

The bait should be cast with the current or only slightly diagonally to it. After the weight has hit the bottom the line bulge should be straightened carefully so as to achieve contact with the bait from the first moment.

When noticing a more obvious signal of a take, one should not delay in hooking, even if it should only turn out to be a false alarm, as the barbel will not delay in making its getaway with the bait and possibly even the hook itself.

A passive method for fishing on the bottom can be improved in its effect with an alternative form of tripping the bottom, i.e. trundling the bait along the bottom. For this the fisherman selects a somewhat lighter, rounder weight, and could possibly also exchange the rod for a lighter one, at least 4—4.5m (13—14¾ft) long with a semi-soft action. The weight must be such that it will be enough to pull the bait down to the bottom, but not to hold it in one place. The water current should slowly trundle the weight along together with the bait with short interruptions in as natural a way as possible. If the weight stops for a moment or two at some obstacle, it should be lifted up a little with a gentle movement of the rod. In this way one can fish across a wider area. It is also possible to fish by pulling a weight against the current, although in this case the movement of the bait will be less natural and the barbel will usually instinctively sense this. This more active

fishing method is only possible in easier terrain in gently dragging currents and at depths of up to 2—2.5m (6½—8ft). Even in this fishing method it would be most effective to assemble the rod and line with the most secure fixing of the hook and weight directly on to the main line. However, the risk of tangling and losing the rod and line nevertheless forces one to fix the lead weight on to a thinner rig. The baits and the way they are mounted on the hook are the same as when fishing on the bottom with a stable weight. They are also cast downstream in the same way and contact must be maintained with the bait at every phase, because even in this case instantaneous hooking is essential.

Less usual, but in some cases very effective, is barbel fishing by swimming the stream in various water profiles, quite often also just below the surface. This can be considered in the sunny, summer season and during sunny autumn months, when barbel break with custom and swim up from the

Rod and line assembly for barbel fishing by swimming the stream in shallow, gently moving waters. A spherical weight expedites the smooth drifting of the bait along the bottom.

bottom, enticed by other fish and coming up to feed on land insects which are drifting downstream. This banqueting by the barbel is typical in some lowland rivers in the period of mass mayfly occurrence.

A lighter, longer rod with a semi-soft action for a 20—50g (0.7—1¾oz) weight, a smaller and lighter reel, a thinner line (0.18—0.20mm/0.007—

0.008in), hook nos. 4—6 and a fine, slender float of natural colour should be used for fishing by swimming the stream. The zinc weights — fine weights or sliding small toggles — are fixed, depending on the strength of the current, up to 40—60cm (16—24in) from the hook. Seasonal baits are best, that is insects which fly at that time of year. One can, however, also fish with universal baits. With a view to the finer tackle, in this case the larvae of both aquatic and land insects are better, and dung worms of the earthworm family. With smaller baits it is even possible to use a no. 8 hook. Because of the thinner line a simple rod and line assembly should be used, with the hook and the weight on the main line, to avoid weakening the assembly with unnecessary knots. Casting is carried out downstream (when wading), or diagonally downstream (from the bank). The angler waits a moment after casting until the float settles down, only then straightening out the line bulge. The line is held constantly straightened, so that it is possible from time to time to check the float to prevent it from running ahead of the bait. The current is stronger near the surface than in the water profile, and sometimes the float is also driven along by the wind. A finger is held on the line in order to follow the take. As far as possible one should concentrate the fishing in shaded areas, reaches shaded by trees, the vicinity of larger boulders, submerged trees and so on. Barbel do not particularly like reaches filled with light, as they feel safer in shady places.

The barbel is a tough fighter. It goes to the bottom and by means of suitable manoeuvring seeks to drag the tackle between obstacles. In the first phase of hooking one should leave the spool a little freer, and definitely not try to pull in the fish hard. The mere fact of being able to hold it on the spot of hooking for a moment may be considered half the battle. Playing should be left for later, when the fish slackens a little. Both when wading and when fishing from the bank, a landing-net with a long handle is necessary.

The barbel reacts to luring in the same manner as other fish species; in stronger currents, however, one does not get very far with the usual methods. The angler can therefore try his luck using bait placed in thoroughly weighted perforated plastic bags, ideally tied on to a string, so that he can later remove it from the water. The effectiveness of luring may be increased by adding chopped earthworms and similar animal baits.

Roach and rudd

A well-known Czech saying, 'small fish are still fish', is endorsed by fans of fishing for roach, rudd and similar small fry. One should never cast aspersions on the sporting value of their favourites; and if one goes for a colossal pike or catfish, years may go by before seeing it. On the other hand, when fishing for roach and rudd the angler can achieve success at almost any time of the year or day. A catch of several dozen rudd using the finest tackle and a very thin line is from the sporting point of view on a par with catching a pike using stronger tackle.

Roach and rudd are fish with a great capacity for survival, and they know how to look after themselves in almost any type of water. With the exception of the swiftest trout courses, they can be encountered practically anywhere. Roach can even acclimatise themselves to the lower sections of the trout belt, whereas rudd will not adapt to too tough an environment, preferring warmer reaches. It is not possible to characterise the typical environmental requirements of these two fish, since they are at home in rivers and brooks, in the smallest and largest canals, in semi-cut-off and cut-off river arms, in all water reservoirs and valley dams, in flooded gravel pits, lakes and so on. When choosing a gathering place they behave with discernment, always seeking out locations with the richest choice of accessible food. In flowing waters shoals of them can be encountered in various water profiles at junctions between more protracted, milder currents and still waters, in sections with more abrupt changes in the riverbed, at junctions between whirling and calm sections, and everywhere where objects carried downstream settle, and together with them also the food fish eat. In still waters they swim about in shallow zones with denser growth — that is, mainly in the vicinity of the banks, and in summer in sections with an elevated bottom. They do not need any special shelters, and feel comfortable even in completely open waters. They spawn in April—May, rudd usually somewhat later than roach. In waters where there are few predatory fish they often over-reproduce in large numbers. In spite of their remarkable feeding activity and adaptability, they grow very slowly. Standard catches usually have an average weight of 0.1—0.3kg ($3\frac{1}{2}$—$10\frac{1}{2}$oz). Record catches starting from 1kg (2.2lb) also deserve recognition for the fact that the fish has managed to live 18—20 years.

Apart from the sporting point of view, we can also consider roach and rudd fishing from a practical point of view. Both fish rank among the most suitable and most accessible fish baits for catching the majority of predatory fish species. When mounted on the tackle they behave actively, as they are required to, and also have great powers of endurance. A fisherman who has mastered fishing for them in any situation will have no problems in obtaining and keeping them as fish bait.

The choice of a specific time of year for roach and rudd fishing is not really necessary. As long as the angler adapts the fishing technique (part of which is of course luring) to the prevailing circumstances, he may catch them successfully practically all the year round. This also applies to the time of day for fishing. These permanently hungry fish cannot afford the luxury of idling during the day, as many other fish species can.

Neither roach nor rudd makes a distinction between plant and animal food. As far as baits of animal origin are concerned, smaller earthworm species (dung worms), bone worms and the larvae of aquatic insects are equally effective and, of plant baits, bread, kneaded into the shape of a small ball the size of a pea, seems to be the most effective. All types of pasta, pieces of dumpling, small peas and baits, of corn and husked grain are also good. The

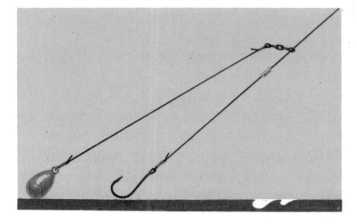

One of the possibilities for assembling the rod and line for roach and rudd fishing on the bottom with the aid of a weight. The hook is attached to the main line, the weight is tied with a loop onto a special thin line.

more experienced angler will not even be surprised at individual catches of older and therefore larger rudd using a small fish or spinner, or a colourful floating wobbler. In the summer months these small fish will even have a pick at insects flying near the surface. So another approach is to try fishing with small artificial flies or with live insects, for example horseflies or grasshoppers.

A basic precondition for fishing success is as fine a rod as possible and as thin a line as possible. Not even a beginner should try a line over 0.15mm (0.006in) thick or a hook over no. 10, and a more experienced angler will certainly choose an even thinner line, 0.10mm (0.004in), a rig up to 0.08mm (0.0032in) and hook nos. 12—16.

At the chosen vantage point the fisherman must first and foremost search the bottom thoroughly with a plummet. He should then concentrate on a section where the bottom is more snaggy, with small holes and elevated parts, or where there is a fault between shallow and deep waters. When luring, one should not exploit the confidence of small fish and lure them at any price to the shallowest bankside sections. Smaller fish are easier to lure; with larger and more experienced ones the instinct for self-preservation usually prevails over gourmet fancies and they will stay in the background. So let us meet the fish half way and offer them bait in those places where they tend to congregate and where they feel most secure. In overgrown, murky waters, a depth of 1—2m (3—6ft) will do; in open waters a greater depth is needed. When luring one should proceed in the usual way. The bait should be compact and heavy enough to reach the bottom quickly and remain both in the required place and in the current. The lure should be presented to the fish before fishing and during the course of fishing only if the interest of the fish in the bait is diminishing. Too frequent luring can lead to excessive concentrations of bleak near the surface, which makes fishing more difficult. In swift reaches, the proportion of earth in the bait is increased, and one must also reckon with part of the bait being carried away, so it is therefore necessary to lure more frequently. Too great a dispersal of the bait is ineffective, the optimal luring area being 2—3m² (22—32 sq.ft).

Roach and rudd are fished for in those places where they prefer to stay, that is mainly in the lower water horizon; in the warmer season even in milder dragging currents, sometimes close to the surface; in autumn and winter at watersheds between currents and still waters deeper down, possibly even right at the bottom. For this reason float fishing is usually chosen. A suitable alternative is chosen according to the distance of the gathering place, the strength of the current and the weather conditions.

The classic walking fishing method, practised, for example, when fishing for chub, barbel and vimba bream, is not essential for roach and rudd fishing. It

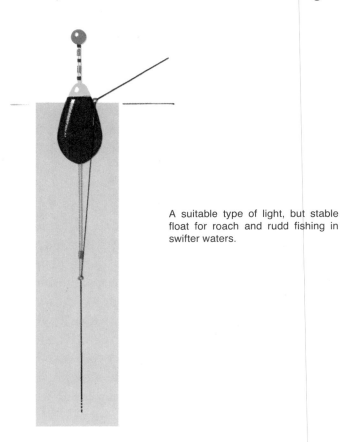

A suitable type of light, but stable float for roach and rudd fishing in swifter waters.

is sufficient to seek out a suitable vantage point and hold the shoal in one place as long as one wants by sensible luring.

The fishing technique, including various ways of assembling the rod and line, is extremely diversified, so we shall focus our attention on the more important tactical fishing variants.

The ideal vantage point is within reach of a 4—6m (13—20ft) long whiprod, which enables one to get even the lightest bait to the required spot without casting. In this case the angler can observe the principle of assembling the simplest and most sensitive rod and line with a weight of up to 1—2g (0.04—0.08oz) and with the smallest float. It is also possible to use the smallest types of bait, mainly the larvae of aquatic insects, which can be cast to a greater distance. A fine, slender hook is attached directly to a 0.10 to 0.12mm (0.004—0.005in) thick main line, and a small, slender sliding weight is fixed with a normal stopper 30—50cm (12—20in) from the hook, or even closer to the hook in stronger currents. The float is attached at one point only, which enables the angler to carry out swift hooking. If the length of the rod and line is 80—100cm (32—40in) greater then the depth of the water, a fixed float is attached; in greater depths a sliding float, a thread being used as a stopper. The shape of the float is determined by the character of the water, and it is always carefully balanced, so that only a small length of the antenna protrudes out of the water. In flowing waters it is usually necessary to overload the float.

When fishing to an average distance, that is 10 to 12m (33—40ft), a classic rod and line assembly is necessary. The fine, long rod should have a semi-soft action for a weight of 10—15g (0.35—0.5oz). A reel is a must, either a smaller fixed-spool one, or a simple centre-pin reel. Casting is partly expedited by the somewhat heavier bait, which holds securely on the hook, for example bone larvae, dung worms, or small balls of bread. The necessary weight should be divided and distributed along the whole length of the line from the float as far as the hook. The main weight consists of a 'torpila', and between it and the hook a smaller auxiliary weight is mounted. In flowing waters the lower weight is again closer to the hook.

In waters with a more extensive shallow or excessively overgrown river or bankside belt, one is forced to fish further off. Here the problem of casting with a light rod and line arises, which can be dealt with by means of a special adjustment. The angler uses a 3—4.5m (10—15ft) long rod for both hands with the butt up to 90cm (3ft) long, sufficiently sensitive, with a semi-soft action and for a weight of 10—20g (0.35—0.7oz). The rod rings are important. They should have an inner diameter of at least 10mm ($\frac{2}{5}$in) and should be fixed on stand-off fittings of the same height, the distance between them not exceeding 25—30 cm (10—12in), so that the thin line will not adhere to the rod. The line, not thicker than 0.15mm (0.006in), is on

the full, shallowish spool of a smaller, fixed spool reel with fast gearing. The float, with an antenna up to 30cm (12in) long, is attached at one point, which accelerates both the sinking of the line below the surface and the required reaction during the take. Most important is the correct distribution of the weight along the whole length of the line, from the float to the hook. When fishing with a firmly fixed float, if the length of the rod is 80—100cm (32—40in) greater than the depth of the water the main weight is placed immediately below the float, thus ensuring its stabilisation in the vertical position. The sum of the auxiliary weights should not exceed three-quarters of the main weight.

Casting must be carried out energetically but with care. The method of casting, either overhead or from the side, depends on the accessibility of the terrain. It is best to cast with both hands overhead, whilst maintaining a 75° angle of the rod during the parabolic flight of the bait. In the last phase of the flight the angler begins to brake a little with his finger on the rod, braking completely before impact on the surface so that the tackle will lie on the water

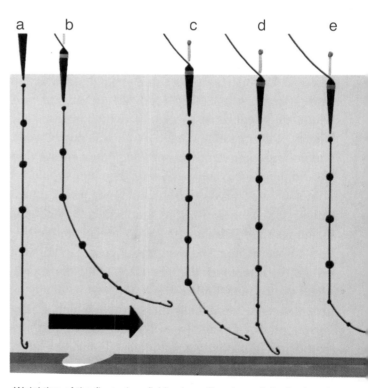

Weighting of the float when fishing in swift waters: a) the basic submersion should be about 25cm (10in) greater than the depth of the water. One weight placed just beneath the float accelerates stabilisation after casting; b—c) after casting, the bait sinks slowly towards the bottom and the float stabilises until reaching the correct position (d); e) when fishing with a checked float, the bait is lifted slightly above the bottom.

without the risk of fouling. If there is a strong wind, he should if possible, adopt a position which will prevent the line from forming large bulges, and even, in extreme cases, casting against the wind. As soon as the float is stabilised he should try, by means of faster retrieving with the rod dipped downwards, to straighten the line and in this way to achieve contact with the bait. Because he is fishing over a greater distance, he must hook energetically by stretching the whole arm. There is no risk of snapping the line, as its elasticity increases with its length.

Fishing in gently flowing waters, where the fish are used to searching for food in the whole water profile, can be attractive. They can also be enticed by effective luring. In this case the bait is only moistened a little, so that it begins to disperse as soon as it has hit the surface. In ideal conditions the angler chooses a spot for fishing which is within reach of a whiprod, a water depth of 1.5—2m (5—6½ft), a mild current and a gentle breeze blowing against the stream, using a whiprod without a reel for fishing near the bank, and for fishing further off one equipped with a centre-pin reel, which facilitates fluent paying-out of the line. The more adventurous angler might try a line 0.10—0.12mm (0.004—0.005in) thick, a line 0.15mm (0.006in) thick of course being more reliable. A slender, fine float with the minimum weight gives the rod and line ideal sensitivity. In this case combined floats with the upper part made of light elder and the lower part made of heavier built cane are especially suitable, attached at two points by means of small rubber or plastic rings.

When fishing directly on the bottom, which is usually the most successful method, the submersion of the float is increased, compared with the depth of the water, by 20—40cm (8—16in), depending on the strength of the underwater current. One is assisted in this by an auxiliary weight placed close to the hook. The weight consists of several smallish balls, evenly distributed along the whole length of the line between the fixed float and the hook. Casting is not done overhead, as the tackle would foul. In the case of gentle side casting with a slight checking of the line just before impact with the water, the bait submerges first, and after this one by one the weights. The float adopts an upright position, a change of which usually indicates a take. When

casting against the stream one often has problems with a large bulge on the line, so it is therefore better to cast at right angles to the stream or slightly diagonally against the stream, so as to have constant contact with the bait. The float is held back in such a way that the bait will roll along the bottom naturally, this also being assisted by a lower weight lying on the bottom. The effectiveness of the bait can be increased by interrupting the rhythm in which it is guided along and by occasionally pulling it up-

a
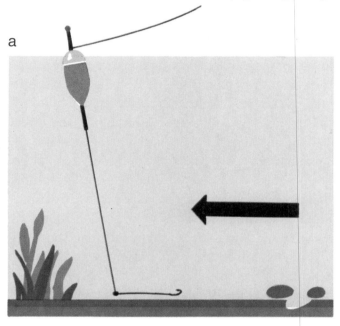

b
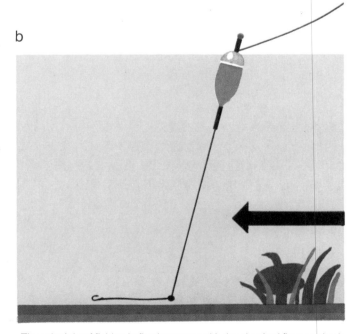

The principle of fishing in flowing water with the checked float method: a) a non-checked float runs ahead of the bait, because the current near the surface is more intense than at the bottom, b) the float must be checked in such a way that the bait will always be ahead, thus achieving a readier reaction to the take of the fish.

wards, then allowing it to sink freely. Combined floats, with the upper part made of elder and a wire keel, are well suited to this fishing method.

In some cases, for example when there is a low summer water level, the fish tend to keep to even stronger, swifter sections. The key to success in this case lies in the most natural presentation of the bait. Food drifting along the bottom stops from time to time, rolling for a moment along the bottom, then drifting again. One cannot, therefore, just leave the bait to drift freely downstream. The speed of the current at the surface is always greater than at the bottom, and the float would always, therefore, be ahead of the bait, which would not keep to the bottom. Moreover, too great a line bulge would prevent the angler from reacting quickly to a take. He must thus constantly work with the bait and direct it, that is fishing by the method of the checked float. It is also necessary to take into consideration that, in swift waters, fish have a different approach to the quarry. Whereas in still waters they act with deliberation and without haste, food carried along by a swift current must be seized by reflex and energetically. This of course also presumes an energetic reaction to the take. The angler can only hook successfully if he has direct contact with the bait, which is achieved by the simplest rod and line assembly. For this demanding fishing method a simple whiprod without a reel, with a line 0.15mm (0.006in) thick attached to the top of the rod, is the ideal combination. Depending on the character of the water, one can fish with a whiprod starting with a length of 4.5 to 5m ($14\frac{3}{4}$—$16\frac{1}{2}$ft), although a longer one is more suitable. By means of omitting or adding parts one can adapt it to various conditions. A special type of float for swift waters should be chosen. It is usually a problem to hit on the optimal weighting of the tackle and at the same time match the requirements for guiding the bait near the bottom or directly on the bottom with the bearing capacity of the float. In stronger currents one must always overload the float, sometimes by as much as 50%. The form of the weight is also adapted to the strength of the current. These requirements are best met by a one-part, drop-shaped, sliding weight. There is no generally valid distance of the weight from the hook, although one should try to keep it to at least 50cm (20in), so that the bait will move naturally and the

fish will not be startled by the weight. In a stronger lower current, which would lift the bait up high, the weight must be pulled down lower.

Chub

In view of the exceptional qualities of the chub, it can be regarded as perhaps the most attractive sport fish. It is willing to adapt to the most diverse living environment, it excels in obtaining food and it has an insatiable appetite practically throughout the whole year.

It is literally a cosmopolitan in its requirements for a living environment. Although its domain consists of more varied submontane courses, the area of its distribution is nevertheless unparalleled — extending from high mountain positions down to the lowlands. It is at home in all types of both enclosed and flowing waters. Given a chance, it shows a preference for localities with sufficient cover, which it uses as its permanent habitation. It is nonetheless able to adapt readily to open waters and it is the only one of the more important fish species which will settle in navigated and naturally devalued sections. In its optimal environment in submontane courses, it constitutes a large proportion of the fish colony, often as much as 30—50% of the ichtyomass.

The chub is omnivorous; larger chub even adopt a predatory approach for obtaining food. It is therefore difficult to find an explanation for its relatively slow rate of growth. It reaches a weight of 1kg (2.2lb) only in its tenth or twelfth year, so the criteria for trophy fish are correspondingly modest. The growth limit is around 5—6kg (11—$13\frac{1}{4}$lb), although one must usually be satisfied with specimens weighting two or three kilos. In the lowlands it spawns as early as the end of April, in submontane regions not until the beginning of June.

Traditional opinion on the proverbial shyness and caution of the chub seems to be rather exaggerated; it behaves in much the same way as similar fish species. When disturbed it seeks refuge in the shelter of its secure hiding-places, although it does not stay there for long and will leave them as soon as the danger disappears. It is active throughout the whole day, keeping mainly to places where there is a likelihood of obtaining a suitable morsel. This is the reason why it mostly swims about in uninterrupted, slightly dragging currents (these also suit it because of their relatively high oxygen content), at watersheds between currents and still waters, above faults on the riverbed and at the edges of whirlpools, where objects carried down by the water settle. With the same intention, in slower reaches, it stays just below the surface. At dusk its courage grows, and it leaves the depths en masse, scouting for food late into the night in shallow, dragging currents. Unlike other fish, it is also active in winter and its intake of food is not even interrupted under ice.

There is an unparalleled wealth of suitable baits for chub fishing, all of which are probably equally effective. If one wanted to list them in order of preference based on statistical fishing results, it would probably emerge as follows: earthworms, small fish, dough, spinner, wobbler, drupe fruits, the larvae of both aquatic and land insects, some offal of domestic animals (liver, spleen), processed and hard cheese, salami, potatoes, scalded wheat, husked grain, corn, bread crust, leeches, mole-crickets, fish tails, bacon, poultry guts, artificial fly, spring and summer maybugs, grasshoppers, locusts, crickets, horsefly. It is also worth mentioning that the biggest chub are fished for with a spinner and fruit. If there were an angler's examination it could consist of a single discipline — chub fishing. The candidate would have to know the whole gamut of fishing methods, from classic fly-fishing, through spinning, fishing on the bottom, float fishing in the water profile, to the attractive dapping method. He would also have to have a grasp of the complete assortment of both common and less usual types of bait and the ways in which they are used.

Both fishing methods and baits may be divided into universal ones — that is, suitable for fishing the whole year round — and seasonal ones. The first group includes sink and draw with artificial lures or a small dead fish, fishing on the bottom and swimming the stream in the lower water profile with earthworms, cheese, grains, husked grains, corn, dough, bread, larvae, or fish tail. Seasonal fishing methods include fly-fishing in the warmer season of the year, dapping and swimming the stream with live land insects in their natural flying season, and winter fishing on the bottom or by swimming the stream just above the bottom, using poultry guts, bacon, liver, spleen, and so on.

Classic fly-fishing can only be considered in more open waters with accessible banks. One makes no special demands of the fly-fishing rod (2.4—2.7m/ 8—9ft, 6—8 AFTMA), choosing relatively large flies, on hook nos. 6—8, with bulkier, hairy bodies (Palmer) and of a colourful appearance, with a predominance of brown, red and green. Fly-fishing is effective mainly when chub are having a pick at food on the surface, tasting drifting pieces of wood or leaves. In this case one fishes with a dry fly; when there is a light breeze and water undulation a wet fly can be used, since chub also seek insects in the water column. One should not go for chub with a fly when there is quite a strong wind, however, as they know that insects are not flying then.

Fly-fishing in smaller courses with densely overgrown banks is also an interesting experience. Here one can fish either from a bank concealed by trees, or find the ideal vantage point in the crown of a willow overhanging the water, where chub are likely to gather under its branches. By climbing up the tree, of course one startles the fish in the vicinity, but if one behaves inconspicuously their curiosity will get the better of them and they will return again straight away. At first a scouting troop of young chub will appear on the surface, after which one will gradually also catch sight of the silhouettes of the largest ones. When they nonchalantly begin to taste objects drifting on the surface, the angler should present them with a fly, but should not allow himself to be tempted by the first opportunity. The large fish remain in the background and only decide to attack the bait when, by lifting the fly, the angler has diverted the attacks of the imprudent young. In the same way it is also possible to fish with live insects — maybugs, grasshoppers, large horseflies and so on. The essence of this fishing method corresponds to dapping.

For spinning, a lighter rod of average length (1.8—2.8m/6—9ft), with a semi-soft action for weights from 10—20g (0.35—0.7oz), a smallish, lighter reel with a shallow spool and a soft line, 0.18—0.20mm (0.007—0.008in) thick, are suitable. Smaller spoons are used, up to a length of 3—5cm (1¼—2in), classic spoons only in swift waters, and spinners also in still waters. Even shorter, stouter wobblers can usefully be employed. The optimal colour shade is silver matte and silver mother-of-pearl; lures which are too polished repel rather than attract. Red beads on the axis of a spinner, or a red trinket on a triple hook of a spinner, or a combination of a spoon and a spinner with an artificial fly or small artificial fish, are also effective.

During sink and draw, one must have regard for the relatively slow reaction of the chub (in comparison, for example, with silver salmon), by slowing down the tempo, but not so much that the fish amuse themselves with the bait. In virgin waters, sinking and drawing is effective under any conditions; in more frequented waters one can succeed only under exceptionally favourable conditions, for example in more dragging currents up to a metre (3ft) deep, or in slightly cloudy water an hour after sunset. In still, generally clear waters, there are minimal preconditions for spinning. In this case a wobbler combined with a fly could be more successful.

For swimming the stream, a light rod over 4m (13ft) long, with a harder action and for weights from 10—20g (0.35—0.7oz), a smallish, lighter fixed-spool reel or centre-pin reel, and a line 0.15—0.18mm (0.006—0.007in) thick are required. It is possible to fish by swimming the stream both on the surface and in the water profile. A take is registered by means of a finger on the line. A float only fulfils the task of keeping the bait at the required depth of the water column. A cautious chub can best be outwitted by inconspicuous floats made of natural materials — uncoloured cork, goose feather and so on.

The size of the hook is adapted to the bait. A dung worm belongs on hook nos. 6—8, larvae on nos. 10—12, a maybug, grasshopper and the like

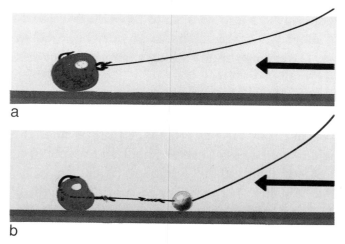

a

b

Rod and line assembly for chub fishing, allowing the bait to drift along the bottom: a) a larger bait, for example a plum, does not require an auxiliary weight, b) a lighter bait, for example a cherry, with a spherical weight.

being mounted on hooks nos. 3—4. When choosing a bait, the seasonal factor should be taken into account. With cherries, one fishes in May and June, with grasshoppers and locusts after the harvest, with plums in the autumn, with earthworms, bread or dough all the year round. The bait chosen of course also depends on the fishing method. With horsefly, grasshopper or maybug, the angler fishes on the surface, with fruits and earthworms both in the water profile and on the bottom. For fishing using a bait drifting along the bottom, more roundish types of fruit, such as cherries, morello cherries, plums and strawberries are most suitable. When using bulkier and heavier baits, it is possible to fish without a weight or float by utilising the flow of the water, for example by allowing maybugs to drift on the surface, or plums in the water profile and on the bottom.

Chub is not usually found in waters deeper than 2m (6½ft), so a light float with a bearing capacity of up to 3—4g (0.12—0.16oz) is always fix-mounted at two points. When fishing with the stream, this enables the angler to fish using the checked float technique, to have constant contact with the bait and to react promptly to a take. A sliding weight is attached by means of a stopper made of tyre valve tubing placed at a greater distance from the hook (up to 50—60cm/20—24in), so that the fish are not startled unnecessarily. When there is a stronger flow of water, the distance of the weight from the hook is reduced, always in such a way that the bait is kept at the required level.

Fishing for chub with live fish bait also has its fans. The fishing methods are practically identical with those for pike-perch fishing, although for chub one can set out with even finer tackle, and with the smallest, 3—4cm (1¼—1½in) long fish. Bleak, roach and goby can serve as excellent bait, although if the angler has the chance, he will obtain 5—6cm (2—2½in) long gudgeon or loach, whose slender bodies have an irresistible attraction for chub.

The classic method of fishing on the bottom is only presented here for the sake of completeness. One will only occasionally fish for chub using this method, mostly as a random quarry when fishing for barbel and the like in late autumn and in winter, when chub have withdrawn to deeper waters out of the main current. The choice of baits at this time of year is limited. If one does not have a supply of earthworms, one can fish with pieces of liver, smaller live or even dead fish, poultry guts and so on. After casting, the angler should not wait for a take for more than 8—10 minutes. If a chub is close by, it will certainly make up its mind within that time and take the bait. If it does not take, try another promising spot and if possible change the bait for a fresh one. This is especially important in the case of strong-smelling baits, such as liver or gut. There are no special requirements for the rod or the tackle as a whole; however, it should be assembled with the maximum sense for the fishing method. A rod about 3m (10ft) long with a semi-soft action, for weights from 10 to 30g (0.35—1oz), fits the bill, equipped with a smallish fixed-spool reel, a line 0.18—0.20mm (0.007—0.008in) thick, hooks depending on the bait, but smaller than in summer, approximately nos. 4—8, divided weight being the best.

Orfe

In the rich bleak family, the orfe must be satisfied with the position of second-best. In terms of the area of its distribution, numerical abundance and sporting value, it lags far behind its brother — the chub. It has very specific demands for a living environment and is not interested in adapting to alternative conditions, only feeling at home in more spacious, submontane and above all lowland rivers. It is somewhat more tolerant in its demands for hiding places. If there is suitable hiding place within its living space, it will take it, but if a hiding place is absent, it feels safe even in open water. In the warmer season of the year it keeps en masse to open water at the edges of dragging reaches and thoroughly utilises food drifting within the whole water profile from the bottom up to the surface. When it is cooler it moves in shoals into semi-cut-off river arms and backwaters, away from the main river bed. More spacious, deeper, dragging canals also suit it, where it settles in places with dense plant cover. Sometimes it even acclimatises itself in enclosed waters in overgrown parts, although avoiding muddy sections. Although it has relatively high demands regarding the quality of the water, like the barbel, given the chance of a richly laid table, it will lower its demands and keep to the outlets of urban sewage and other waste products, where the hope of a richer morsel beckons.

It is considered to be a more thermophilic species. In autumn it withdraws to the depths, but during a milder winter, even if the edges of the river are frozen, it will not interrupt its eating pattern, although reducing its intake. In winter it is surprisingly active. It is more choosy than the chub about what it will eat, tending towards less bulky morsels, with the larvae of aquatic insects prevailing in its diet. It readily accepts, however, other edible elements drifting downstream, for example plant seeds, and will also be happy with the finer parts of aquatic vegetation. A welcome, although not a decisive supplement to its diet are land insects, for which it will rise as far as the surface. Small fish form a negligible part of its food, so fishing with small fish is not included in the list of orfe fishing methods. It will of course sometimes catch a small fish, as will a carp.

Orfe spawn at the end of April or in May very noisily in abundant shoals in shallower, calmer water. It must live nine to ten years to reach a weight of 1kg (2.2lb), so that trophy fish 2—4kg (4.4—8.8lb) in weight have a colourful past behind them.

Orfe will bite most reliably in May, then without much variation throughout the whole summer. There is no need to be discouraged, however, from autumn or winter fishing, assuming that one lures sensibly. In urban courses under sewage outlets one can even fish without luring.

By comparison with other white fish, orfe fishing is distinguished by special rules. Whereas other fish species take the bait more decisively and energetically, the orfe can behave surprisingly indolently. It will not condescend to hurry for a quickly drawn bait, and too slow a bait would seem suspicious to it. Of the basic fishing methods, swimming the stream and fly-fishing are equally effective.

Anyone who wants to specialise in orfe fishing by swimming the stream should invest in a special rod, which must be as light as possible, since one will be fishing with the rod in the hand. A length of 3.5—4.5m (11½—14¾ft) is enough, for a weight of 10—30g (0.35—1oz). A soft action is necessary in this case, however, as the orfe has a very delicate small mouth. A line 0.12—0.18mm (0.005—0.007in) thick is sufficient, and a smaller type of reel (a centre-pin reel is not essential), with a shallowish spool.

Fine, small hooks are used, no. 6 for earthworms, no. 8 for dung worms and so on, no. 10 for wheat grains, husked grain, peas and larvae. The rod and line is assembled using the method suitable for flowing waters. A weight — small weights or coils of sheeting — is fixed on to the line from the hook as far as the float, depending on the character of the water, the lower lead weight being 20—40cm (8—16in) from the hook. The float — always a type suitable for flowing water — is as a rule fix-mounted at two points.

Both animal and plant baits are effective. Of the animal baits, one can use earthworms, the larvae of land and aquatic insects and land insects in season — grasshoppers, crickets, horseflies. Of plant baits one can try out soft peas, small grains of semi-ripe corn, husked grains, wheat, pieces of bread, pasta, dough and groats. With live baits one should take care that they stay active on the hook for a long time. Once can also try suitable combined baits of the sandwich type, e.g. a small dung worm with a bone worm and the like. An earthworm only

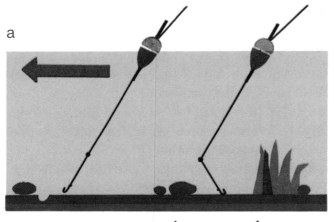

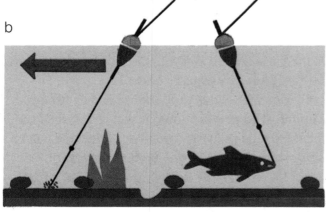

Fishing for orfe and similar current-loving fish species in swift waters by the checked float method: a) the bait gets caught in an obstacle (the so-called false take), during which the position of the float does not change; b) the take of a fish is signalled by the changed position of the float.

112

needs to be pierced by the hook once, as the orfe does not tend to denude hooks. The tip of the hook should be free whatever kind of bait is used, as otherwise one risks failure when hooking. When selecting baits for various conditions we can recommend, for example, bone larvae in summer and the beginning of autumn, when there is a constant water level and clear water, and earthworms early in spring and in late autumn, and generally when the water level is rising and when the water is cloudy. This should only be taken as a general guide, however. It is always best when starting to fish to experiment for a few minutes with various baits until one finds the most effective one.

It is also necessary to experiment with the depth at which the bait is drawn. In general one should bear in mind that in the warmer season fish tend to stay closer to the surface, in cooler weather gradually moving to the lower levels of water, if not actually to the bottom. The drawing of the bait is complicated by the water current in which one usually tends to look for orfe. Fishing is carried out using the system of checking the float, but in a different way from what one would normally expect. When fishing for other fish species, the float is only checked sufficiently to prevent it from running ahead of the bait and so that bulges do not form on the line. The bait moves at the same place as the current and one does not check it. When orfe fishing, taking into account its indolence, one must from time to time in addition to the float also check the speed of the bait. The advantage of this method lies in the fact that it is easier to avoid obstacles and catching up the hook. It is not possible to dogmatise about how much to check the bait; every angler must learn this patiently for himself. Until mastering this method, one should fish from accessible banks and carefully, step by step, go with the rod and line so that one is always fishing at the same distance. Later the angler may even try fishing from a single vantage point, gradually extending the fishing distance. The line is paid out by hand, preferably too little rather than too much, so that the swift current will not pull it down and bulges will not appear on it.

In the case of orfe, fishing on the bottom is the least promising, as it places the bait at a level where the fish do not normally have their hunting ground. It could perhaps be tried in late autumn, when the supply of food in the water is becoming scarce and hunger forces fish into greater activity. A small thin fish fillet should be tried as a bait.

Spinning with an artificial lure may only be considered in one case out of a hundred, on the assumption that the angler has found a locality where trophy specimens live. Common 30—35cm (12—14in) long fish are not yet big enough for a spinner, and will hardly try to go at the smallest young fish. If one is after a large fish, one fishes for it in a similar way as for chub — that is, using a finer, shorter, casting rod and with the smallest artificial lures.

In smaller courses, where it is possible to find a good cover on the bank, one can fish for orfe by dapping with a 5—6m (16½—19½ft) long, sensitive rod. It is fished for in the same way as chub, but with smaller types of bait and, wherever possible, with natural ones, for example summer maybugs, smaller green or brown grasshoppers and horseflies.

With a slight change in fishing technique, it is also possible to use insects for classic fly-fishing, mainly if there is a chance for wading. If the angler is not sufficiently experienced, he can try allowing the insect to drift along the surface with the stream, whereas a more experienced one would fish against the stream. The use of artificial flies is of course not excluded, although it is not necessary to use an imitation if there are ample live insects in the open air. Live insects are used mainly in season, when fish commonly encounter them. Bread crust can also be used as an effective universal bait, and should be tried when the angler sees that the orfe are seeking prey as far as the surface. To make casting farther off easier, the crust is dipped for a moment in water after being mounted on the hook. During the flight through the air it dries out and rests easily on the surface.

Grass carp

Of the group of East Asian herbivorous fish species which were successfully introduced into European waters during the 1960s, only the grass carp may be considered to be an undoubtedly successful contribution to sport fishing. In its original habitat, more open, dragging, lowland rivers are its domain. In European conditions it acclimatises itself above all to enclosed waters, where it fulfils the important role of biological regulator. Its task is to keep down the excessive growth of plants growing below and to some extent even above the surface.

With the exception of the character of its diet and conditions for reproduction, the grass carp may be considered identical in its requirements for a living environment with the thermophilic carp. The ideal habitat of the grass carp is warm, shallow, richly overgrown lowland waters. By virtue of its generally undemanding and adaptable character, it can nevertheless also withstand harsher climatic conditions, readily reducing its demands as to the warmth of the water, and its feeding activity will continue even in extremely low water temperatures, around 6—7 °C (43—44.5 °F). As regards food, it is adaptable in its requirements. If it has a choice, it will mainly eat fine, young shoots of underwater plants, although hunger usually forces it to graze on hard vegetation growing above water. In waters where the fish are given extra food, they can easily become spoiled. Plant foodstuffs — corn, groats, bread, pasta and the like — taste as good to it as animal ones, for example, earthworms, fish fillets and insect larvae.

Its sporting value is also increased by the fact that it does not allow itself to be thrown off-balance by fluctuations of temperature, the phase of the moon, the direction of prevailing winds and similar factors. The grass carp is also active in the late evening hours, and sometimes even at night. The result of its extraordinary feeding activity is its exceptionally rapid growth and its potential for attaining gigantic proportions considering European conditions. In its original habitat it grows up to 40—50kg (88—110lb), and so far everything points to the fact that in European waters it will find even more favourable conditions.

If the angler wanted to be precise when grass carp fishing, he would of course fish for it with baits which are as similar as possible to its natural diet. Reality is different, however, and plants only figure minimally when it comes to trophy catches. An evaluation of the effectiveness of baits in the case of trophy catches indicates that so far we probably do not know how to fish for it. Grass carp catches have so far essentially occurred randomly during carp fishing. It emerges from experience that the grass carp can most probably be caught using corn, various doughs, mainly with a high proportion of cornflour, bread and boiled potatoes. Besides other baits, such as peas, husked grains and cereals, even baits which are atypical for grass carp fishing can be used, however — for example, fish fillets, earthworms, or spoons. We assume that the technique for grass carp fishing will continue to develop, and that thus also the assortment of baits will be enriched by typical items, for example, boiled carrots and a rich selection of dry land and aquatic plants.

The most successful seasons of the year for grass carp fishing are the same as for the carp. Fishing is most successful in July and August, although the grass carp is not so sensitive to the cold as the carp, and should theoretically bite even in the colder season. Frequent grass carp catches when fishing for carp may be explained by the fact that these species share the same living space, have similar tastes, and can therefore be fished for in a similar manner. One must nevertheless take into account certain special characteristics of the grass carp.

The chief difference lies in the mentality of the two fish species. The partially domesticated carp behaves in every situation in a somewhat cultivated manner, whereas the untameable grass carp is impulsive and temperamental, and will become startled at the slightest disturbance and go into a frenzy. Mass hysteria among grass carp can even be caused by the noisy casting of a heavy bait into the vicinity of a shoal, by stamping noises on the bank and so on. Maximum caution and concentration are therefore essential when fishing.

The grass carp seeks food mainly in the water column, predominantly in the upper profile, and under normal circumstances does not go near the bottom. One can react to its behaviour in two ways: either adapting to the grass carp and fishing for it in the upper layers of the water, or trying to entice it to the bottom by means of suitable luring. One selects the alternative according to the character of the habitat. The grass carp has a terminally positioned mouth which is not adapted to picking food out of the deeper layers of mud. In water with a softish, muddy bottom, therefore, one selects fishing in the water column or on the surface; but if the bottom is harder, one may then try fishing there as well. One must also bear in mind the same conditions when luring. In case of a harder bed one lures directly, whilst for a soft bed lighter lures may be considered

(soaked pieces of bread with the crust, pieces of cake, and so on), or green plants. Plants should be dug up with the roots and earth, so that they will not float on the surface. Tufts with earth sink straight down, and the green parts remain free even on a muddy buttom. Luring is necessary when fishing for the untrusting grass carp. One must also reckon with the fact that its reaction to luring will not be instantaneous, as it is with the carp. The angler may lure with all the baits used, chiefly with a rich assortment of cultivated field-produce (clover, lettuce, tufts of peas, chopped green leaves, haulms of root vegetables and so on). Young milk corn, and groats of corn and other flours are also suitable. Aromatic additives, such as vanilla, aniseed, Peruvian balsam and so on increase the effectiveness of the lure.

Although in general we have critical objections to the use of feeding-troughs, when grass carp fishing they are tolerated as a necessary evil. For on many occasions it is not possible to reach further off shore to the grass carp's domain with the bait by any other method. The bait inside the feeding-trough should not be too dense, so that part of it will be released as soon as it hits the surface, dispersing over a wider area and throughout the whole water column. Too cohesive a bait would only be released from the feeding-trough at the bottom, which has little effect when fishing for grass carp.

In contrast with general principles, a stronger and thus less sensitive tackle is tolerated when grass carp fishing, depending, however, on the character of the water. In easier, more open waters, in which one can allow a hooked grass carp to manoeuvre perhaps within a hundred metre circle, even fine carp fishing tackle may be used. If one has mastered fishing technique and makes sufficient use of the flexibility of the rod, one can play a grass carp with a line 0.25mm (0.01in) thick. In the difficult conditions of excessively overgrown waters, a stronger tackle will be necessary. The tackle must be assembled carefully and particular care should be given to tying on the hook, the tang of the hook being rounded off and possibly tied on with two knots. The thickness of the line must match the rod; grass carp do not mind thicker lines from 0.40 up to 0.50mm (0.016—0.02in). A critical item of tackle is the float, which can have a disturbing effect especially in the case of noisy casting. Size is thus kept to a minimum and bright colours are avoided.

When assembling the tackle, the angler should avoid more complex assemblies that would require more knots. The ideal assembly is as simple as possible, with the hook, weight and float on the main line. Its only weak point is the knot on the hook, so that one should choose a type of knot which will only minimally weaken the strength of the line.

A special grass carp rod should be 3.5—4.5m (11½—14¾ft) long and relatively bulky for a weight of over 100g (3.5oz), with a soft to parabolic action. As far as reel types are concerned, multiplier reels are best, fixed-spool ones only if they are larger, bulkier models with a spool capacity of 150—180m (490—590ft) of line up to 0.50mm (0.02in) thick and they should have a perfect brake system. The strongest hooks are used, sizes 1/0 to 2/0.

In still or only slightly flowing water it is best to fish with a float. When fishing closer to the bank the float should be fix-mounted at one or two points. When casting further off a sliding float is better, as it reduces the risk of fouling the tackle, and also achieves a longer cast. In swift waters a slender 'torpila', fixed 40—60cm (16—24in) above the hook, functions best as a weight. In calmer waters a divided weight is mounted. Pieces of soft sheeting or wire are therefore better, simply fixed by means of pieces of matches.

In swift waters or in the case of great distances and a harder bed, fishing on the bottom with a weight may even be considered. However, the angler should not in this case reduce the demands on the resistance of the tackle, although the rod can be shorter, 2.5—3.0m (8¼—10ft). The rod and line is assembled in the usual way. If a feeding-trough is mounted at the same time, with a weight of 80—100g (2.8—3.5oz), an auxiliary weight is not necessary.

There is considerable room for improvement in fishing methods both on the surface and just below the surface. The grass carp likes to keep to the surface water profiles, constantly checking events on the surface with an inquisitive glance. It will certainly be captivated by suitable morsels floating with a natural movement on the surface. These may be tufts of green plants, sometimes also bread crust; like the carp, grass carp can be enticed by the interest of small fish in a bread crust. When casting to a short distance, or with the aid of the wind and undulation of the water, it is possible to fish using only bait without a weight. Bread crust can be as large as 2×2cm ($\frac{3}{4} \times \frac{3}{4}$in), and should be dipped in the water shortly before casting. However, it is only possible to fish in this way using fine tackle (line up to 0.20mm/0.008in), so that the angler must first resign himself to the risk of losing a larger quarry. This risk can only be excluded by using stronger and thus less sensitive tackle, which demands a change of fishing method.

In this case, two alternatives may be considered, the first based on the practical experience that a small floating transparent glass ball is not suspicious to a grass carp. Depending on the water content of the small ball, it may be used simultaneously for two functions — as a bait and as a float. So as not to give the grass carp even the slightest cause for suspicion, the small ball is fixed at some distance from the hook — approximately 50—60cm (20—24in). A grass carp can be put off by a noisy impact of the tackle on the surface, so the angler should forego accuracy when casting. It is better to cast to one side and guide the bait to the chosen spot with the aid of the wind or water movement.

When fishing in more open waters, where the

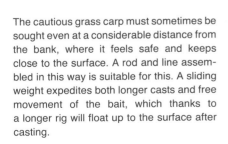

The cautious grass carp must sometimes be sought even at a considerable distance from the bank, where it feels safe and keeps close to the surface. A rod and line assembled in this way is suitable for this. A sliding weight expedites both longer casts and free movement of the bait, which thanks to a longer rig will float up to the surface after casting.

115

cautious grass carp is often to be found more than 60m (200ft) from the bank, one can only succeed in casting with the aid of a sufficiently heavy weight. The weight must be sliding, and fixed in such a way that the bait (bread crust) will come up to the surface after being cast. The length of the rig is therefore somewhat greater than the depth of the water. If the bait starts to sink after a while, it is replaced with a fresh one. A take can be observed from the movement of fish around the bait, although to be on the safe side one can also use a bite detector.

Up to a point, the shyness of the grass carp is to be welcomed. It will only collect food if it feels absolutely safe, but because of this the take is usually emphatic and fast, sometimes so much so that it can carry off a carelessly secured rod and line on which the reel brake has been activated. Sometimes it will even hook itself. In both easier and more difficult terrain, regardless of the size of the expected quarry and the strength of the tackle, one should always fish with at least half reserve on the reel brake setting. The angler should also not allow himself to be lulled by the suspiciously tame behaviour of a grass carp immediately after hooking, when it can seem to him that the fish has given up. Either this is a fighting tactic on the part of the fish, or more likely it is taking some time for it to become aware of danger. A calm reaction after hooking is always a prelude to an ensuing fit of fury from the grass carp. All at once it will shoot off like a torpedo, which can easily overtax even the most resilient line or rod. The angler should definitely not try to take the initiative into his hands. Like it or not, the fish must be given its head, although the angler should try to keep it at a greater distance, so as to make effective use of the flexibility of the rod and line. Similarly the angler should not lose his head even in more difficult terrain. It is better to risk the lesser evil of the grass carp becoming tangled in the vegetation than losing it early on during hopeless attempts at forced braking. When the fish has exhausted its strength, the angler can pull it out of vegetation. One must also take care when trying to get it into the landing-net. A grass carp which has apparently given up can suddenly spring to life, and if the angler allows himself to be taken by surprise, it will snap the line and be off.

116

FISHING FOR PREDATORY FISH

Silver salmon

The silver salmon is something of a rarity in the family of peace-loving carp-type fishes. Although it does not have a mouth equipped with teeth, as one would expect of a true predator, it is nevertheless quite a ruffian and is unrivalled in its rapacity. It sometimes gives the impression of hunting not so much from hunger as for pleasure, as if thriving on the alarm it creates among shoals of defenceless bleak.

It has two basic demands with regard to its environment; it needs the most spacious possible living area and the greatest possible variation in its surroundings. It does not seek out cover, feeling safe in open water further from the bank. It flourishes in more open submontane and lowland rivers. It selects the most varied reaches as its living space, in which sudden breaks in the water flow occur, for example under locks, in whirlpools under larger obstacles, under transverse dikes, and both at the junctions and tributary estuaries of rivers. In summer it also likes to keep to the swiftest reaches just below

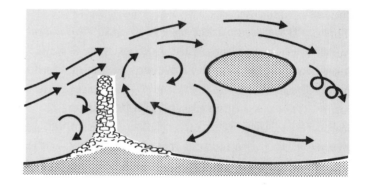

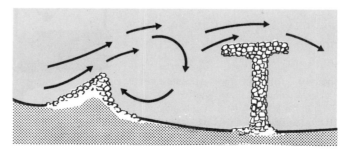

Favourite haunts of the silver salmon in lowland courses with banks reinforced by stony barriers.

the surface, to satisfy its high oxygen requirements. In autumn when the water cools down it withdraws from the surface to greater depths, although avoiding sections with an excessively muddy bed. Although the silver salmon is a typical river species, it can readily adapt to more open non-river waters, behaving there just as tempestuously as in flowing water.

It spawns in April and May. Owing to its predatory way of life it grows faster than other fish, reaching a weight of 1kg (2.2lb) as early as its fifth or sixth year. Five or six kilo (11—13lb) silver salmon are considered to be trophy fish. There used to be reports of twenty kilo (44lb) specimens some time ago, and even today one can catch an eight or ten kilo ($17\frac{1}{2}$—22lb) quarry.

The silver salmon is enjoying increasing popularity within the sport fishing community. It is definitely only a sport fish species, as its gastronomic value is dubious; it has dry, bony flesh. Its attractive features are its imposing appearance, the possibility of fishing for it all year round using all possible fishing methods, and the wide choice of both natural and artificial baits and lures. The true sports fisherman particularly appreciates the challenge of the silver salmon as it is not easy to catch.

Despite ranking among the most cautious of fish, the silver salmon is a real provocateur in the water. The daily pattern of its life consists of incessant, nervous circling just below the surface. Nevertheless it is not permanently on robbery raids; there are moments when it even behaves peaceably. Its erratic moods can easily be discerned from the behaviour of small fish species in the vicinity. It is hard to explain how these small fish discern the silver salmon's mood, but sometimes they scatter in despair even at the sight of its shadow, while at other times they scarcely notice it when it is circling round them.

The most favourable time for silver salmon fishing is the second half of the season, mainly August and September. Poorer results in spring and later in autumn, however, cannot be attributed solely to the reduced appetite of the silver salmon. They are more likely to be the fault of fishermen who do not take into account changes in the behaviour of silver salmon in the cooler season and who do not adapt to these by changing the fishing method. Silver sal-

mon may be fished for throughout the day, even when it is completely dark.

Sink and draw is the most effective fishing method. In a contest among the various types of artificial lures, probably the one that stands up best is the home-made spoon. Silver salmon is also frequently fished for using fish-bait, earthworms, bone larvae, dead fish on the bottom, and fish tails and fillets.

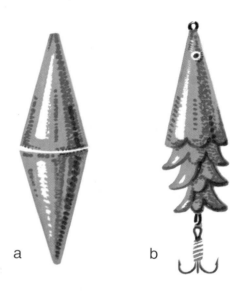

An excellent simple bait for silver salmon can be made of a weight of elongated shape (a), or in the shape of a spoon (b).

The silver salmon must not be allowed time to think about the bait. Practice has proved that in many waters it has been spoiled by excessive sinking and drawing and that it has been turned into a 'professor' with a superb instinct for distinguishing baits. One should not even set great hopes on fishing with fish-bait mounted in the classic way on a float. Success is more likely to be achieved by the exchange of usual, and therefore compromised, fishing methods for less common ones, and standard baits for unusual ones. Simply put, one can only get the better of silver salmon if one is prepared to be throughly innovative.

When choosing tackle, the angler should not be misled by the blustering impression given by the silver salmon. He must go for it gently, in kid gloves, choosing the finest tackle, presenting the bait as naturally as possible and sometimes even using trickery. Any fine casting rod will do for sinking and drawing with normal baits. When fishing with a special silver salmon lure (a combination of a spoon and artificial flies), one needs a stronger, more flexible rod about 3m (10ft) long with a semi-soft action for a weight of 20—60g (0.7—2.1oz). In view of the need for longer casting and considerable overloading, preference is given to larger rings on taller stand-off fittings. An average sized fixed-spool reel with a shallow spool having a capacity of 120—150m (390—490ft) of a line 0.20 to 0.25mm (0.008—0.01in) thick should be sensitively balanced with the rod. For sink and draw, small baits of all common types should always be chosen, and even the simplest baits prepared by the angler himself can be effective. The type, shape and colour of the bait are chosen according to the water level, visibility and behaviour of the silver salmon at the time. Besides classic spoons and spinners, slender floating wobblers are also successful in summer.

When the water is perfectly clear in sunny weather one must tactically surprise the silver salmon. It is better to wait with rod and line at the ready, until nosing out a spot where a disturbance breaks out from time to time, at more or less regular intervals. Although the silver salmon is restless and has a wide action radius, it does have favourite spots to

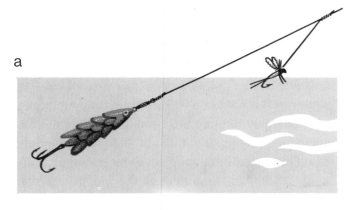

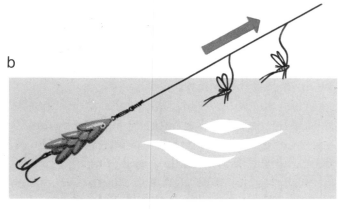

A combination of a spoon and a fly for silver salmon fishing: a) with one fly, b) with two flies.

which it returns. Its arrival can be realiably discerned from a typical undulation of the surface in a V shape and from increasing alarm among small fish. If a bait suddenly lands in its vicinity, it will attack this disturber of the peace if only to punish it for its audacity. From personal experience we can recommend giving preference to fishing by sink and draw on summer days with changeable, overcast weather. While the sun is behind the clouds, the angler waits with the rod and line at the ready. As soon as the sun comes out, he casts to the spot where the silver salmon are. There have also been some good results from fishing during morning fogs.

In reduced visibility, when the water is slightly cloudy and the surface is disturbed by waves, success may also be achieved by means of systematic spinning, that is by systematically combing the surface water profile. The lure is drawn with an interrupted tempo, in still waters more quickly, in flowing waters more slowly, and it does not matter if the bait skips over the surface from time to time.

The method of combining spinning with artificial flies has proved particularly successful for silver salmon fishing. The spoon consists of a 15—25g (0.6—1oz) weight with an elongated shape and eyes for mounting. At a certain distance from this unusual spoon, the angler attaches two silver salmon flies in such a way that the lower one will move just below the surface and the upper one on the surface itself. The effectiveness of the weight can be increased either by using a sound effect, by cutting its upper part into a blunt shape and cutting several transverse grooves on the surface, or by visual effect, when the terminal hook is made more conspicuous by means of a red or brightly coloured cotton thread or small piece of rag. With a combined lure the distance of the components from one another is important. A weight is always at the end of the line, a lower wet fly being tied on a loop 30—35cm (12—14in) from the weight, the upper dry fly on a slightly longer loop after a gap of another 40cm (16in). Of course the exact distribution also depends on whether one is drawing from a high bank or at water level.

Silver salmon flies, unlike trout and grayling flies, may be as simple as possible, detailed execution being unnecessary. It is sufficient simply to tie two

small white, 4—6cm ($1\frac{3}{4}$—$2\frac{1}{4}$in) long hen feathers onto the shank of a hook no. 1—2 in such a way that it is concealed on both sides, and possibly to decorate the fly with a collar of white down attached to a ring. A fly may also be prepared from goose or duck down, or even of plastic, cotton threads and the like. Most advantageous in all methods of preparation, however, is a preponderance of white and lighter shades. A heavier fly for casting farther off is also prepared on a similar principle and is also suitable for fly-fishing even with a normal casting rod. The actual small body of the fly is formed from lead sheeting covered in a thin layer of cork. The cork is wound round with silvery or golden thread, this making the small body more conspicuous. The small tail and perhaps a collar are made of down in the same way as the previously mentioned flies.

The technique for fishing with a combined lure is identical to that employed for classic spinning. Depending on the accessibility of the terrain, casting is carried out either from the side or overhead, slightly checking the lure just before it hits the surface, so that it will land gently and smoothly. In the first phase after impact, the rod is raised and the line is retrieved quite quickly until all the lures settle at the required depth. The guide is always the upper fly, skipping along the surface. In this fishing method one should not be too hasty, waiting from time to time and casting only when and where the silver salmon are most in evidence.

Fly fishermen have the best chances of success when silver salmon fishing. Nevertheless in the case of silver salmon, flies do not constitute such an important dietary element as they do for trout and grayling, the fly possibly reminding the silver salmon more of a small fleeing fish than an insect. Not only the technique must be adapted to this fact, but also the choice of flies. When fishing for salmon-type fish one attempts to imitate as closely as possible an insect which is just flying overhead; we do not have to pamper silver salmon, preferably choosing flies which are fantastic rather than natural, although not forgetting that it likes lighter flies made brighter with silvery or golden foil.

In more modest waters, where one can manage with shorter casting, the angler selects a more resilient fly-fishing rod 2.5—3.0m (8—10ft) long with a softer action for a fly-fishing line nos. 7—9. In more

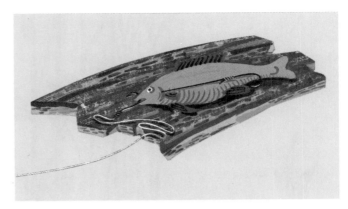

One must sometimes use tricks to catch the cunning silver salmon, for instance by allowing the bait to drift on a piece of tree bark towards the fish.

open waters even two-hand rods 3.5—4.5m ($11\frac{1}{2}$—$14\frac{3}{4}$ft) long with parabolic action can be used. The first 80cm (30in) of the rig is of 0.40—0.45mm (0.016—0.018in) thick line; it is enough if the second, lower part, on to which the flies are tied, is made of line 0.30—0.35mm (0.012—0.014in) thick. Apart from the largest flies on hooks nos. 1—2, smaller flies on hooks nos. 6—8, and even streamers, bucktails and similar lures may also be employed.

In emphasizing the effectiveness of even the simplest flies, we do not wish to dissuade fly fishermen from their faith in perfect flies, of which we can recommend, for example, the universal Silver March Brown and White Palmer; for overcast weather throughout the whole of the season, White Moth and Yellow Drake; for spring and autumn, Cardinal; for sunny summer days, Red Palmer and so on.

When fishing with fish bait — ideally with 6—7cm ($2\frac{1}{4}$—$2\frac{3}{4}$in) long bleak — the silver salmon has time to think, and usually detects the slightest inconsistency in luring. One can rarely succeed when fishing using the classic method with the aid of a common float. One has a better chance with a small glass ball or without a float, allowing the small fish-bait to drift with the current. Sometimes the fisherman tries going for silver salmon with a trick. At first he allays its suspicion by floating downstream, towards the spot where it currently is, bits of bark, feathers, small twigs and so on. After a while the silver salmon stops taking notice of these drifting objects and the fisherman can then use them as a float. It is also possible to allow fish-bait placed on a bowl-shaped piece of bark to drift downstream. At the required place it is then jerked into the water by a movement of the rod.

a

b

In open water, the pike feels vulnerable, and given a chance will seek out suitable cover. Young, less experienced pike give preference to the tangle of aquatic plants, sometimes even in the direct vicinity of the banks (a), while older fish feel most at home under the cover of the crowns of fallen trees (b).

In a similar way — without a float — one can also fish with live insects: maybugs, grasshoppers, locusts, larger horseflies and the like. If one has plenty of baits, one can first of all whet its appetite with several pieces. If the banks are overgrown and the fisherman can find a good hiding place there, he can also achieve success by dapping. One gets the indolent silver salmon into the mood, for example, by luring bleak with a slice of bread. There are good conditions for silver salmon fishing until the water freezes, when the angler then seeks it in deeper, gently flowing reaches. Sometimes it departs for semi-cut-off river arms for the winter, although swimming out for food to watersheds between flowing and still waters. During this period the most successful method is usually sinking and drawing with dead fish-bait, mounted in an arched shape, which increases its effectiveness for sink and draw. How-

122

ever, one can also practise fishing on the bottom with a small fish. Cool water reduces the activity of silver salmon, so that the tempo of the bait is slowed down while sinking and drawing. Making use of artificial lures is problematic in winter, amongst other things because the water is too clear.

Pike

With regard to its habitat, the pike can be classified as a true cosmopolitan, as it is able to adapt itself to the most varied types of environment. It can cope equally well with brooks and small rivers, the largest lakes and valley reservoirs. The exceptionally large habitat of the pike extends from the belt of brackish waters, where salt water mixes with fresh, as far as the lower boundary of the climatically harsher trout belt. It can therefore be caught among lowland thermophilic fish species as well as in the neighbourhood of trout. For this reason, the pike is considered to be one of the most attractive sport fish species. On the other hand, the pike makes high demands on adequate cover within its territory. It will definitely not acclimatize itself to open waters without opportunities for cover. The occurrence of pike can thus only be expected in places where there are fallen trees in the water, deeper water hollows, stony barriers, free standing large rocks, small islands of vegetation both below and above the surface, and so on. In flowing water it avoids the swifter reaches. Given a chance to choose its habitat, it will seek out calmer, more open, meandering reaches, whirling currents downstream from transverse stony barriers, places under the overhanging branches of riverbank trees and shrubs and the like.

The pike seizes its quarry sideways, but when devouring it turns it round head first.

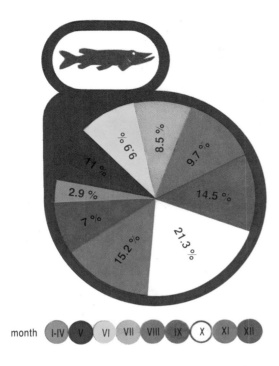

The effectiveness of pike fishing at various seasons of the year.

month I-IV V VI VII VIII IX X XI XII

In its way of life, the pike is rather a territorial fish, interrupting this habit only in the spawning season, although even then not undertaking migrations over long distances. It spawns early in spring, as soon as the ice thaws, in the peripheral overgrown parts of banks submerged by the spring flood. Its living and hunting territories are essentially identical, and its behaviour stereotyped. It is characterised by a stubborn patience. Perfectly adapted to its environment in its colouring, it can wait, apparently indolently, for hours at a time for an opportunity for a suitable quarry, which enters its field of vision oblivious of any danger. It always attacks its prey only after thorough preparation, making full use of the element of suprise. It is able to attack with lightning speed thanks to it powerful tail, which is futher reinforced by the dorsal fin positioned towards the rear.

With its specific requirements for dietary components, the pike fully meets the criteria for predatory fish species, an adequate amount of available fish thus being of vital importance to it. A large mouth equipped with teeth, a spacious gullet and sack-like stomach enable it to seize the prey, which can be as much as half its own length in size. It chooses its food on the basis of bulk, and prefers fish of more elongated, slender body shape. This also explains the frequent cannibalism of the pike. Frequent cases of a prey or bait being attacked even by a fully sated pike lead one to suspect that the motive for its voraciousness is not solely the feeling of hunger, but also an inborn rapacity. Sports fishermen of course accept these characteristics of the pike with gratitude, and they also appreciate the fact that its feeding activity is not so sensitively dependent on seasonal swings of temperature, as is the case, for example, with the feeding activity of the catfish or pike-perch. The fishing season can thus be prolonged into the late winter months. The cooler season of the year is even said to be the optimal fishing season, as smaller fish are withdrawing into the depths and hiding places at this time of year, and the famished pike, because of this lack of food, is willing to attack any even slightly acceptable looking bait. The temperature of the water obviously also affects the metabolism of the pike, which is more interested in food when the temperature is higher. One could come to the conclusion that the above is contradicted by the lesser chances of catching pike in the summer months. In summer, however, the pike has an opportunity to select its food in conditions of plenty and hunger does not compel it to attack lures which make a less natural impression. In summer, therefore, the angler gives preference to fishing for pike with fish-bait. One should never

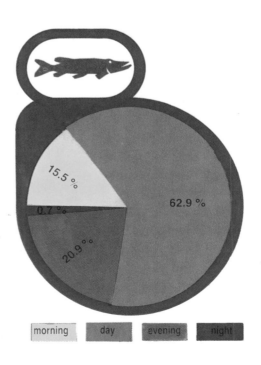

morning day evening night

The effectiveness of pike fishing depending on the time of day.

123

The effectiveness of various pike fishing methods.

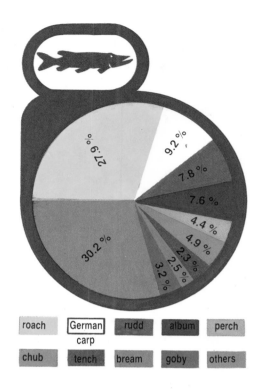

| roach | German carp | rudd | album | perch |
| chub | tench | bream | goby | others |

Illustration of the effectiveness of various fish-baits for pike fishing.

underestimate the voraciousness of the pike, if only since it is precisely because of this characteristic that the fish grows very well and can reach gigantic trophy proportions. It usually reaches the weight of one kilogram (2.2lb) as early as the third year of its life, and an adult pike will put on up to 1—2kg (2.2—4.4lb) a year. Current record catches are of the order of 20—25kg (44—55lb).

The opinion prevails among fishermen that the pike orients itself mainly by sight and partially by the senses of the lateral line, so it is likely that only a moving prey will attract its attention. The fishing methods for catching pike are based on this assumption, relying mainly on the principle of active movement of the lure. In recent years there has been a swing towards fishing for pike with non-moving dead fish-bait. This is justified among other things by the fact that, when seeking food, the pike is also able to orient itself by the senses of taste and smell. The proponents of this fishing method promise catches of the largest pike, which are difficult to achieve using the classic methods. It is thus probably worth a try.

As regards the best time of day for fishing, it is not necessary to stick rigidly to morning and late afternoon. Similarly, optimists who do not let themselves be put off by lack of success in the morning

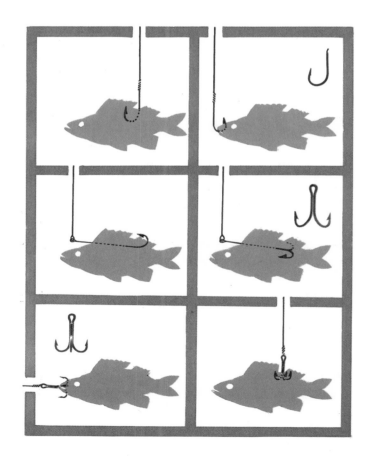

Basic methods for mounting fish-bait for pike fishing.

124

A more delicate live bait is pierced gently through the mouth with the hook.

Less common method for mounting live bait for pike fishing on the bottom with an auxiliary float.

may achieve a good catch during the day. Nocturnal successes are few: after all, the pike hunts with its eyes.

As far as baits for pike fishing are concerned, live fish-bait are definitely the most successful. This one-sided orientation has inevitably had negative repercussions in terms of the surprisingly low effectiveness of the most sporting fishing method — sink

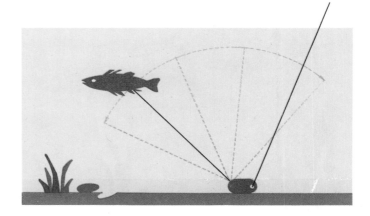

For a trophy pike, the fish-bait is presented on the bottom in such a way that it will have a sufficient action radius. The stopper is placed up to 100—120cm (40—48in) from the hook.

and draw using various types of artificial lure. Conclusions about the suitability of fashionable wobblers are not realistic, as the evaluation of results is so far not sufficiently representative. The layman will certainly be surprised at the large number of trophy catches achieved using atypical baits, such as corn, peas, pasta and so on. This cannot be explained by a tendency on the part of the pike towards vegetarianism, as all such catches occur by chance when fishing for carp or other fish species. One can also assume with some certainty that the pike took a moving bait while it was being lifted up or when it was moving in swift water. The bait can move even in still water if smaller fish play with it, which will attract the attention of a pike.

When choosing fish-bait, one should definitely stick to the principle of slender body shape. The actual selection of the species, however, depends on local conditions. The influence of the fish-bait species on the size of the catch cannot be assessed unequivocally, although in this respect we recommend concentrating attention on the German carp, the perch and the carp-bream.

In spite of some objections from the sporting point of view to fishing for pike and other predatory fish using live fish-bait, it is certainly the most effective fishing method. The principle is simple. The fish-bait is sewn on to a single, double or triple hook, possibly on to a system of several hooks, using a steel rig, weight and float. The actual assembly of the rod and line may be one of several possible variations. The fish-bait-stranded steel wire-snap weight-float system, by means of which the angler fishes mainly in the upper layers of water, to depths

125

A classic pike float usually has dimensions which will enable it to keep the presented fish-bait within a limited space, which to a certain extent reduces the effectiveness of the bait. The use of these floats is only justified in difficult waters full of obstacles.

A smaller float facilitates movement of the fish-bait and increases the effectiveness of the bait.

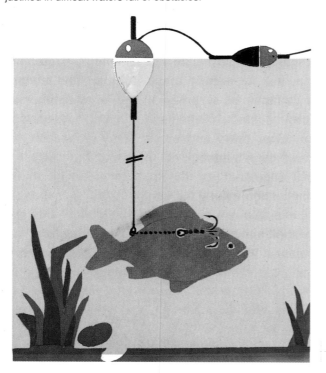

In excessively difficult, usually heavily overgrown surroundings, the rod and line can be assembled with an auxiliary float, which prevents the line from fouling in obstacles.

If the angler has definitely nosed out a place where a cannibal is lurking, the fish-bait can also be localised in this way.

The paternoster system, suitable for pike fishing in terrain with obstacles: a) overall view (1 — basic float, 2 — auxiliary float, 3 — line 0.30—0.40mm (0.012—0.016in) thick, 4 — wire or plastic tube, 5 — main weight), b) detail of wire rig.

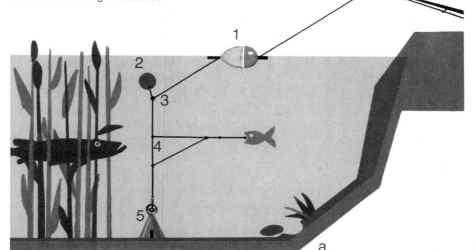

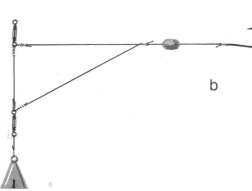

of 100—150cm (40—60in), is the most frequently used assembly. For fishing in greater depths, in which larger fish are expected, the float is fixed between the fish-bait and a small weight, which prevents the fish-bait from becoming hidden in obstacles.

In the summer season, mainly in the late afternoon and in the morning, the classic ledgering method is also used. Roach, rudd and perch are suitable for this. A float is not used at all, and a sliding, smallish weight is attached no less than 1m (3¼ft) from the hook, so that the fish-bait has sufficient opportunity to move about. A larger perch may also simply be impaled on the hook under the dorsal fin without using a weight or float, especially in deeper waters. A minimally weighted perch will itself choose which layer of water it goes to. For pike fishing with live fish-bait carp rods with harder action are also suitable. These facilitate more accurate casting of the bait further off and, above all, guarantee reliable hooking in the hard bony pike mouth. Stranded steel wire is essential, nevertheless it must not excessively obstruct the movement of the mounted fish, nor should it be too hard. Under normal circumstances a line 0.30mm (0.012in) in diameter is used; in more difficult conditions, where the angler is obliged to use greater power, a line 0.35 to 0.40mm (0.014—0.016in), thick is needed. Double and triple hooks are definitely more reliable, both when hooking and when playing the quarry, although increasing the risk of more serious injury to the fish. As far as possible, therefore, one should try, mainly for ethical reasons, to fish for pike using a single hook. We regard the use of large, so-called pike floats, which restrict the movement of the fish-bait, as a bad habit. The pike, as we already know, has a relatively limited hunting territory and does not stray from it, waiting patiently until a bait lands within it. The fisherman should therefore try to make this fishing method more active by leaving the fish-bait as much freedom as possible, so that it will move actively within the maximum range and at various depths. It does no harm if from time to time it drags a smaller float down as far as the bottom, then tired by the resistance of the float, allows itself to be carried up, trying again to escape, perhaps to one side. Too large a float arouses in pike a suspicion of the bait, which moves up and down on it as if on a seesaw. A large float may be permitted as a last resort if one is fishing, for example, at a small open spot among dense growth.

The choice of a fishing alternative using live fish-bait depends on the given situation. In the warmer season of the year during the day the fish-bait is presented at a shallow depth or even on the surface, while in the evening and towards morning it pays off to try it at a greater depth. In the cooler season the angler likewise seeks pike mainly at greater depths. There are several possible ways of fishing using dead fish-bait. In waters with a hard bottom, one fishes on the bottom with the tackle weighted with a weight but without a float. In muddy and overgrown waters, only a fish-bait drawn along the bottom can be considered, either using a float or some other technical device, such as for example small polystyrene balls in the mouth of the fish-bait, or blowing air into the body cavity of the fish-bait. In contrast with fishing with live fish-bait, hooking must be instantaneous.

The relatively poor results of fishing for trophy pike by sinking and drawing artificial lures should not put one off this fishing-method. The sink and draw technique is the same as for other fish species. Every lure should be 'alive' in the water and attract the attention of the predator by means of its natural behaviour. Sink and draw must be carried out in such a way that the pike is not given any reason to pause to consider the lure. Successful fishing catches using simple home-made lures prove that the shape and detail of their technical execution do not matter. The colouring of the lure is much more important, as some colours provoke the pike to flee rather than to attack. Innovation of the lures used is also important. Any rough and ready innovation has a chance to be successful for a time. Classic spoons, rotating spinners and all types of wobblers and twisters are pretty well equally effective. The choice of lure also depends on the conditions. Classic spoons are used in flowing waters, spinners in still waters, floating wobblers in summer and sinkers in cooler waters, the colour shade being chosen according to the weather. The fan-like method of sink and draw should be followed, first casting to one and then to the other side of the vantage point, then combing the whole accessible area by means of gradually prolonged casts.

Mechanical, monotonous sinking and drawing is a bad habit. The lure is checked slightly and the line bulge straightened after casting and before impact with the water, so as to obtain contact with it. It does not matter if the lure sinks deeper in the first moment, as it is desirable to change both the direction and the depth while sinking and drawing, which can be achieved by a change both in the rhythm of retrieving and in the way the rod is held. When the fisherman observes that a predator is pursuing the lure, he must not slow down the tempo at which he is drawing it, as this could awaken doubts in the predator. On the contrary, the doubts of the pike are dispersed by a sudden acceleration or unexpected change of direction. The angler must concentrate fully until the last centimetres of the draw, and a take can often surprise him in the moment when he is already lifting the lure out of the water. At this moment one changes the rhythm of drawing and the predator decides at the last moment to seize the fleeing quarry.

Nevertheless, one should not fish by sink and draw at any price. After sinking and drawing for several hours with no success in unsuitable conditions, even the greatest optimist becomes lethargic and inertly guides the lure more or less monotonously, which offers a good opportunity for pike to learn how to give a wide berth to a suspicious object. One should only sink and draw, therefore, when there is good reason to expect success, and one must be kept constantly on the alert by the occasional interest of predators in the lure.

By way of conclusion, one more word of advice for the unlucky: try a combination of spinning and fishing with live fish-bait. First, the chosen spot is combed according to instructions using a spoon. If success is not achieved, the tackle is remounted with live fish-bait, which is cast to the spot where the trajectories of the spoon casts intersected each other. The preceding sinking and drawing may have aroused the interest of pike in the vicinity and one of them may have pursued the spoon but changed its mind about attacking it. It is now alert and will probably take the fish-bait. If it does not, have another go tomorrow . . . .

Pike-perch

There is a notion, which has been handed down over the years, that the pike-perch represents a kind of privileged, noble class among lowland fish species on account of its excessively demanding nature with regard to its environment. This may have been true at one time, in the conditions of clear virgin waters; the pike-perch of today, however, in attempt to survive has already greatly reduced its aristocratic proclivities. If it has a chance to choose, of course, it will give preference to more open, deeper, unpolluted waters rich in oxygen with a harder, gravelly, sandy or clay substrate and with sufficient opportunities for taking cover. Therefore this is where the angler should focus on looking for it. Where the opportunities for choice are limited, however, it will also adapt to muddier waters, as long as it is able to find there deeper reaches with suitable hiding places and an adequate supply of food. Thanks to its adaptability the pike-perch may be considered a fish species which provides excellent prospects from the sport fishing point of view, another contributory factor being the relatively wide area of its distribution. Since in winter it has a substantially reduced metabolism, the pike-perch ranks more among the lowland fish species, although it is able to get by successfully even in more northerly, climatically harsher conditions, in which it lives in

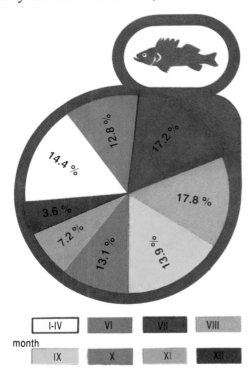

Success of pike-perch fishing depending on the season of the year.

128

the vicinity of salmon-type fish species. In flowing waters it avoids the swiftest reaches, and it prefers to keep to deeper, slightly dragging parts in the warmer season. In autumn it withdraws to deeper backwaters or semi-cut-off arms of rivers away from the mainstream. It has also taken a liking to more open, deeper canals and similar waters. Pike-perch should nevertheless not be sought only in the deepest sections of the water. For it is a practical fish and so, like it or not, it is obliged to stay mainly in places with sufficient food, this being scarce at the greatest depths. Among the positive characteristics of the pike-perch is the fact that it will make do with any kind of substrate for venting eggs, which it moreover also protects, so it is able to take care of its offspring. In lowland waters it spawns at 8—12 °C (46—54 °F), in harsher conditions at 6—8 °C (43—46 °F).

In view of its method of feeding, it is somewhat of an exaggeration to characterise the pike-perch as a predator. It does not change over to a predatory feeding method until the second or third year of its life. Given a chance, it will of course give preference to fish, although when short of food it is able to shift its orientation readily, even to larger aquatic insects and other aquatic animals. It will not even disdain a small dead fish. Its small mouth and gullet, however, will only permit it to seize smallish prey (the optimal size being about 8—10% of its own bulk). It adheres consistently to its daily routine, withdrawing into hiding places in the depths during the day, only manifesting more pronounced activity in the early morning and late afternoon. Thanks to excellent orientation by sight, it sometimes hunts late into the night, and sets out to hunt in the morning while it is still dark.

The pike-perch clan maintains a characteristic family cohesion in all situations, such as when settling a common territory and when hunting. Fish of even five to six different age-groups may be grouped in one clan, younger fish probably forming isolated groups. In a suitable territory, the pike-perch clan may number up to several dozen fish ranging in weight from 0.5 to 7kg (1.1—15.4lb).

The choice of suitable hunting territories is subject both to the requirement for suitable prey and to pike-perch hunting tactics. A shoal of pike-perch hunting together tightly encircles the quarry, this

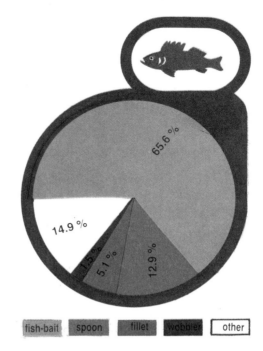

Effectiveness of various pike-perch fishing methods.

being the reason why the hunting territories are sometimes situated as far as the bank, at other times near an obstacle. After the circle has been closed, one pike-perch makes a lightning attack at the surrounded small fish, which try to flee in panic, thus becoming easy prey for the predators in wait around them. The feeding activity of a pike-perch is unsurpassed, and it is able to gorge itself on food during a productive hunt. In so doing, it compen-

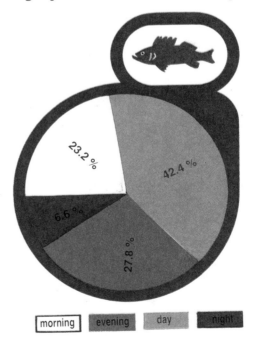

Results of pike-perch fishing at various times of day.

sates to a certain extent for its weak point, which does not allow it to seize larger quarry. It is interesting that the pike-perch has a slow growth rate in comparison with its appetite. It reaches the weight of 1kg (2.2lb) only in the fifth or sixth year of its life, and rarely exceeds a maximum final weight of 10kg (22lb).

The sport value of the pike-perch is somewhat reduced by the fact that after hooking it gives up very quickly and after several feeble attempts at resistance will allow itself to be fished out only too easily. The rules of the game when fishing for pike-perch are doubtful. It can happen that under apparently ideal climatic and water conditions the fisherman combs with the bait dozens of ideal places where one could swear to the presence of pike-perch, and still he comes away with nothing. When he is already starting to lose hope, the pike-perch suddenly make their presence felt and hungrily go for the bait one after the other. At such moments the colour or shape of the spoon really does not matter — the main thing is for the fish to have something to attack. This invasion, however, is usually

In canalised courses, pike-perch haunts are sought out, for example, by the vertical sinking of a fish fillet using a rod of appropriate length.

short, and as a rule it is followed by a lengthy period of calm.

Pike-perch can be fished for with equal success throughout the whole fishing season, that is from May until the end of December. On average the first half of the season, until the end of August, is usually the more successful. The most reliable bait for pike-perch is a small live fish, the effectiveness of spinning, however, being defended by German fishermen in particular on the basis of their results. Pike-perch catches using animal baits (earthworms, dung-worms, larvae, and so on) are considered normal in view of the omnivorousness of the fish, whilst relatively frequent catches using plant baits must, as in the case of pike, be regarded as coincidence. As regards fish-bait, pike-perch particularly like roach and goby and then rudd, bleak and German carp.

The results of fishing at various times of the day contradict the view of the nocturnal way of life of the pike-perch. The supposed indolence of the pike-perch during the day is only due to the fact that it is bothered by excessive sun and light, from which it hides in the shade. It does not always have to be the deepest nook: in summer it also likes to hide in shallows in the shade of broad water-lily leaves or small islands of reeds. In the period of increased feeding activity, it leaves its shelter and keeps to places with sufficient suitable smaller fish, so that it will also make its way into shallow, riverside areas. It behaves in a similar manner in the daytime and both before and during a storm. Excursions for food are relatively short, although it hunts very productively — and this is the very time for pike-perch fishing using all the usual methods and all common baits. This period should be utilised for sink and draw fishing with a dead fish-bait, as well as with all types of artificial lure. Live bait is also reliable bait at such moments, but should not be allowed to sink as far as the bottom, being kept to a depth of about 50—100cm (20—40in) with the aid of a float.

In the phase when pike-perch are passive during the day, the bait must be presented to the fish right under its nose; sinking and drawing is of little use, and also unrealistic on account of many obstacles in the water. One should therefore fish with natural baits — live or dead fish — using a passive method either without a float with the bait on the bottom, or with a float which will keep the bait at the required depth. Pike-perch may be provoked into activity by moving the bait up and down. This is always a risky fishing method and one must be prepared for possible loss of the tackle, or even of the quarry.

If the fisherman chooses his tackle on the basis of the minimal combative spirit of the pike-perch, he will then be able to manage for most fishing methods with ordinary carp tackle, and for sink and draw fishing with any finer casting rod. Anyone who wants to get the most out of the attractive method of moving the bait up and down, however, should definitely invest in a special rod up to 5—6m (16—20ft) long with a harder action. In their day, simple bamboo whiprods with the simplest centre-pin reel were suitable for this fishing method. In easier waters, even larger catches can safely be played using a line 0.22—0.25mm (0.009—0.01in) thick, lines 0.25—0.30mm (0.01—0.012in) thick being justified mainly when fishing in a dense network of obstacles, when the fisherman is compelled to use greater force when playing the quarry. Both for practical and ethical reasons, preference is given to single hooks of various types and sizes. The risk of losing the hook may be eliminated by using hooks with a protected point. Triple hooks are only justified

In canalised courses, pike-perch families keep to the hiding-places formed by the boulders with which the banks are reinforced.

when using artificial lures, and stranded steel wire is not used.

The most effective universal pike-perch fishing method is fishing with live or dead fish-bait, which is suitable for all waters and during all seasons of the year. Fine carp rods over 3m (10ft) in length are appropriate for this method, although the ideal rods are 4—6m (13—20ft) long with a fine but rather hard tip, which will keep a hooked pike-perch in check, even in a mesh of obstacles. Since the angler is casting mostly to shorter distances a simple reel will do, although a fixed-spool reel is necessary for sink and draw. The principle of minimal use of weights and floats should be observed. Live bait is mounted simply by the back or mouth, more complex systems for mounting bait not being necessary. We proceed from the assumption that the pike-perch attacks the quarry from behind. Single hooks, sizes 1—4, are used. It does not matter if the hook seems excessively large in comparison with the bait, although for the sake of more secure hooking one should take care that the point is free. The size of the fish-bait should be chosen carefully. Smaller, 5—6cm (2—2¼in) long fish are exceptionally effective for pike-perch, the disadvantage of these, however, being that even smaller specimens will also try to go for them. A small pike-perch will rarely go for a fish-bait 8—10cm (3—4in) long, leaving them to larger fish. When choosing the species of fish-bait, one should take into account which fish species usually live in the immediate vicinity of the pike-perch. In deeper, more open waters, the pike-perch is accompanied mainly by perch and ruff, in shallower waters by white fish.

The variations of fishing with live fish-bait are adapted to the character of the territory and the behaviour of the fish, and one should adhere to the principle of presenting the bait to the immediate vicinity of the pike-perch. In the cooler season, as well as in summer during the day, the less active pike-perch should be sought in deeper reaches and the fisherman should try to be as active as possible when fishing. In the period when pike-perch manifest increased feeding activity, the fisherman follows them to shallower reaches where the smaller fish are, and he can also choose a less active fishing method.

In rivers, cut-off river arms, and other natural

waters, the pike-perch territories are usually predominantly in riverside parts, water hollows below underwashed banks, in the exposed roots of riverside trees and below trees submerged under water. In canalised waters, pike-perch settle riverside reaches reinforced with free-standing boulders and whirling reaches under stony barriers leading transversely into the stream. The depths of the water in the territory is not decisive, even 1.5—2m (5—6¼ft) will do, shade and a general feeling of safety being the determining factors for pike-perch.

In this difficult terrain, it is only practically possible to fish by lifting the bait up and down. The requirement of getting the bait as close to the fish as

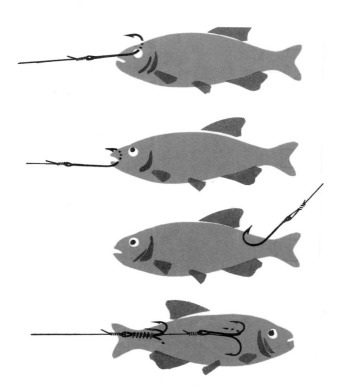

Methods for mounting dead fish-bait suitable when fishing for pike-perch and other predators.

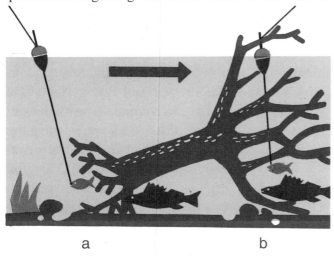

a   b

The mounting of live bait when seeking out pike-perch haunts among the roots and in the crowns of submerged trees: a) the bait placed in front of the hiding-place, b) the bait is placed directly into the hiding-place, the line being thrown over a branch protruding above the surface.

possible can only be met by a sufficiently long rod, which facilitates manipulation of the bait directly from the bank. The chosen spot should be systematically combed within as wide a radius as possible and in all water profiles. The angler always starts from the bottom, lifting the bait up a little with short jerky movements. As long as pike-perch are actually there, and if they have an appetite, they will soon make their presence felt after observing the bait. Lengthy, stubborn waiting for a take is a waste of time and the fisherman is better to try a couple of metres further along, or at another vantage point. He must carefully observe the bait at each phase of fishing, as it sometimes happens that an over-full pike-perch will take a while to consider it, following

it from the bottom, but only attacking just below the surface.

For experienced fisherman it can be interesting to fish for pike-perch in deeper, slowly flowing water near hiding places which the fish can find among the roots or branches of a submerged tree 15—20m (50—65ft) from the bank. A pike-perch hiding among the roots will take a live bait which one allows to drift slowly towards where it is. A second method is somewhat complicated; the bait is cast 10—15m (32—50ft) upstream from a submerged tree and about 3—4m (10—13ft) behind it. Then it is allowed to drift as far as the level of the crown of the tree, the line being flicked over the branches

Preparation of fillets from larger, white fish.

132

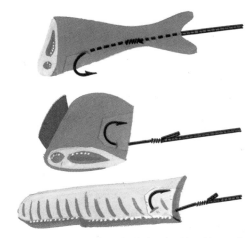

Mounting of the fillet on a single hook with a larger shank.

protruding from the water and the bait pulled a little towards the hiding place of the pike-perch among the branches. When the quarry is being played, the caught pike-perch must be extricated through the branches of the tree, which can only be accomplished by a fisherman who has perfect control of his tackle and is acquainted with the laws of mechanical physics. In both cases 4.5—5.5m (14¾—18ft) long rods with more resilient but sufficiently flexible tips are used, and a line 0.30mm (0.012in) thick. A float is attached at two points in such a way that the bait will move 25 to 30cm (10—12in) above the bottom.

In valley reservoirs and similar more open waters, the pike-perch usually has inexhaustible options for choosing its territory. It is therefore bound to choose the ones which are ideal for it, these mostly being situated further off-shore, for example in construction remains, the channel of a former river-bed, remains of trees and so on. In such places, of course, one can only be successful when using a boat. Fishing is usually carried out by lifting the bait up and down and absolute silence is essential when doing this, as in such an environment the pike-perch can be highly suspicious and cautious. It can even be disturbed by the unusual shadow of a boat or trembling of the water. For this reason the angler does not steer the boat too close to where the fish are, mooring a little away off, the greater distance being compensated for by a longer rod. Here of course one can also fish using more passive methods, such as with fish-bait on the bottom or in the water profile.

During the period of increased pike-perch feeding activity, that is towards morning, late afternoon, at night in summer and even in daytime during storms, the angler seeks the fish in their usual hunting territories, that is, in shallower, overheated waters, where there are smaller fish. Here mainly sink and draw is used, although fishing with a shallow presented fish-bait may also be successful.

One can also fish with dead fish-bait, fish tail or fillet using the same methods.

For pike-perch fishing by spinning the same rules apply as when fishing for other predators, the lures, however, being smaller, up to 10—12g (0.35—0.42oz) in weight. The success of sink and draw depends more on the careful drawing of the lure than on its shape and colour. In poorer visibility and in muddy water, lighter, silvery lures are better, in sunny weather darker copper or lead colours. The effectiveness of lures may be increased by using red beads, pieces of red cotton thread, or plumelets dyed red. In flowing waters, classic spoons of all types may be employed; spinners are better in still waters, either simple or combined with a small fish made of soft plastic, possibly adorned with a red trinket. Smaller types of sinking wobblers are also appropriate; in deeper, more open waters vertical sink and draw using a 'marmyshka' is usually effective. Reports of the success of twisters and various imitations of insects, larvae, earthworms and even special deep-sunk flies, are hopeful.

The pike-perch take varies. Sometimes it seizes the bait without one even noticing it, at other times it surprises the angler with a boisterous take. It will always take an artificial lure more energetically, whereas it will first chew a natural bait in its mouth, which is indicated by an irregular bobbing of the float. Hooking is not carried out until the moment the pike-perch begins to make off with the bait so that it can swallow it in peace. Although the pike-perch does not have a combative spirit, this does not mean that one should underestimate it during playing. A large pike-perch needs to be tired like other fish. Although it will not try to escape to a greater distance, it will nevertheless desperately try to withdraw to the safety of the depths in the first phase after hooking. It is enough, therefore, if one can keep it on the spot where it was hooked, as the elastic line and flexible rod tip will tire it after a while and it will allow itself to be pulled up to the surface

135

One-piece wobblers for fishing for smaller predators — trout, perch, pike-perch.

relatively easily. A sudden change of pressure can occasionally cause shock and the death of the fish.

Perch

The absurd but true case of a perch taking its own eye, which the hook has torn out during a preceding unsuccessful hooking, can only be explained in one way by the layman: that this is an insatiable, easily caught, voracious fish. Although the perch may be regarded as insatiable, it is not so easily caught. It is the young ones that are naive, a larger, and especially a very old perch being a cunning fox that one gets hold of more by accident than design.

The characteristics of the perch are more or less identical to those of the pike-perch, although the perch is even more adaptable and various types of water suit it, assuming that they are not excessively muddy and have favourable oxygen content. It is not demanding either with regard to a substrate for venting eggs, which it sticks in stages throughout the course of the whole spring to various objects in the form of bead-like formations, thus being able to take effective care of its young. It is an indiscriminate carnivore which will gather even dead quarry, not even stopping its feeding activity in winter. The growth rate of the perch is exceptionally variable. In

its case one can apply the rule: 'small water, small fish, large water, large fish'. In waters with limited space, especially when there is over-reproduction of the species as a result of the absence of predators, it grows very slowly and develops a typical, stunted population. In more open waters, assuming that its population is kept down by sufficient numbers of other predators, it grows rapidly and can even reach more than 2kg (4.4lb) in weight. It is by then already a merciless cannibal, effectively participating itself in regulating the numbers of its own species. The ideal biotopes of the perch are deeper, more open and clean lakes and water reservoirs in submontane regions. It also has a very good tolerance of harsher climatic conditions.

It may be fished for throughout the whole year, although summer fishing from June to August is most effective. Artificial lures for spinning, earthworms, fish-bait and larvae predominate among the lures used. Classic spoons, spinners, twisters, wobblers and even some special types of artificial fly are equally effective as regards artificial lures. It is surprising that fish fillet, which has proved so successful with the related pike-perch, does not figure among the range of baits.

The territories of larger perch are very difficult to determine. Basically they tend to keep to deeper waters, although this depends on the season — in winter to the greatest depths near the bottom, in spring during spawning closer to the surface, as they also do in summer. It is not possible, however, to be precise about the rules of their behaviour, as they behave as they feel like at the time. Under the same weather conditions they may be either at a depth of 30m (100ft) or close below the surface. One thing is certain, however: their appetite is constant, and if the fisherman once succeeds in ascertaining their location, he can possibly make up in a single fishing trip for a whole unsuccessful season.

The restless character of the perch provides one with an opportunity to attract it mainly by indirect luring, that is by means of luring small fish, a concentration of which will arouse the interest of predators. At the beginning of spring, alevins are lured with fine, surface groundbait, small fish later being lured closer to the bottom. In both cases, a substance which will intensely cloud, possibly even colour the water is added to the bait. Luring for larger

137

perch is carried out further off and also in deeper water.

Direct luring with pieces of earthworm, small fish, larvae and so on, is carried out only if one intends to fish for several days at a chosen pike-perch territory. A combination of spinning and natural bait, as in the case of pike fishing, is another variation for luring. A hopeful spot is first thoroughly combed using a suitable artificial lure, which will attract the attention of predators and put them in a combative mood. They will then be more ready to take a fish-bait. In frequented waters this solution is usually the only answer.

The perch is an attractive fish species on account of its exceptional versatility, which makes it possible to fish for it using diverse fishing methods. Nonetheless it has also inherited from the pike-perch its poor combative spirit, so that one can manage fishing even with the finest tackle.

For sink and draw, a fine, 2—2.4m (6½—8ft) long rod with a semi-soft action for a weight of 10—20g (0.35—0.7oz), and a smaller, lighter reel with a shallowish spool for 120—150m (390—490ft) of line with a thickness of 0.18 to 0.20mm (0.007—0.008in) is chosen. Practically the whole range of artificial lures for sink and draw may be used, as well as some special systems and some types of wet artificial flies. Lures should be correspondingly small, their effectiveness being increased by a blood-red trinket at the end of the hook, or with red beads on the spinner axis. A perch will soon see through lures which are too shiny.

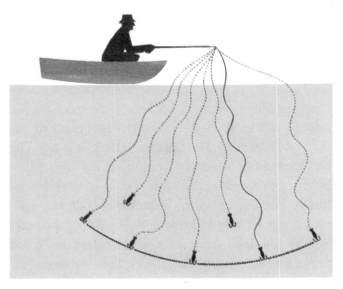

Method of fishing by vertical sinking and drawing from a boat.

The technique for drawing the lure is identical with fishing for other fish species — a drawn lure should imitate the movements of a sickly small fish. In the case of the perch, however, preference when drawing is given to the lower water profile, a slower drawing tempo generally being chosen, and the fisherman moves the lure vertically as often as possible. After casting, the lure is allowed to sink freely to the bottom, and the fisherman then guides it upwards in a parabolic curve by means of faster retrieving, slowing down the tempo when reaching the peak of the curve and allowing the bait to fall slowly towards the bottom along the falling part of the parabola. This method requires longer casts, preference therefore being given to heavier baits, which may occasionally be weighted.

A perch take is most likely in the vicinity of obstacles, since like the pike-perch it enjoys a feeling of safety under cover. The movement of the lure must be observed constantly. If the perch show suspicion, which will manifest itself in observation of the lure, the angler must definitely do something, changing the bait for a less usual one, or changing the path of the drawn lure into a more pronounced, more upright parabola, possibly changing over to the method of vertical drawing.

In more open, deeper lakes or valley reservoirs without a substantial number of obstacles, sink and draw may be carried out from a boat, using both artificial and natural lures. Here finer, up to 3m (10ft) long rods for fishing on the bottom should be used. Tackle with a weight situated 60—100cm (24—40in) from the lure, is cast to the required distance from the boat, the depth at which the lure is drawn being controlled by the speed at which the boat is moving. The rod should be firmly fixed and if the brake mechanism of the reel is carefully set the fish may even hook itself.

Fishing using vertical drawing is probably best suited to the character of the perch. The lure is allowed to fall to the required depth of its own accord, sometimes even as far as the bottom, and is then lifted up with short energetic jerking motions, and again allowed to sink downwards with oscillating movements. In this way, the angler gradually combs through a greater area. This method may only be employed in waters at least 8—10m (26—33ft) deep, ideally from a boat, and occasionally even from steep banks under which there is sufficient depth. When fishing from a boat, a special short rod is used; when fishing from the bank, a longer rod normally used for dapping. Larger types of slender shape are chosen from among possible lures, for example kosaks, eskimos, spherical spinners, as well as special perch flies. Even special deep water rigs with suitable natural bait may be considered. From the range of natural baits, small live and dead fish are equally effective, as well as fillets or fish tails, earthworms and larvae.

In waters where there is a risk of losing the hook in an obstacle or in aquatic vegetation, only fishing with a float can be considered, for which any fine, long rod over 3.5m (11½ft) with a semi-soft action for a weight up to 10—20g (0.35—0.7oz), any smaller type of reel, the line thickness being from 0.18—0.22mm (0.007—0.009in), depending on the difficulty of the terrain, and a hook commensurate with the bait (no. 4 for earthworms, 6—8 for larvae) are suitable. Whether to attach a divided or nondivided weight and fixed or sliding float depends on the circumstances, the swiftness of the water and the depth. When fishing in flowing waters, casting is carried out so that the bait will gradually drift to a greater distance. In still waters the bait is activated by occasionally pulling and lifting it up. The bait should not be left in one spot for too long, as the perch either take immediately or not at all. The first take is as a rule a hopeful sign, and after casting fresh bait to precisely the same spot, the angler may even fish out the whole related clan.

During the day, the catfish prefers to keep to a safe hiding-place in submerged trees.

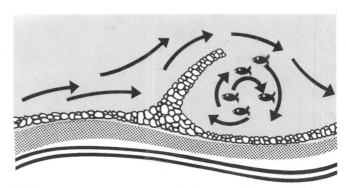

Catfish haunts in more open, canalised courses lie in reaches downstream from transverse stone barriers.

When fishing with fish-bait, preference is given to smaller ones, up to 4—5cm (1½—2in) in length, which may be a small perch, bitterling or bleak.

In open waters when fishing at a distance, one can only be successful using the classic method of fishing on the bottom. The tackle is assembled with the aid of a sliding weight, so that the predator will not be disturbed during the take. Earthworms or smaller fish are chosen as bait. In flowing waters, casting is either carried out to a watershed between the current and still water, or to a fault between shallow and deep water, where possible in such a way that the current will activate the bait. The bait is only left in one place for any length of time at a particularly promising spot. Elsewhere, the angler tries to activate fishing by tripping the bait along the bottom at intervals of two or three minutes. In this case, fish fillet or tail seems to be a more effective bait.

In more unusual cases, fishing with the aid of a paternoster with two rigs may also be considered.

In the summer season after spawning, when perch keep to the upper layers of water, it is even possible to fish in lakes and dams by combining the methods of sink and draw from a boat with vertical sink and draw. Fairly flexible, thinnish metal wire (copper wire 0.6mm/0.024in in diameter) is used instead of line, and a 2—3m (6½—10ft) piece of line 0.25—0.28mm (0.01—0.011in) thick as a rig. The bait may either be natural (tail, fillet, earthworm) or artificial (a smaller spoon, or one of several special lures). The angler holds the tackle in his fingers, alternatively rowing and energetically lifting the tackle with his hand during the short intervals. When perch fishing using artificial wet flies, the angler attempts to imitate the movement of aquatic animals, either of fry or the developmental stages of aquatic insects (nymphs). Assuming that the bait is drawn naturally — skipping and shaking both from side to side and up and down — the angler can expect to be pleasantly surprised using this fishing method.

Catfish

The catfish has strict environmental requirements, the area of its occurrence therefore being relatively restricted. It ranks among the thermophilic species and its habitat may be found in more open, deeper and warmer lowland waters. It has similarly strict requirements as regard possibilities for taking cover. It only occurs regularly in natural, sufficiently varied, meandering courses. Given a chance to choose its territory, it will settle mainly in deeper water hollows under the high, clay banks of the meandering course, root networks of riverside trees, or the crowns of submerged trees at the required depth. It also favours reaches at faults between swift and still waters, the estuaries of backwaters, semi-cut-off river arms and river junctions with varied beds. It also occurs everywhere where there are water whirlpools, which bring it food. It does not feel at home in canalised courses, where it can most often be found in reaches where there are stone barriers along the banks, as well as in whirling depths under transverse stone dikes. Its dwellings are always to be found away from the mainstream, although in summer it also hunts in the stream. Fairly open water reservoirs, varied cut-off river arms, gravel pits, more open reclamation canals at least 2m (6½ft) deep, and so on also suit it well. It is even possible for it to acclimate itself to harsher climatic conditions (up to 400m/1,300ft) above sea level), although in such cases it has difficulty withstanding the long winter, grows slowly and has no chance of spawning naturally. It matures sexually later than other fish species, not until the fifth or sixth year of its life. It spawns in pairs at a temperature of over 22 °C (72 °F); that is, only from the middle of June, ideally when it is stormy.

It is distinguished from other species by the exceptionally wide range of its diet. Thanks to its physical proportions, it can even try to go for a bulkier quarry. It is not choosy and will consume literally any meaty food it encounters while wandering around if it is accessible in terms of size. A basic component of the catfish diet is of course fish and

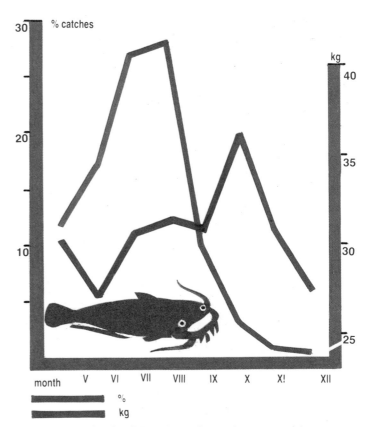

The success of catfish fishing depending on the season of the year.

other larger aquatic animals, and during torrents it enjoys eating dry-land animals which have drifted downstream. Larger catfish specimens will even go after aquatic birds, musk-rats and so on. The water temperature affects its appetite. It survives the winter in a latent winter sleep practically without food, awakening only after fairly substantial spring floods. At the end of autumn, when the water temperature drops below 8 °C (46 °F), it will once again seek out its winter dwellings. Within the relatively short vegetation period, the catfish lives with exceptional intensity, as if trying to make up as soon as possible for its winter stoppage of food intake. It is particularly avid during spawning. By that time it is able to consume up to 60 % of its overall yearly amount of food, and by autumn it will then store in its body sufficient energy for the winter season.

The result of the rapacity of the catfish is its intensive growth and ability to reach gigantic proportions. Reports from the past of 300kg (660lb) catfish have been authoritatively proved and record catches weighing almost 100kg (220lb) have also been verified from the recent past. It should be noted at the outset, however, that the catfish grows slowly at first, reaching the weight of 1kg (2.2lb)

141

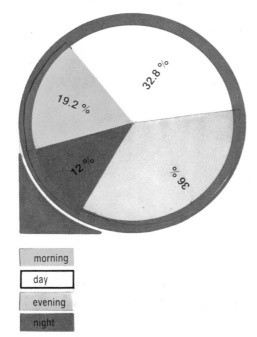

morning

day

evening

night

The effectiveness of catfish fishing at various times of day.

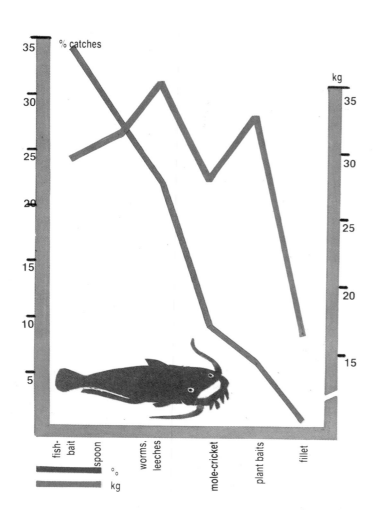

The effectiveness of various catfish fishing methods.

only in the fourth or fifth year of its life, after that, however, growing very rapidly. 50kg (110lb) specimens are usually about 26 years old.

Horrendous stories, some of them even claiming man-eating tendencies, circulate about the rapacity and aggression of the catfish. It is not necessary, however, to make the catfish into a monster. Under normal circumstances, the catfish will give man a wide berth. Isolated cases of it being aggressive only occur if the catfish feels cornered and cannot save itself by escaping. Even I myself have as a result of carelessness become a target for an attack by a catfish. A male guarding eggs on an artificial nest mistook my hand submerged under the water for a fish. Out of habit we are accustomed to characterising the catfish as a typical nocturnal predator. It spends the days under cover, becoming active only at twilight, that is, after sunset, and towards morning. It only changes its daily routine during the period of summer storms when, expecting rich quarry to drift downstream, its appetite lasts the whole day. At one time the catfish probably observed these rules. However, nowadays it often interrupts its daily siesta. One should also correct the theory of the surly, solitary catfish which will not tolerate any relatives in its vicinity. It only behaves in this way in cases where there are so many suitable spots in the river that every fish can choose its own. Usually, however, there are not enough such suitable spots, and the catfish is therefore compelled to restrict itself to communal hostels and hunting territories.

The optimal season for fishing for catfish is definitely the first half of the period of vegetation growth, ideally just after spawning. At that time the catfish is exceptionally active, its aggression being increased by summer storms and oscillations in barometric pressure. July and August are the most hopeful months for fishing. Poorer catches during the second half of the period of vegetation confirm that cooler water does not suit the thermophilic catfish. At the end of October, fishermen should leave the catfish alone, so that it can settle down for its winter sleep in peace.

One should give careful consideration to the question of the most suitable time of day for fishing, as statistical results frequently do not correspond to logic. Fishing during the evening hours is usually successful; morning and night-time catches are poorer, however, whereas daytime fishing is often surprisingly successful. Daytime catches are usually also of greater weight. All this partly contradicts the view that the catfish is a typical nocturnal predator. The catfish also has a right to its whims, and it is not possible to fit it into a mould. Its daily activity need not be dependent on a storm, and the catfish may also sunbathe just below the surface in stable weather. Although it is true that the catfish spends the day digesting its morning quarry, there are few which would turn down a fragrant morsel that happened to fall right under their nose. The secret of daytime fishing success lies predominantly in the art of finding the hiding-place of the catfish and choosing the appropriate fishing method.

The lack of choosiness of the catfish is an advantage for the sport fisherman, and the widest range of baits can be used when fishing for it. Apart from the most common ones, such as both live and dead fish-bait, fillets, earthworms, leeches, the larger larvae of aquatic insects, grasshoppers, locusts and so on, pieces of liver, spleen and coagulated blood are for example also suitable. There were times when we even fished successfully using pieces of home-made soap, mice, smaller birds and so on. The predatory catfish will of course also take many types of artificial lure. In spite of the wide choice of lures, it is necessary to point out tried and tested specialties for catfish fishing. Loach, German carp and burbot are the best fish-baits, mole-crickets being

without parallel among insects, probably because of their specific smell, then the mayfly in the period of swarming, and of other lures coagulated beef blood combined with liver a few days old, possibly with spleen. One should not overdo the size of the bait. There are far fewer real giants than there are average-sized catfish, although if the angler is sure that there is a giant in the vicinity, he may even bait with a carp-bream or chub weighing up to 1kg (2.2lb).

Loach is given preference among fish-baits. The slender shape of its meaty body and excellent movement when mounted on the hook will provoke even a half-dead catfish. The body shape of the burbot likewise fully meets requirements. The German carp also moves superbly and has remarkable endurance, being suitable mainly for fishing on the surface; when baited deeper in the water, it tries to act inconspicuously, preferring to hide. Also mobile, and therefore conspicuous, are the perch and ruff (in neither case is it necessary to cut off the dorsal fin, as the catfish can easily cope with them). More resilient species should be chosen from among white fish, so that they will survive the rigours of being on the tackle, for example roach, rudd, carp-bream and chub. The smaller and more delicate bleak, bitterling and goby should be left for pike-perch and pike fishing.

Fishing with a spoon can also be successful. The angler can set out for catfish both with classic spoons and spinners, although he can rely equally even on home-made spoons. There is no need to doubt the effectiveness of wobblers, twisters and so on. Preference should be given to larger, heavier artificial lures, colour only being able to play a part in good visibility. At twilight, when spinning is most likely to be considered, the catfish will hardly notice the colour of its quarry.

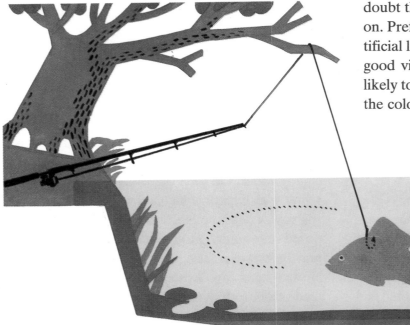

A characteristic method for presenting fish-bait (ideally the German carp) at a definite catfish haunt.

Fish-bait presented when fishing for catfish just above the bottom.

Earthworms and dungworms are universal baits in all types of water, in any season of the year or at any time of day, moreover bringing the greatest likelihood of the largest catches. The excessive and unwelcome interest of other fish species in these baits can partly be reduced by choosing the largest specimens. Probably once in every ten attempts the omnivorous catfish can be caught using atypical, mainly plant baits, as apart from meaty food, boiled potato, potato dumpling, corn groats, bread dough and so on also figure on its menu.

A stouter catfish is fully aware of its strength and will never give up without a fight. It will struggle bravely and tenaciously; its escapes are well thought-out, and it knows how to distribute its strength economically. It alternates two tactical, regularly interchanged variations of the fight: it either makes continuous assaults with furious lashing of the line with its tail, or during the course of the fight it lies down on the bottom. Although the angler must not underestimate the catfish, he can venture for smaller specimens up to 10—20kg (22—44lb) using just ordinary carp-fishing tackle. When spinning, one can rely on an average casting rod used for pike fishing. One cannot pursue a catfish with brute force alone, as it must be played patiently and with skill.

Rods of course must be as resilient as possible, that is, large, with harder action and suitable even for a weight of more than 100g (3.5oz). For sink and draw, a 1.8—2.8m (6—9ft) long rod should be chosen; for fishing on the bottom 2.8—3.5m (9—11½ft); for tripping the stream and swimming the stream up to 4.5—5m (14¾—16½ft) long. As regards

reels, a medium-sized multiplier reel is the most reliable, whilst of fixed-spool reels one should use only those made of the best materials and technically the best executed, equipped with a particularly solid spool with a capacity of at least 150m (490ft) of thicker line. Particular emphasis is placed on good quality, appropriately sized hooks. Catfish specialists even nowadays rely only on hand-forged hooks. The line must correspond to the type of rod. For spinning, swimming the stream and tripping the stream, a line 0.30—0.35mm (0.012—0.014in) thick will do, as a stronger one would be impractical for this fishing technique. For fishing on the bottom, a line 0.40 to 0.60mm (0.016—0.024in) thick is chosen, depending on the terrain.

Like the pike-perch, the catfish can either be 'sat out' or 'walked out', the choice of fishing method depending on its behaviour under the given conditions and on the character of its location. After an opulent morning banquet, the catfish withdraws to a sheltered lair, so that it can digest in peace and apparent passivity. At that time access to it is more difficult, and sink and draw fishing brings with it a high risk of frequent losses of baits in obstacles, so that of the active fishing methods only tripping the bottom, the technique of which is the same as when pike-perch fishing, can be considered. A precondition for this is to be able, by means of a long rod, to reach the place immediately above where the fish is, better chances of success thus being contingent upon fishing from a boat. When fishing at a distance, the angler must mostly resort to fishing on the bottom, and in relatively shallow waters must even fish with a float. In both cases the baits should be as natural and as convincing as possible, and the angler must also try to get them as close to the catfish as possible, into its field of vision. Live bait is top of the list, and a bunch of moving earthworms is also effective. The attention of the catfish may also be attracted by aromatised baits, especially in cloudy water. On such occasions it is better to present it with liver or spleen a few days old, a plucked sparrow, a dead mouse, or a small dead fish with exposed intestines. Mole-crickets, grasshoppers or mayfly, however, also give off a provocative aroma. Normal baits can also be aromatised in an infusion made from rotting meat, blood, cheese and so on.

In the period of increased activity, that is 2 hours

The loach ranks among the most effective baits when fishing for catfish, keeping well even on a single hook.

before and 2 hours after sunrise and in the evening from sunset until complete darkness sets in, the catfish sets out for places with abundant food. In more varied waters these are usually shallower, sometimes even riverside parts, in monotonous deeper waters the upper layers of water. In shallower waters it always seeks out food above the bottom. Its attention is drawn to suitable food on the bottom by its sensitive senses of smell and taste, which are situated mainly in its long whiskers, and it registers small fishes moving in the water column in front of it by means of sight, and along its flanks by means of the lateral line.

Sometimes the catfish will interrupt its daily routine and set out during the day on wanderings, even when it is not stormy, sunning itself just under the surface and sometimes showing off like a dolphin. At such moments, a couple of casts with a spoon are definitely worth trying.

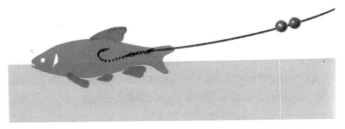

The loach can also be mounted by sewing it on to a triple hook.

The necessity for a carefully assembled rod and line is dictated both by the imposing nature of the fish and by the usually difficult terrain, fraught with obstacles. The catfish is strong, but not stupid, and is particular about fine tackle. It will react with suspicion to excessive resistance, spitting out even the most enticing bait. Therefore the tackle should be assembled as simply as possible, without any unnecessary knots. The hook equipped with a tang, the sharper edges of which must be blunted, is firmly tied. Under normal conditions, a classic rod and line assembly is chosen, the hook being tied at the end of the main line, and an appropriate, always

The catfish likes to take a bite at a sandwich-type bait.

sliding weight being fixed above it by means of a thick stopper. The shape of the weight is subject to the character of the water, and flat-shaped weights are generally more advantageous.

Hooks are usually the Achilles heel of the catfish tackle. When fishing with the majority of fishing techniques using natural baits, one can fully rely on stronger, perhaps even thicker simple hooks nos. 1—2 up to 4/0, with shanks of various lengths. Hooks with longer shanks are suitable, for example, for mounting a bunch of earthworms, and even two mole-crickets, two or three leeches and so on will fit on them well. A bunch of earthworms may of course also be mounted on a double or triple hook. The choice of hook should therefore be left to the angler's preference. Smaller and more sensitive fish-bait should be mounted gently, being pierced with a simple hook just under the place where the dorsal fin starts. A fish mounted on the hook in this way will hold well, is not tired and is active in the

145

water. The angler must of course also take into account the possibility of the catfish getting away with pulling the fish-bait off the hook. Larger and more resilient fish-baits, for example, loach, German carp, as well as larger roach and rudd, are mounted on a triple hook by sewing them through without the risk of the fish losing the opportunity of movement. The needle is guided just under the skin along the back, so that its musculature is not injured, and is pulled out just before the place where the dorsal fin starts; then a triple hook is tied on and pulled back with the whole shank under the skin. Two curves of the hook encircle the flanks of the fish, the third one pointing straight upwards. A double hook is less reliable for sewing through, as after a while it can work loose and twist round a little, the points will not protrude as they should and hooking is uncertain.

Baits of the sandwich type may be practical, assuming a combination of baits which have different effects — one for example being effective with its movement and colour (earthworm), the other with its aroma (liver a few days old).

On the basis of experience, fishing with two rigs on one rod and line cannot be recommended, as the two baits are only a few centimetres apart, and sometimes even become tangled. Two hooks are more likely to mean an unnecessary risk of losing the quarry. During playing, a loose hook may catch itself in some obstacle and the whole tackle will come off. One should also carefully consider fishing using two rods, mainly in cases where the angler is

The short-sighted catfish can be fooled by the simplest bait — a piece of cigar-shaped weight attached to a triple hook.

146

A special rig used by fishermen in the Danubian lowlands when fishing for catfish using a sound-whistle.

alone and there is no-one to help him. If the catfish are taking, one has enough to do even with one rod, and if they have no appetite even a dozen rods will not help. When fishing by swimming the stream in flowing water, the use of two rods is practically out of the question, because the angler must be in constant contact with the bait to be able to hook in time.

When assembling tackle for fishing by sink and draw, one can proceed in one of two ways, either by tying the bait directly on to the main line, or by means of a stronger rig. The first method meets the basic requirements for simplicity and reliability, but also has a weak point: because of the excessive overloading of the rod and line by drawing heavier baits, the last few metres of line in particular start to suffer after a while, the line thus losing its elasticity and resilience. This process is intensified when playing the quarry or extricating the tackle. From time to time, therefore, the angler must discard the end piece of the line (the damage to which may not be discernible) and in a jiffy the spool is half-empty. It is thus better to choose a rig of stronger line, which will better withstand the overload. So as partly to compensate for the weakness of an extra knot, the angler decides for a rig up to 5—6m (16—20ft) long — it is always easier to change a worn out piece of rig.

Although the catfish is not regarded as a particularly sharp-sighted fish, the angler should nevertheless not underestimate it either, so that when choosing the colour of the lure the following generally recognised principles are taken into account: good visibility means darker, more matte colour shades, and in reduced visibility lighter, more conspicuously coloured lures are chosen; however, lures which are too shiny have an off-putting effect. The necessity for lures to imitate a living creature as closely as possible is doubtful, as an attacking catfish is not interested in counting the scales on an artificial fish, or in being delighted by the eyes of an artificial mouse. There are greater hidden resources and reserves in the technique of sinking and drawing than in the detailed execution of the lure.

The catfish fulfils a sanitary function in the water superbly well, concentrating above all on the elimination of diseased and thus more sickly fish. It will unfailingly pick out such a fish in a shoal and focus its attention on it. A more sickly fish hangs behind a shoal of healthy fish, from time to time desparately trying to catch up with it, but tiring quickly and sinking downwards until it recovers again. A drawn lure will be successful if it behaves in the same way. Perfect drawing of the lure may seem easy at first sight, but mastering it requires the right touch and gift for it. One should particularly beware of stereotypes, and maintain — depending on the conditions — frequent changing of the rhythm and depth of drawing.

The characteristic method for catching catfish is fishing by means of a sound whistle, the principle of which lies in inducing both a sound and a pressure effect when submerging and pulling the whistle out of the water. The angler holds the whistle in his hand at an angle of 30°, submerging it under the water to a depth of 8—10cm (3—4in). The effect itself is achieved by an energetic, arched pulling movement out of the water, being caused by the sudden release of an air bubble caught under the rounded, concave ring of the whistle. The sound, but chiefly the pressure waves, spread through the water to a great distance, perhaps signalling to indolently resting catfish that their relatives are banqueting on the surface. It is also possible that the sounds of the whistle imitate the splashing sounds of jumping frogs. Whatever it is, the catfish really react to these

A fighting catfish resorts to lashing the line with its powerful tail.

sounds and set out on a hunt. There is no need to overdo this luring; one should try it two or three times, one shortly after the other, in one spot, and if nothing happens it is better to try again a little further on. The method of sound luring is most effective in virgin waters, if these still exist. The actual technique when sound luring is that of swimming the stream, of course, only with the aid of a boat. Only a shorter, especially resilient rod and a resilient rig should be used. The depth of submersion of the bait is chosen according to circumstances, and in the case of especially productive luring the catfish will venture into the direct vicinity of the boat and may even bump into it. Baits may vary, preference being given to mole-crickets, loach or rotting liver.

Of the less usual methods, we should mention fishing 'on a gibbet'. A small fish, usually a palm-sized German carp, or even a somewhat larger carp-bream, is pierced with a single hook under the dorsal fin and presented in such a way that it will hardly touch the surface. The fish of course desperately tries to get under the water, and makes a great deal of splashing noise. A sufficiently long rod is es-

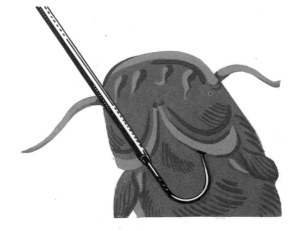

The only reliable method for landing a catfish is to use a gaff.

149

sential for success, the fisherman using it to get the bait to the required spot. The rod must be well secured, so that the catfish will not pull it away during hooking. The brake of the reel is released and the assembly may even be fixed to a reverside tree. Fishing 'on a gibbet' may only be considered in swifter waters with high underwashed banks and sufficient deeper hiding places, in which one may expect catfish lairs.

Vertical sink and draw with artificial lures is essentially identical with fishing by tripping the bottom.

Experience with playing other fish species is not of much use with the catfish, which has to be played differently. The carp is startled when hooked and makes off at lightning speed, while the pike and trout jump out as if out of their minds, thereby rapidly exhausting their strength. The catfish stays cool even in the most critical situations, does not squander its strength and fights to its last breath. It can even free itself with a gaff hook already in its body. In the first phase of combat, the catfish tries to get 'home', as if knowing that he can best rid himself of the tackle in the tangle of obstacles. The angler should not give way to panic and try to stop it at any price, only checking it sensitively in such a way that he always has a reserve of at least 20% of the line on the spool. As the line is paid out, the tackle gains resilience and he can then try to divert the catfish from its set course slightly to the side by exerting greater pressure. After 20—30m (65—100ft) it will stop of its own accord and lie down on the bottom. The angler, however, should not now sit back and relax, because the catfish is still far from being tired. He should likewise not try to lift the catfish up by force. It is best to try 'morse code', that is, plucking the taut line with a finger with the rod pointing directly towards the fish and the occasional pumping movement. It will seem to the angler that it takes ages and the presence of the catfish is only betrayed by clouding of the water and bubbles escaping from the mud. After a while the catfish will change its mind, raise itself and make another attempt at escape, then lying down again. It will draw from its reserves another tactical variation — positioning itself with its head pointing straight down towards the bottom, burrowing in the mud and furiously lashing the line with its powerful tail. It is difficult to give

150

advice on what the angler should do in this phase, whether to keep the line taut or to slacken it a little and thus lose contact with the fish. The chances are even in both cases. After an unsuccessful attempt at freeing itself, the catfish will set about moving again and this situation may repeat itself several more times, until the angler gains the impression that the catfish's energy is inexhaustible. As the fish tires, so too the angler loses strength. After a while, sometimes even after a few hours, the angler is finally able to pull in the catfish with the rod and line, lift it out of the water and see it in all its glory.

Eel

The life-cycle of the eel, which until recently was shrouded in mystery, is worthy of our admiration. They originate in the Sargasso Sea and after three long years of arduous migration from their place of birth across the vast expanses of the Atlantic the young eels reach the shores of Europe. Then, after a short rest which is used for acclimatisation from salt to fresh waters, come further laborious journeys inland, sometimes of hundreds of kilometres against the river current. Finally, and after ten or twelve years, they undertake the formidable journey back to their native waters to spawn and die.

The adaptability of the eel is also remarkable, as it is generally regarded as a thermophilic fish species which survives the winter season in an inactive state, but in spite of this penetrates higher, cooler, submontane regions. Of course, the warmer lowland muddy waters suit it better, enabling it to have

The apparent passivity of the eel during the day is only superficial. A bait suitably presented to the vicinity of its haunt can provoke it to attack even at high noon.

The voracious eel can be enticed with a bulky meaty morsel, perhaps even one that smells. A bunch of large earthworms can be attached to a hook with a long shank.

a longer active period and bringing rich sources of food. The eel makes no distinction between flowing and still waters, and will acclimatise itself anywhere, though avoiding excessively swift reaches, and in submontane courses settling in the calmer, deeper backwaters in meanders.

The eel is light-shy. It does not show itself during the day, so the selection of its living space depends on accessibility of the darkest possible hiding places. The depth of the water is not decisive, and in the summer season it is possible to find its dwellings even in shallowish, bankside parts of the water in the dense tangle of vegetation. In open waters with insufficient hiding places, it feels safer at a greater distance from the frequented banks; it withdraws to the depths and likes to take every opportunity to burrow its way into the mud, from which only the head and part of the tail protrude.

Both types of eel — the narrow-headed and broad-headed — have a relatively large mouth and gullet, therefore giving preference to bulkier morsels. The importance of fish in eel nutrition is often overestimated. During its short vegetation period, when it manifests increased feeding activity, it cannot afford the luxury of choosing its food and will consume anything meaty which it comes across. Small fish are therefore an occasional variation of its menu, the basis of which consists of bulkier aquatic animals, for example larvae, slugs, beetles,

frogs, and so on. The intensity of growth of the eel is not proportional to its voracity. After a ten- or twelve-year stay in fresh water, it grows to an average of 1—2kg (2.2—4.4lb). Trophy fish over 3kg (6.6lb) in weight mostly come from enclosed waters from where they have no chance to escape, and are usually 15—16 years old. A record European eel weighting 7.8kg (17lb 6oz) came from the Ebro river in Spain.

When sport fishing for eel, the choice of the correct vantage point is more important than the fishing technique, which is fundamentally based simply on fishing on the bottom using natural meaty baits. The spring temperature conditions compel the eel to seek food in shallow, warmed parts of the water, sometimes even in the vicinity of the banks, where the depth is less than 1m ($3\frac{1}{4}$ft). In summer, when even the deeper waters gradually warm up, eels have a chance for wider dispersal. At the end of the vegetation period, it again moves from the rapidly cooling shallows to the relatively warm deeper waters and can be sought at depths of as much as 10 to 12m (32—40ft).

Both traditional views and the statistics of trophy catches confirm that the late evening hours are the most successful time for fishing. However, many anglers consider this view to be unnecessarily conservative. During the day, the eel keeps to its hiding-place in order to feel safe, although this does not mean that it will necessarily forego an accessible morsel. As regards the question of a suitable time of year for fishing, the answer is unequivocal. One has good chances immediately at the beginning of the vegetation period, just after the water has warmed up to 12—13 °C (54—56 °F). The most suitable time for fishing is in July; in the second half of summer catches gradually fall off, and from October onwards the eel withdraws to deeper nooks. Essentially the eel is only fished for with earthworm or fish-bait, of which mainly smaller fish, most often goby and bleak, are used. Among less typical lures, only two count — fish fillet and the spoon.

The sporting value of eel-fishing is to some extent thrown into doubt by the fact that the angler does not have to, and indeed cannot, go for eel in 'kid gloves'. A hooked eel cannot be played with too much deference, as circumstances compel one to use force and guide the quarry to safety as soon as

153

possible. The voracious eel, which is trusting of bait, cannot be put off the take with a more resilient, hardish rod with a semi-soft action over 3m (10ft) in length, for a weight of 30—60g (1.0—2.0oz), nor by a relatively thicker line (0.30—0.35mm/0.012—0.014in). Simple hooks of sizes 2—6 are suitable, depending on the bait. Stranded steel wire excludes the possibility of an eel biting through the line, and also helps the angler when playing the quarry in the tangle of vegetation.

The use of relatively large and heavy baits (for example a bunch of 5—6 earthworms) will enable one to fish to a shorter distance with the simplest possible tackle assembly, dispensing with both weight and float. If fishing further off, a sliding weight is a must, and the tackle is assembled using one of several basic methods, depending on the conditions (the shape of the weight and the way it is mounted depend on the current, and on the character of the vantage point). When fishing in excessively muddy waters, preference is given to float fishing, possibly even with a dead fish-bait lightened either with air or polystyrene, in which case a greater distance is left between the hook and the weight. Baits are impaled on the hook in a simple manner, so that the earthworms or fish-baits are not injured too much and will be sufficiently active. The eel does not hunt so greedily that it will denude the tackle.

An eel take is characteristic for the fact that when gulping down the bait it helps itself with movements of the whole body. A sharp tugging at the tip of the rod or float is a signal that in a moment the angler can expect a continuous drag, to which he must react with immediate hooking. Sometimes it is enough just to hold the rod firm, as the hook is already sitting in the gullet of the fish. In case of premature hooking, when the hook is sitting only in the mouth, the chances in combat are in favour of the eel. Then it tries to adopt a position with its head pointing straight towards the bottom, winding its tail around the line and easily freeing itself from the hook. The eel should be pulled out energetically from the very first moment, so it is not given a chance to burrow its way into obstacles.

One should never handle a caught eel directly near the water. It can find dozens of possibilities for saving itself even from apparently impossible situations. Do not try to hold it with bare hand, always either use a rag or first roughen the hand with sand. The storing of eel in nets or buckets is also risky, and the safest quarry is a dead one.

Recently much publicity has been attracted by the question of reliable detection of the take in difficult conditions of visibility. The most reliable signalling device is of course an experienced hand. Anyone who is afraid, however, of being overcome by drowsiness when fishing, can help himself with any one of many technical innovations — phosphorus floats, bells, rattles, and even signals that light up.

Burbot

Knowledge of the regularities of the life and habits of freshwater fish species can only be utilised with reservations when acquainting oneself with the burbot. The life cycle of this unique, originally sea fish (the rest of its relatives, the codfish species, live in the sea) is arranged exactly the other way round. Whereas other fish species live more intensively when the temperature of the water is higher, their activity being restricted in winter, the burbot is most active at the lowest temperatures, and in the summer season falls into a somewhat lethargic state. Therefore the optimal habitat for the burbot is cooler waters in harsher climatic conditions in the submontane zone, where it reaches elevations of up to 1,000m (3,300 ft) above sea level. It nevertheless has a wide area of distribution and quite often also settles lowland waters. When choosing its territory, it has two basic requirements — high quality of water with correspondingly high oxygen content, and sufficient options for taking cover. It finds hiding-places in deep, dark nooks in the tangle of roots, in holes in clay banks, in crevices between rocks, in holes in underwashed bridge pillars, in cavities under locks and so on.

It leads a concealed existence throughout the whole year, leaving its hiding-places only at dusk, except during summer storms, when it will prowl for quarry in the cloudy water during the day. It spawns in December—January at temperatures close to freezing point. It is one of the most fertile of the sport fish species, venting over a million eggs directly into the water. It is carnivorous, orienting itself by means of the senses of taste and smell while searching for quarry, and it will not disdain decomposing

food. As a predator, it is of course also able to seize smaller fish, and in trout waters is usually considered to be an undesirable element, as it likes to feed on the eggs and alevins of salmon-type fish species. The larger larvae of aquatic insects, small crayfish, slugs, frogs and so on predominate on its menu. Its sanitary function in the water is to a certain extent welcome, and does not have to be looked upon negatively in trout waters. In cooler, more open north European lakes, it can grow to a massive 20kg (44lb), in central European conditions even 2—3kg (4.4—6.6lb) specimens are considered to be trophy fish.

The real burbot fishing season begins as early as November, lasting in warmer lowland conditions until the end of March, and at higher elevations can be prolonged until as late as the end of May. The ideal time of day for fishing is from dusk until late in the night; on cloudy days, when it is snowing and barometric pressure is dropping, there are suitable conditions for a catch even in the early afternoon hours.

The choice of baits poses no problem, as one can be sure that the burbot will investigate any bulky meaty bait, whether it registers it by sight or by its highly developed senses of taste and smell. If the angler really wants to attract the burbot's attention, he will get in a supply of smaller fish for the fishing season. They need not be live, and can even be processed frozen. A supply of earthworms will also pay off. If the angler has to have recourse to other baits, however, these need not be considered merely as a last resort. Poultry guts, pieces of liver, spleen, kidneys and so on will also be a delicacy for the burbot.

One should anticipate the territory of burbot in reaches with sufficient hiding places. In flowing waters, these are mainly found in the bankside sections, in which the water is at least 1½—2m (5—6½ft) deep, but still, excessively muddy backwaters can be ruled out as the water in such places has a low oxygen content. The bankside sections of courses, reinforced with free standing rocks, are also promising, as are spots under transverse barriers, under which whirling depths form. The situation is more complicated in lakes, dams and other enclosed waters. Here one can also be guided by the burbot's environmental requirements, therefore looking for it further offshore.

When sport fishing, the angler proceeds from the fact that the burbot is not in the habit of moving too far away from its hiding places. It will prefer even the most modest quarry right under its nose to a distant delicacy, however enticing. The bait must thus be presented right in front of its mouth, that is either on the bottom or just above it. Fishing methods are limited to fishing on the bottom with or without a float. The angler mainly fishes without a float if the burbot territories are further offshore.

A normal carp-fishing rod is used, as well as the usual type of reel; a thicker line (up to 0.25mm/0.01in) is used, and one should not hesitate to use hooks nos. 2—4. A weight is attached depending on the length of the casts, although usually only one.

The decision to assemble simple tackle, with a hook, stopper and sliding weight directly on the main line, or to assemble the tackle with the lead weight on a special thinner rig depends on the accessibility of the terrain. The rod must be well-secured, as one is fishing in extreme conditions, in the dark and in frost, and apart from this a hungry burbot can pull the rod and line into the water with lightning speed. Mostly, however, it takes gradually, trying to swallow the bait on the spot, and only then swimming off. A suitable detector, for example a sound detector, is a necessary tackle accessory.

When fishing at a shorter distance, the angler avails himself of the advantage of longer, if possible lighter rods, with which he fishes from the hand, thus being able to present the bait to the burbot precisely and effectively. When fishing, he tries to be as active as possible, combing the various spots with the bait; as far as possible, the bait is either allowed to drift downstream, or is tripped downstream. The bait is guided just above the bottom, or is allowed to drift freely downstream along the bottom, lifting it up from time to time. Even a promising sport should not be combed for longer than 4 or 5 minutes. If a predator is there, it will certainly make its presence felt within that time. If one is fishing predominantly by swimming the stream, a float is essential. It is fix-attached at two points, a divided weight is chosen and the individual weights are distributed in such a way that the water current will not lift the bait too high. In all cases the rods should be equipped with rod rings of large diameter, so that one does not have to worry about icing up when casting.

The burbot is always straightforward and the angler therefore does not delay with hooking, so that the hook will not get stuck as far as the gullet. A hooked burbot defends itself with jerky movements and tries to save itself in a hiding place. In the first phase of combat, therefore, it must be held more energetically, so that it does not entangle the line in obstacles. After that one can fish it out relatively easily.

FISHING FOR SALMON-TYPE SPECIES

Salmon-type fish species, the blue blood of the fish empire, were born under a lucky star. When describing their characteristics, one can only use superlatives. Their bodies have a truly ideal form, strictly in accordance with the laws of hydrodynamics, emphasised by extraordinarily bright colouring, which is nevertheless always in harmony with natural conditions. Their sporting value is second to none, and not least they have superb gastronomic qualities. Even Nature itself is on their side — the scenery of mountain and submontane torrents forms the most dignified environment for them.

River trout

Clean, cool mountain and submontane torrents with hard, gravelly or stony substrate and a high content of freely combined oxygen are home for the river trout. The trout is basically a territorial fish, and will give preference in any type of water to reaches with sufficient possibilities for cover. As it grows, its requirements for the size of its living environment also increase. Younger, one to two year-old fish will also settle the monotonous, canalised reaches of courses, being satisfied with even the slightest hiding places, for example near a large rock on the bottom, or in irregularities on the bottom. Adult fish do not feel safe in these waters, however, only settling them here and there, mainly under cascades and so on. During the day the trout remains either under cover or in deeper water in the vicinity of cover, becoming more courageous at twilight and swimming out for food even as far as dragging shallows. Feeding possibilities also play

158

a role when it is choosing a territory, as the trout likes to keep to more varied sections where the water will bring it food. Larger trout prefer a solitary way of life. In smaller brooks, as a rule a single trout reigns in one pool. In brooks in which the rate of flow is highly variable, the trout is sometimes compelled to change its usual rhythm of life. When the water level is extremely low, it migrates downstream into deeper water, but as soon as the rate of flow increases it will happily return to its original territory.

The trout is carnivorous. The alevin feeds on minute plankton and benthos, while more mature fish have a diet which steadily becomes more varied. Apart from the basic elements — that is, larvae and aquatic insects — its diet is made more interesting with the gathering of insects which have drifted downstream either under water or on the surface, and the trout will even seize insects flying here and there above the surface. The latter form a negligible component, however, of its diet as a whole.

The growth rate and body proportions attained by the trout depend on the suitability and size of its living environment. In the harshest submontane torrents with a long and severe winter and a short, not particularly favourable growing season, which offers only modest feeding possibilities, the trout attains a length of barely 25cm (10in) and will not live more then four or five years, although it is distinguished on the other hand by its large head and beautiful colouring. In the more favourable conditions of spacious mountain courses with more water, it can reach up to 40—50cm (16—20in) in length, 1 to 2kg (2.2—4.4lb) in weight, and can live up to 7—8 years. In the southernmost part of the areas in which it occurs, in rich courses at the trans-

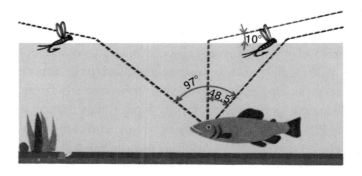

Field of vision of the trout from the bottom to the surface.

ition from the submontane zone into the lowlands, it can live even longer than ten years and will attain a weight of 3—5kg (6.6—11lb). In valley reservoirs and larger lakes, one can also encounter fish reaching a respectable 15kg (33lb), although in this environment they gradually change into the sea form of the species. The trout spawns from the end of autumn until the beginning of December. If it does not have suitable conditions for venting eggs at its territory, it will not hesitate to undertake a relatively long migration against the stream. Several hundred large eggs are vented by the female into an oval nest, which she has carefully deepened out and cleaned beforehand, in a small, swift brook. After spawning the parent fish generally return to their original territory.

Its relentless feeding activity and wide spectrum of food make the trout an exceptionally attractive sport species, which can be fished for by using various methods and a wide choice of both natural and artificial lures. It is just because of these sporting virtues that trout populations are often very seriously endangered. With intensive fishing using mainly natural animal baits, it is possible to wipe out virtually the entire population in smaller trout courses. Every prudent fisherman must therefore accept with understanding the increasingly strict regulations for trout fishing and for salmon-type fishing in general, which restrict the assortment of baits and the maximum quota of daily catches, as well as prolonging the close season. It might therefore be sensible for the future of trout to ban all natural, mainly live baits and permit fishing only with the aid of artificial lures, that is, classic fly-fishing and classic spinning. Fishing for this aristocratic creature with earthworms or grasshoppers should be regarded as beneath the angler's dignity.

The ideal season for trout fishing is generally considered to be spring, when the water tempera-

ture reaches 8—10°C (46—50 °F) and the trout are famished after the long winter. Statistics reveal that from the middle of April until the end of May more trout are caught than in the whole of the remainder of the open season. It is nevertheless interesting that relatively heavy specimens are caught at the end of the season. Spinning is the most successful of the possible fishing methods.

In the first instance, however, we should focus our attention on the most aristocratic and most elegant method for trout fishing — fly-fishing. Trout may be fished for both with dry and wet flies, as well as with nymphs and streamers. A more experienced fly-fisherman can catch successfully throughout the whole season; a beginner, however, should restrict himself to fishing under the most favourable conditions. The beginning of the season is usually best, but only in relatively warm weather, when the vegetation is in full bud. At that time the insects begin to swarm more intensively, and the trout are gradually getting used to them. Sufficiently varied courses of average size are ideal for fly-fishing by wading. Success depends of course on the water level, and fly-fishing in cloudy water cannot by considered at all in practice. The best conditions are brought by the period directly after rain, or even better after a storm, when the water gradually begins to cloud. The weather must always be taken into consideration. In stable summer weather, the angler has a better chance for success early in the morning and from late afternoon until darkness has completely set in, in lower barometric pressure or when the sky is partly overcast, throughout the whole day.

Procedure when casting an artificial fly.

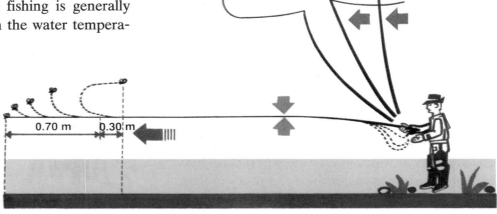

0.70 m   0.30 m

159

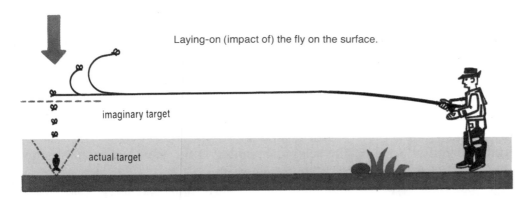

Laying-on (impact of) the fly on the surface.

imaginary target

actual target

When choosing the fishing method, one is guided by the immediate circumstances. If trout are gathering food from the surface, moving in distinct circles, preference should be given to fishing with a dry fly. In swift waters this circling is not perceptible and a wet fly proves more advantageous. In this way one is able to fish in mountain torrents practically throughout the whole season. In deeper and more open waters under similar conditions, one fishes with either streamers or nymphs.

The choice of a suitable fly is one of the most debated but at the same time least researched issues of fly-fishing. It is not possible to recommend a type which is guaranteed to be successful. The most sensible fly-fisherman probably has a butterfly net among his equipment, always ascertaining before fishing which insect species are swarming at the time. He can also dissect the first catch and find out on the basis of the stomach contents what the trout are enjoying the taste of at that moment. As regards the general rules for the choice of flies, depending on the season of the year and the immediate conditions, we shall restrict ourselves only to a brief guide. At the very beginning of the season, one should choose smaller and more matte flies, later in spring gradually larger and lighter ones of brown shades, in summer gradually even larger ones, then at the beginning of autumn again gradually smaller ones which are brownish in colour. During a sunny day, smaller, lighter, shiny flies are used; in less intense light, that is, in the late afternoon, in the morning and when the sky is overcast, larger flies with less conspicuous colouring are better. In markedly reduced visibility, late in the evening, the lightest possible flies, even completely white ones, are chosen. The precise imitation of insects is only necessary in clear water when using dry flies; in other cases both exact imitations and the many fantastic flies are usually equally successful.

160

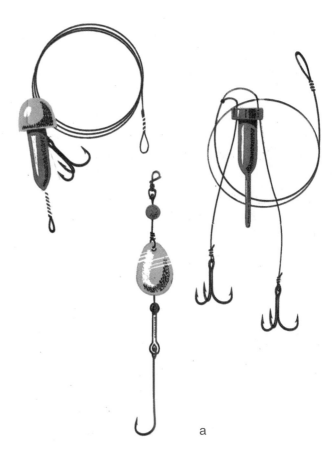

a

Basic systems for trout fishing by sinking and drawing.

b

When fly-fishing one must bear in mind the shyness of the trout; therefore fish at a greater distance, ideally 10—12m (33—40ft) from the bank. The actual fishing technique is adapted to the accessibility of the terrain. Casting is always carried out gently, so that the fly hits the water first, and only then the rig and fly-fishing line. If the cast is not successful, the angler pulls in the line and tries again. It is best to cast dry flies against the stream, or possibly diagonally downstream. After casting, the fly is allowed to drift freely downstream, so as to give a natural impression. The fly-fishing line is always shortened, either by retrieving or pulling it in by hand, so that one can react immediately to a take. Whether to fish with one or two flies is a matter of habit. The take of the fish is observed by sight, ideally with the aid of polarised glasses.

A wet fly is cast slightly diagonally against the stream, and after impact is likewise allowed to drift downstream. It will move at various depths in the water, carried along by the lower currents. The take will be felt in the hand.

Fishing with nymphs, which can under certain circumstances be even more successful, differs in a number of details from wet fly-fishing. The nymph, which imitates the larvae of aquatic insects, especially the mayfly, represents the daily bread-and-butter of the trout, and the fish therefore has the greatest confidence in it. Hence the nymph can be used in all waters, even still waters, and at any time of the year or day. The ideal time for fishing with a nymph is of course during the season when insects naturally fly in large numbers — depending on the climatic conditions, from May to July. At this time of year, the nymphs rise up from the bottom to the surface, where the trout hunt them, so the fishing technique has to fit in with this situation. In other seasons of the year, nymphs move more along the bottom, or are carried down to this depth by the water. A nymph may be cast both down and upstream. Unlike a wet fly, which is allowed to drift downstream freely, one tries to guide the nymph towards the spot where the trout are hunting.

Although when using a streamer one could fish with a light, fly-fishing rod, a somewhat longer — approximately 2.8m (9ft) — rod with a relatively hard action is more advantageous. A streamer is

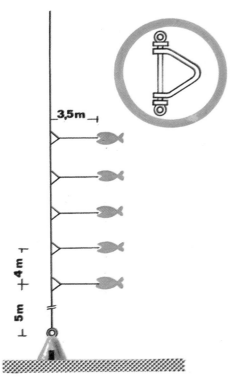

Seehund system for depth fishing for lake trout.

cast in the same way as a fly, and after it has sunk to the bottom, the lure is tripped along with jerky movements as when sinking and drawing, hooking also being carried out in a similar way.

Trout fishing by spinning is essentially identical with fishing for other predatory fish species. If expecting an average catch, one chooses a light, fine casting rod 2.2—2.8m (7—9ft) long, a line up to 0.20mm (0.008in) thick and a small type of fixed-spool reel. For fishing in more open waters, where it is necessary to fish further off and where one can also expect larger catches, one must be equipped with correspondingly more resilient tackle. Drawing can be carried out both with a wide range of all types of artificial lure and with dead fish-bait mounted on

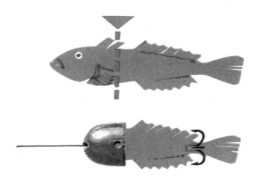

One of the methods for preparing a Miller's Thumb as bait when trout fishing by sink and draw.

163

a special system. Small lures are chosen and the drawing technique depends on the character of the water. In still water, drawing is carried out with variations of tempo, although in swifter reaches one can afford a slower tempo, so that the trout has time to attack.

In rare cases, if because of the inaccessibility of the terrain one does not succeed either in fly-fishing or drawing, it is even possible to try fishing with dead fish-bait — a gudgeon, goby or Miller's thumb 5—6cm (2—2$\frac{1}{4}$in) long. One can fish using a common casting rod, although a larger, no. 1—2 hook should always be chosen, so that it will not penetrate as far as the gullet of an under-sized trout. The fish-bait (although a tail will do) is mounted simply, ideally by the mouth, and is allowed to drift freely downstream unweighted. The line is paid out very carefully, so that one is in constant contact with the bait. A trout take of a fish-bait is usually very energetic, and can be recognized unmistakeably by a tugging at both the line and rod. The angler should not delay in hooking. The trout swallows the bait with a gulp, and at the point of hooking it is definitely more humane for the hook to catch it in the mouth, and not penetrate as far as the gullet.

Sea trout

Sports fishermen have been used to speaking of the sea trout as a separate species. In fact, however, we are dealing here with a form of the river trout which has adapted to life in the specific conditions of more open, deeper and colder lakes, valley dams and similar waters. The adaptability of the trout to a change of living environment is exceptional. When the river trout, characterised by its bright, intensive colouring, strays from a mountain torrent to a dammed lake, it changes into the typical lake form known as the sea trout within a short time. It is not the body shape which changes but the colouring. It acquires a monotonous silvery colour, darker on the upper side of the body than on the flanks, with darker, pronounced spots, whilst the red spots of the river trout disappear completely. The much larger environment of lakes provides the fish with more favourable feeding possibilities. Because of this, the trout grows more quickly, and gives a stouter, meatier impression.

Sea trout keep to the depths for most of the sum-

mer, even inhabiting lakes more than 100m (330ft) deep. Only at twilight will they dare to approach the surface in search of quarry. Along the belt by the shore, they keep mainly to tributary estuaries at the beginning of spring, not penetrating the tributaries until the end of autumn during the spawning migrations.

As the sea trout grows, its food requirements increase, and the adult fish becomes a true predator, which dictates fishing methods and baits. One has the best chances of a good catch from the beginning of the open season until the end of May, as long as one keeps fairly close to the shore, mainly at tributary estuaries. At such times it is fished for using traditional methods either with fish-bait or a wide range of artificial lures — spoons, spinners, Devon minnows, wobblers and so on, as well as with bulkier wet flies. In the course of the season, when the sea trout keeps offshore and at greater depths, sinking and drawing may be considered. At the beginning of the season, before the water has warmed up too much, the fish are sought closer to the surface, whilst during the course of the summer it is preferable to try fishing by deep spinning, for which the same range of artificial lures is used.

Rainbow trout

The acclimatisation of the North American rainbow trout to European waters at the end of the 19th century amounted to a jackpot for both sport fishermen and trout breeders, mainly for the reason that the rainbow trout, unlike its aristocratic relatives, can if need be reduce its demands to an unbelievable extent and adapt itself to given conditions. As a salmon-type fish, it will of course assert itself fully in all trout waters, perhaps with the exception of high mountain torrents. Surprisingly, however, it will also assert itself superbly in the less noble environment of both flowing and enclosed waters, not only within the submontane zone in the barbel belt, but sometimes even in distinctly lowland conditions. The breeding combination of carp with the rainbow trout is now already quite a common one. One can also reckon with rainbow trout in more open, deeper lowland waters with maximum temperatures of up to 25°C (77 °F), as long as they have sufficient oxygen content. Deeper gravel pits and similar types of water, supplied by the cooler tributaries of

spring sources, are a most suitable environment.

In terms of their way of life and food requirements, rainbow and river trout are very similar, which means that they compete with each other both for space and food. In such a case the omnivorous and generally more aggressive rainbow trout usually manages to oust the landlord. For this reason it is necessary to see the future of the rainbow trout mainly in waters which no longer fully suit the more demanding river trout — most probably at the lower boundary of more open trout courses, in the whole of the grayling belt, and in some places possibly also in the barbel belt. Particularly suitable conditions for the rainbow trout can be found in enclosed but wide waters, as long as they are relatively clean and cool, and have a favourable oxygen content. There, with a sufficient supply of food, the rainbow trout will feel well-off and, what is most important, it will give up its typical wandering tendencies. The rainbow trout does not usually spawn until March or April, and is somewhat more fertile than the river trout. Under favourable living conditions it grows quickly, and in an optimal environment it can grow to a weight of 10kg (22lb) as early as the fourth year of its life. The most it can reach is a weight of 20kg (44lb) with a length of 1m (3¼ft).

It is fished for using essentially the same methods as for river trout. As it is more aggressive, one can be more certain of a catch. It is particularly voracious just before winter sets in, and in autumn can be fished for superbly using all types of artificial fly. It is also possible to fish for it in winter through holes drilled in the ice.

Huchen

The huchen's positively ideal hydrodynamically shaped, powerful body predetermines it for habitation in the swiftest rapids of submontane rivers, where it settles continuous, more open reaches with sufficient horizontal and vertical variation. It poses kingly demands with regard to the choice of its territory, taking account both of the feeling of security and sufficient suitable food. Therefore it is best suited to deeper parts with rapids followed by dragging sections. A welcome addition in the territory are obstacles directly in the stream-line, for example large boulders or tree trunks, near which the huchen

a

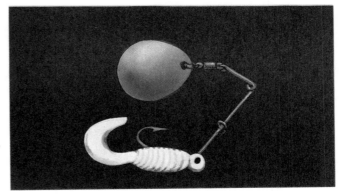

b

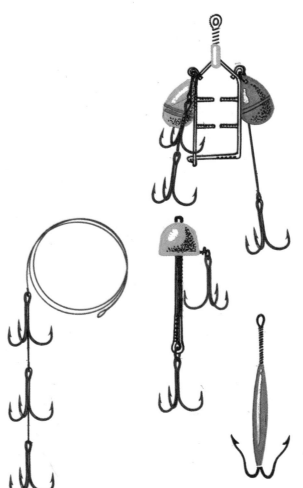

Systems suitable for huchen fishing.

167

feels safe and from where it will dart out for a quarry at lightning speed. It is also demanding with regard to its neighbours, and prefers carp-type fish with slender bodies — that is, broad-snout, chub and barbel. The clearer, swifter reaches of the barbel belt and lower parts of the grayling belt are thus the huchen domain.

The huchen spawns from April to May, and before spawning undertakes migratory journeys upstream into shallower torrents with gravelly substrates. After the early period of its growth, when it can only resort to minute plankton and benthonic food, it very quickly changes over to a predatory method of feeding. Apart from fish, it will attack anything living that happens to find its way into the water within its territory. An adult huchen is a peevish solitary fellow, and will not put up with any competition in its vicinity. By virtue of its obstinate rapaciousness and the fact that its appetite remains on the same level practically throughout the whole year, it grows faster than its relatives, reaching a respectable size. There are confirmed reports from the submontane zone of the Danube from the second half of the last century of gigantic huchen weighing 60—80kg (132—176lb). In present-day conditions of excessive pressure on the part of sports fishermen and the gradual devastation of the living environment, the huchen of course has a more difficult time, but in spite of this it can still reach a weight of over 30kg (66lb). The sport value of this 'Queen of the Waters' needs to be evaluated soberly, however, and one is at a loss to say whether it is appropriate to advocate fishing for it at all. In fact it would be better to think about how to secure its existence, or possibly increase its numbers, so as to be able to continue to boast of this beautiful fish even after the year 2000.

The optimal time for huchen fishing is at the beginning of winter, when the general shortage of accessible quarry compels it to attack at any even remotely suitable opportunity. Although the locally tolerated fishing method around the Danube using live bait is effective, because of the possibility of serious injury to smaller, undersized fish, one should voluntarily exclude it from one's repertoire. One can happily do so, as sink and draw fishing, either with a dead fish-bait mounted on a special system, or with common artificial lures, is excep-

tionally effective for catching huchen. Classic Heintz spoons and similar spoons, as well as spinners and wobblers, are adequate for this purpose. The huchen, like other predators, attacks the quarry instinctively, and does not have time to evaluate the detailed execution of the lure. In contrast with this, however, it is perfectly able to distinguish any unnatural detail in the movement of the drawn lure. It will only trust the lure if it moves in the water as if alive. If considering special artificial lures, various types of lamprey tail are worth trying.

Huchen fishing specialists equip themselves with special tackle, which consists of a casting rod, possibly even for both hands, which should be substantial and have a hard tip which will expedite reliable hooking; from among possible reels, multiplier ones are more reliable, whilst from among the fixed-spool ones, only larger types of the best quality should be used. The line should always be over 0.35mm (0.014in) thick, and the lure (dead fish-bait or spoon) over 15—18cm (6—7in) in length. The rod rings should be of a large diameter, so that they will not frost up in winter. Apart from a valuable trophy, the huchen also attracts fishermen for reason of its gastronomic value. Unlike the trout, for example, even the largest huchen has delicious, juicy meat.

Grayling

The fans of grayling fishing represent an elite caste in the society of St. Peter's guild. Many of them respect one fish alone — the grayling — and only one sole fishing method, fly-fishing exclusively with artificial flies. The special characteristics of the grayling are further accentuated by the fact that a belt of submontane rivers and brooks has been named after it as the Grayling Zone.

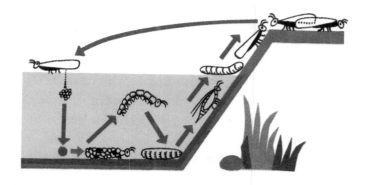

Scheme of *Chironomidae* life-cycle.

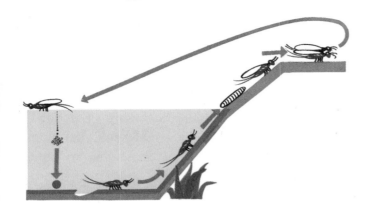

Scheme of *Plecoptera* life-cycle.

The submontane reaches of brooks and rivers of sufficiently varied character, where swifter reaches alternate with prolonged, slightly dragging currents and with more extensive still places in deeper backwaters are the domain of this fish. The grayling is a social fish, living in large communities, keeping mainly to open water, so it does not have special requirements with regard to opportunities for taking cover. It will therefore hold its own even in monotonous, canalised courses, assuming that these have sufficient water and rapids, although it will also adapt to still waters. After a long stay in more open valley reservoirs, it will develop into a stouter, meatier lake form. It will not tolerate a deterioration in the environment or polluted and chronically clouded water, and is exceptionally sensitive to an oxygen deficit. It spawns from April until the beginning of May in the milder currents of smaller submontane courses and on gravel substrates. It has a relatively short life, normally only living four to six years and growing to a weight of 0.3—0.5kg (10½—17½oz). Even grayling longer than 50cm (20in) and heavier than 1kg (2.2lb) are considered to be trophy specimens, and only sporadically do fish occur weighing 2—2.5kg (4.4—5.5lb).

The relatively small mouth of the grayling suggests that the basic components of its diet are small animals. The fact that fly-fishing is supposed to be the most effective method for grayling fishing could mislead one into thinking that flies constitute a large proportion of the diet of this fish. In fact, however, what is known as benthos, that is insect larvae living on the bottom, are the basic source of nutrition for the grayling. The most common are bank-bait larvae, which can form up to 90% of the grayling diet in some waters. Another important component of its diet are hatching insects, which are accessible to fish during the last metamorphosis of the larva into the imago. Food flying close to the surface, although intensively gathered by the grayling, is basically only a welcome seasonal variation of its menu, if only for the fact the grayling gathers mostly only the tiniest flies, the nutritional value of which is minimal.

The grayling ranks among species which have an exceptionally high level of feeding activity. It will not ignore even the smallest quarry drifting downstream which it will easily register with its keen eyesight. In cloudy water it seeks food on the bottom, in clear water making use of the whole water profile. Adult grayling, like some other carp-type fish species, will occasionally even seize smaller fish, although this does not justify characterising them as predators. Similarly, one cannot reproach the grayling if it occasionally samples the eggs of other fish, as these pay it back in the same way.

Having agreed in the introduction to this section that a true fisherman will only go for grayling with the fly-fishing method, we should also stand by this when describing the fishing method. Catching a grayling in cloudy water using a dung or bone worm holds little pleasure, and to a certain extent involves a degradation of the noble origins of this beautiful fish.

Fine tackle should be chosen for grayling fishing. This does not imply an underestimation of the combative qualities of the fish, as the grayling, although it gives a generally refined impression, can nevertheless fight courageously. But the angler has to take into account its fine mouth, which could easily tear with harsher treatment. The actual choice of rod depends on the character of the water and the fishing method. If fishing in ideal conditions, that is in brooks up to 1—1.8m (3¼—6ft) deep with wading possibilities and open banks, where one casts to a distance of 10—15m (33—50ft), a rod 2.4—2.5m (8—8¼ft) will do. In more open waters, when one is obliged to cast further off, a rod about 2m (6½ft) long should be chosen. Where one will be fishing predominantly with a wet fly, the rod needs to be somewhat more resilient and hard, whilst for a dry fly, on the other hand, it should be softer and finer, although the average fly-fisherman will of course go in for a universal rod.

On the basis of this, one then also needs to match the selection of a fly-fishing line. It is definitely not necessary to have the most exclusive, and thus the most expensive, fly-fishing line. If fishing in small brooks, where one is obliged to restrict oneself to short casts, even the simplest parallel fly-fishing line will be adequate. When fishing with a technically more demanding method, preference is given to better quality fly-fishing lines — when wet fly-fishing to a sinking fly-fishing line, and in the case of dry flies to a floating one. The angler, of course, still has a chance to select technically better quality fly-fishing lines, such as a combined one with a sinking end part only, or possibly an amphibious adaptable one, which is greased when fishing with a dry fly so that it will float, and when not greased will act as a sinking fly-fishing line. There are no special requirements as regards a reel, which may be either mechanical or automatic.

There are two opposing views concerning the choice of effective artificial flies. Some anglers see in the grayling a sly cunning fox, which will discover even on the tiniest fly every difference however slight from the natural model. Proponents of this thesis have a butterfly net among their equipment, as well as instruments for dissecting fish, carefully ascertaining before starting to fish which insects are swarming, and what the grayling are after at that moment. If they are to be able to meet the whims of the fish, their equipment must include several hundred imitations of diverse insect species. Others see the grayling as a capricious fish, which one minute will not take even the closest imitation, and the next minute will go like a wild thing after a fantastically unnatural fly type. The truth probably lies somewhere between the two. One can easily ascertain the entomological knowledge of the grayling by observing it while hunting. It will rise slowly and elegantly from the bottom to the surface for a natural bait and unhurriedly swallow the fly, returning in a dignified manner to its original spot. If there is something about the fly that it does not like, however, it will follow it as if irritated, touch it with its mouth closed and return to the bottom.

The grayling fly-fishing season has two distinct peaks, the first being immediately at the beginning of the open season, when the fish are exceptionally famished after spawning and the long winter. During the warmest summer months, when there is a surplus of natural food, it takes a more suspicious attitude to artificial lures. The second peak of the open season starts at the beginning of autumn, when the nights begin to turn really cold; that is, as early as the second half of September in more northerly latitudes, in October in warmer conditions. Warm autumn days after night frosts are the best, after the mist over the water has dispersed. Fishing success is of course also affected by peripheral factors, such as the level and purity of the water, the weather conditions at that moment and so on. At the beginning of the season one can rely on the grayling being active all day long. On hot summer days it is usually most active early in the morning and evening, during the day only if the sky is partially overcast. In summer, especially during the day, grayling can even be sought in stronger currents. In autumn it is active throughout the whole day, and in colder weather particularly around noon. Overcast, gloomy autumn days are less favourable, although the grayling rather likes silent drizzle when there is no wind.

Whether to choose a dry or wet fly depends on the circumstances. With a dry fly, one fishes mainly when the grayling are obviously hunting, that is when they are circling, which generally can be observed only in calmer reaches of the course. Experienced anglers, especially with the aid of polarized glasses, will try dry fly-fishing even in swifter sections. Fishing is either carried out systematically, that is by gradually combing the section being fished with the fly, or by observing the circling of the grayling, picking out a fish and concentrating attention directly on it. The fly is cast diagonally downstream, a little behind the spot where the grayling is, and is allowed to drift down freely in such a way that a substantial bulge will not form on the fly-fishing line. In this way, the angler can react readily to the take, which he registers by sight. Hooking is carried out gently at the moment when the grayling has taken the fly and is heading back towards its home spot. It is very important to choose the right vantage point for fishing, as the angler must have the possibility to manipulate the rod when casting and needs to conceal himself. Many anglers consider the grayling to be a trusting fish, which one can approach to within grasping distance. Although there are cases when a grayling bites only a metre away from the angler, more often it is disturbed from its untroubled routine by any conspicuous movement on the bank, or the mere silhouette of the fisherman. It is thus always better not to put oneself on display or give the fish reason for increased vigilance.

Under more difficult conditions, in swift waters, under cascades, or in whirling reaches — that is, everywhere that one has problems observing the dry fly — preference should be given to fishing with a wet fly. It can also be used in more still waters when the fish are not hunting close to the surface and when one has had no success with a dry fly. This usually happens less intensively, and when the grayling are busy seeking food on the bottom.

The angler usually fishes downstream with two to three flies. The flies are cast at right angles to the current, and guided in such a way that the end fly will be submerged, the first suspended one will float on the surface and the second one will skip above the surface. Sometimes, however, it is a good idea to try fishing with all three flies submerged at various depths in the water. After casting, the flies are again allowed to drift downstream of their own accord, and the fly-fishing line is held constantly loose without any substantial bulging. The take is best observed if the angler follows the movement of the flies under the surface, or possibly even of the fish around the flies, with polarized glasses. Nevertheless he must choose a vantage point where he will have the sun behind him, holding the rod almost upright, in extreme cases registering the take even from the movement of the rig or fly-fishing line. Takes of a wet fly are usually more energetic, although one should not hesitate to hook immediately, because the grayling will quickly recognise its mistake and get rid of the fly.

In the event of not being able to make up one's mind about which fishing method to choose, it is also possible to try a combined method of dry and wet flies. A wet fly is naturally attached at the end, a dry one on a rig.

Hooking and playing grayling must be carried out gently. A fine, thin hook (mostly size nos. 14 to 20), which can, however, easily tear through the fine mouth of the fish, is used, with a thin, relatively delicate rig — about 0.15mm (0.006in). Although the grayling defends itself courageously, it does not deviate into obstacles during combat and makes use only of the strength of the current. A landing-net is necessary to fish it out of the water. Freeing the fish from the hook with moistened hands with the aid of a clamp or small pliers is normal procedure, and in the case of fish which are let back into the water it is essential.

The angler's brotherhood tends to blame every fishing failure on the capriciousness or moodiness of the fish. But are we really so foolish as to suspect these creatures of malicious intent? It makes more sense to seek the reason for failure elsewhere. An unsuitable choice of fishing tackle or bait, as well as the wrong choice of fishing method, and not least one's own lack of skill — imperfect mastery of fishing technique or unsuitable behaviour at the water — can all contribute to such failures.

Every sport fisherman should try to utilise as well as possible both his own and others' experience in order to improve his knowledge, to learn as much as possible about the way of life of fish, and to develop his skill when fishing. However, fishing ethics must not be forgotten, nor should the correct sporting attitude towards fish, for fixation on making a catch would throw into doubt the value of sport fishing. It is not after all essential to make a catch at any price. One would do better to regard a caught fish as a bonus to the wonderful experiences one has during fishing. Each one of us waits for his big fish, but one should not lose heart if it does not come. Maybe tomorrow, maybe the day after tomorrow, or in a year's time . . . .

Plates

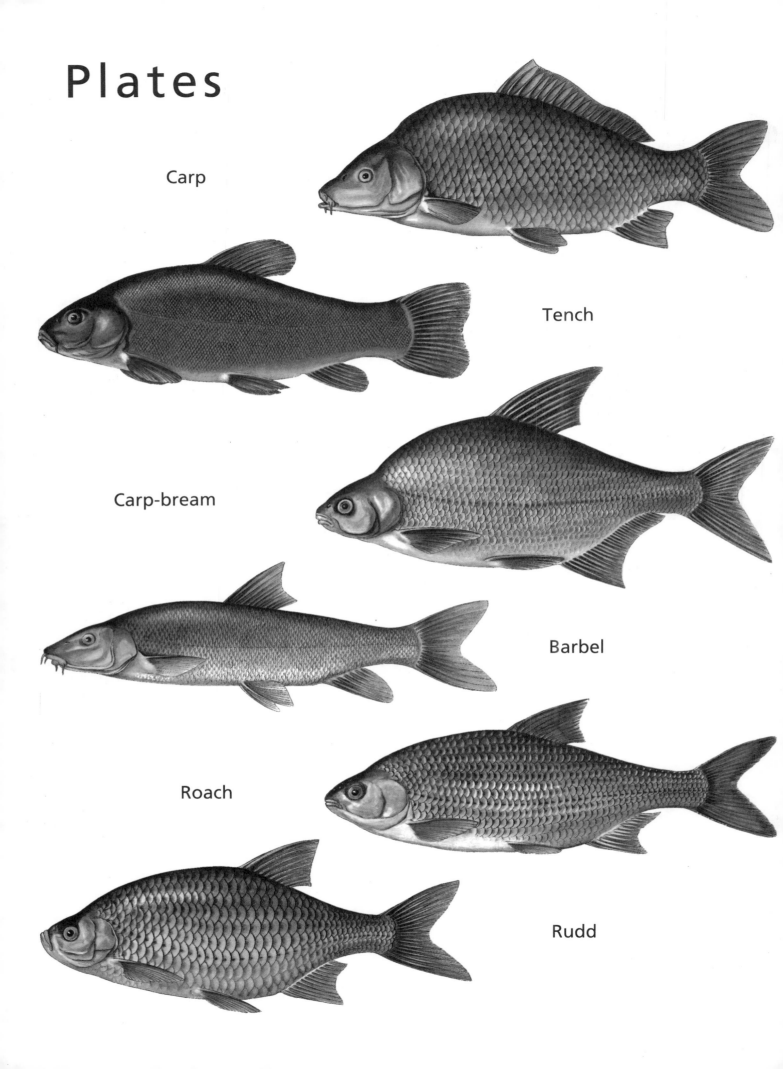

Carp

Tench

Carp-bream

Barbel

Roach

Rudd

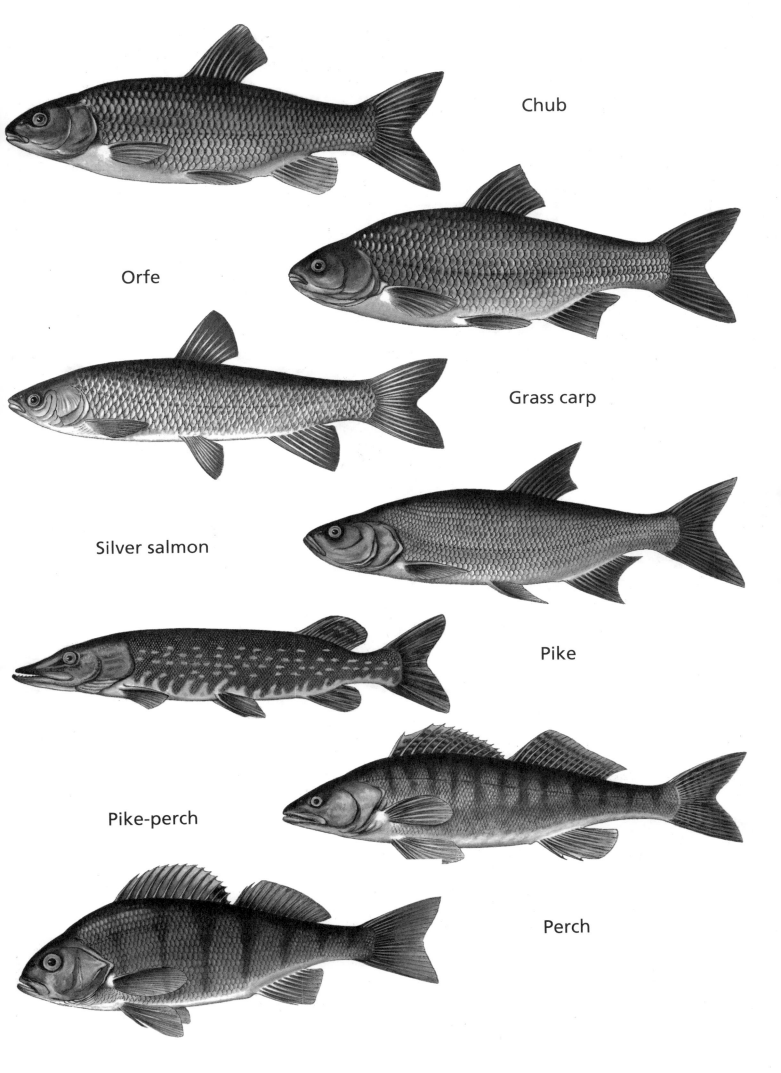

Chub

Orfe

Grass carp

Silver salmon

Pike

Pike-perch

Perch

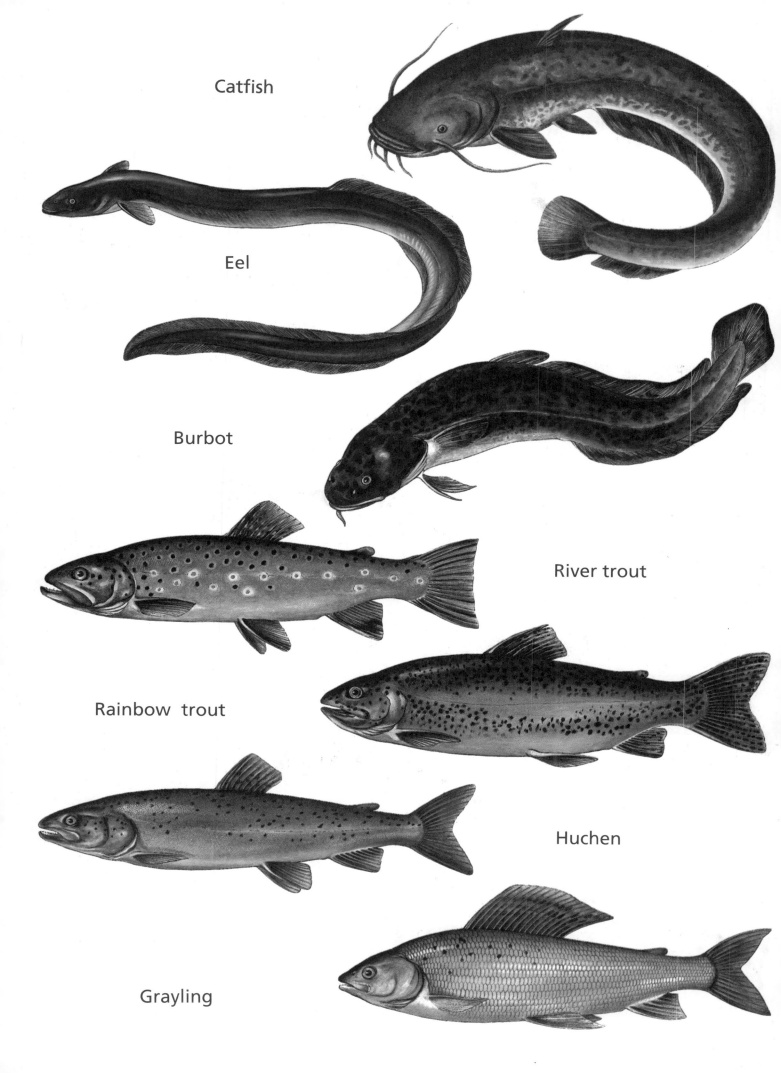

Catfish

Eel

Burbot

River trout

Rainbow trout

Huchen

Grayling